KOREAN
MADE SIMPLE

A beginner's guide to learning the Korean language

GO! Billy Korean

Korean Made Simple: A beginner's guide to the Korean language
Volume 1, Edition 1

Written by: Billy Go
Edited by: Michelle Chong and Wooseok Lim
Published by: GO! Billy Korean

Audio files for this book are available for free download from gobillykorean.com.

Cover and inside illustrations by: HeeJin Park (heejindraws.tumblr.com)
Hangul letter blocks by: Sarah HaEun Jeong (esperes.weebly.com)

Copyright © 2014 GO! Billy Korean
http://www.gobillykorean.com
All rights reserved

Printed by Amazon Kindle Direct Publishing (KDP)
Available from Amazon.com and other retail outlets
ISBN: 1497445825
ISBN-13: 978-1497445826

DEDICATION

This book is dedicated to *you*, the learner. If it weren't for people like you who are interested in learning the Korean language, this book would not exist. Thank you for being interested in Korean, and for your support in purchasing this book. My only hope is that this book will serve as a strong, first step toward your personal language learning goals – whatever those goals may be. Good luck in your studies.

TABLE OF CONTENTS

	Preface	vii
	Introduction to Hangul	15
	More Hangul	41
	Introduction to Sound Changes	51
Chapter 1	Saying Hello	57
Chapter 2	Likes and Dislikes	65
Chapter 3	Simple Sentences	69
Chapter 4	Wanting and Not Wanting	75
Chapter 5	Verbs	83
Chapter 6	More Verbs	91
Chapter 7	Asking Questions	103
Chapter 8	More Questions	115
Chapter 9	Adjectives	125
Chapter 10	More Adjectives	133
Chapter 11	Colors	147
Chapter 12	Numbers	163
Chapter 13	More Numbers	177
Chapter 14	Negative Sentences	199
Chapter 15	Korean Markers	213
Chapter 16	Telling Time	225
Chapter 17	Shopping	243
Chapter 18	Relationships	255
Chapter 19	Informal Korean	265
Chapter 20	Past Tense	281
	Answer Keys	297
	Appendix A. Typing in Korean	309
	Appendix B. Hangul Chart and Names of Letters	311
	Appendix C. Sound Change Rules	313
	Informal Korean Conversations	323
	Special Thanks	331
	Glossary	332

Preface

So you've decided to learn Korean! I congratulate you on your decision, and welcome you on your new journey. As for me, I first learned Korean while living in Korea in 2005. Upon returning home, I chose to major in Korean at my university in 2008, and it's been nonstop fun ever since. I'm happy with my decision to pursue Korean education as a career, and hope to be able to help many others see their Korean abilities improve as we study this wonderful language together here in this book.

What to Expect

This book was designed with you, the learner, in mind. As such, I'm assuming that you have never studied Korean before, and will begin teaching from the very basic of basics, working our way up from there.

First time language learners, Korean beginners, and curious minds of all ages – yes, even those of you who may think "I'm too old to learn a language" – were in my thoughts while writing this book. This book was designed specifically for *you*.

If you've already studied some Korean before, that's great! Don't worry. I have you in mind as well. In addition to covering the basics, I always make sure to add in a little more in each chapter. Through my personal and academic studies of the Korean language, I'm finding the majority of resources out there for teaching Korean often fail to present concepts in their correct forms – to put it simply, I find lots of mistakes in Korean being taught in other textbooks and on web sites. As such, it's likely that you'll learn something new through this book, even if you've already studied Korean before up to any level.

Preface

Concepts are laid out in their simplest way possible at first, for the beginner. "*Advanced Notes*" sprinkled throughout each chapter add information that beginning Korean courses might not teach at first, but are still important. Sometimes these will even contain advanced-level material if I feel that it's something that even beginners should know. "*Culture Notes*" will deepen your understanding of the Korean language, because you can't speak Korean well without knowing a thing or two about Korean culture. I didn't even know where Korea was on a map before I started studying the language (Note to self: North and South Korea are very different!).

Do not expect to be speaking fluent Korean by the end of this book. There is simply too much that needs to be covered before you will be able to converse in Korean without any difficulties. However, I promise that if you follow this book well and *practice* what you learn, you will be able to gain quite an extensive introductory knowledge of the Korean language through this book. *And*, you will be able to fill in the gaps that most Korean learners face later on in their studies.

And I'll be there the whole way, holding your hand through each lesson – figuratively, of course. I'm not really going to hold your hand the whole time (I'm sorry, but that's just creepy).

How to Use This Book

This book builds upon itself with each chapter. I recommend that you take your time going through each lesson, *in order*. Don't move on to the next section until you feel comfortable with the last one. Each lesson builds upon knowledge learned from the previous one, so skipping a lesson could lead to problems understanding concepts in later lessons; this negative result would obviously compound the more lessons you skip. In short, do all of the lessons and all of the exercises in order, or at least do all of the lessons if you're in a rush and feel confident enough to skip the Practice sections.

If this is your first time learning Korean, I recommend reading each "Culture Notes" section, but skipping the "Advanced Notes" sections, as these are not designed for first time learners. If this isn't your first time studying Korean, I recommend reading the additional "Advanced Notes" in each chapter. In addition, if you've already read this book once before, I would also recommend reading the "Advanced Notes" sections on your second time through.

As you complete each chapter, refer frequently to the vocabulary lists in the back of the chapter, or the Glossary in the back of this book as necessary. If you are having trouble understanding a sentence, or creating a sentence for the Practice sections, it might only be due to not knowing the appropriate vocabulary word.

Preface

Take notes along the way as you complete each chapter. Practice reading, writing, and speaking as much as possible. If you have a friend who can speak Korean, practice speaking and listening *frequently*.

In addition, if you notice a grammar form you are not familiar with, I would recommend proceeding through the book more *slowly*. This book builds upon itself, so if you have missed something, and if it does not appear in the chapter you are currently reading, it may have been skipped from a previous chapter. There is no need to rush through the basics of the Korean language. It will take time to become familiar with using the Korean alphabet, and to become used to hearing the sounds of the language – this is normal. Once you have learned the basics, it will become much easier, and faster, to move forward and acquire new concepts.

Also make sure to download the free audio files for this book at gobillykorean.com.

How to Study Korean

I'm not the authority on how *your* brain will learn this language the best, but I do have a few suggestions. Try some of them, and use what works for you.

1. Quiz yourself frequently on words you are learning, or have somebody else quiz you.

2. Force yourself to create sentences using the words and grammar forms that you are learning.

3. If you are fortunate enough to live in an area with many Koreans (such as in Korea, or a major city), make friends and practice speaking the language as much as possible.

4. Keep a regular study schedule. Even if you only have 30 minutes a day, 5 days a week, stick to it. 30 minutes a day for 5 days is better than studying 150 minutes at once. Shorter, frequent study is also easier to manage if you have a busy schedule.

5. Write vocabulary words you learn on sticky notes, and place them over things and places that they correspond to. For example, you can write the Korean word for "pencil" on your favorite pencil, or the word for "friend" on your best friend's forehead.

Preface

6. Grammar is more important than vocabulary. A beginner with a strong understanding of basic Korean grammar will sound worlds better than a walking dictionary that can't construct a coherent sentence.

7. Brush Up Your English Grammar.

"This is a Korean book! Why do I have to learn English grammar?" Many concepts in Korean are much easier to explain and understand if you have a basic grasp of English grammar. Could you learn that the Korean word 사과 meant "apple" in English, without knowing the English word "apple" beforehand? As such, you'll need to be familiar with words such as *verb*, *adjective*, *noun*, and others, in order to better learn the Korean language. Here are a few English concepts I use in this book which you should be at least familiar with before starting:

Subject / Object / Noun / Adjective / Adverb / Verb

I'll also be covering necessary grammar words as they come up throughout the book, but knowing what they are in advance will help make concepts easier to digest once we get there.

Welcome to Korean and Korea

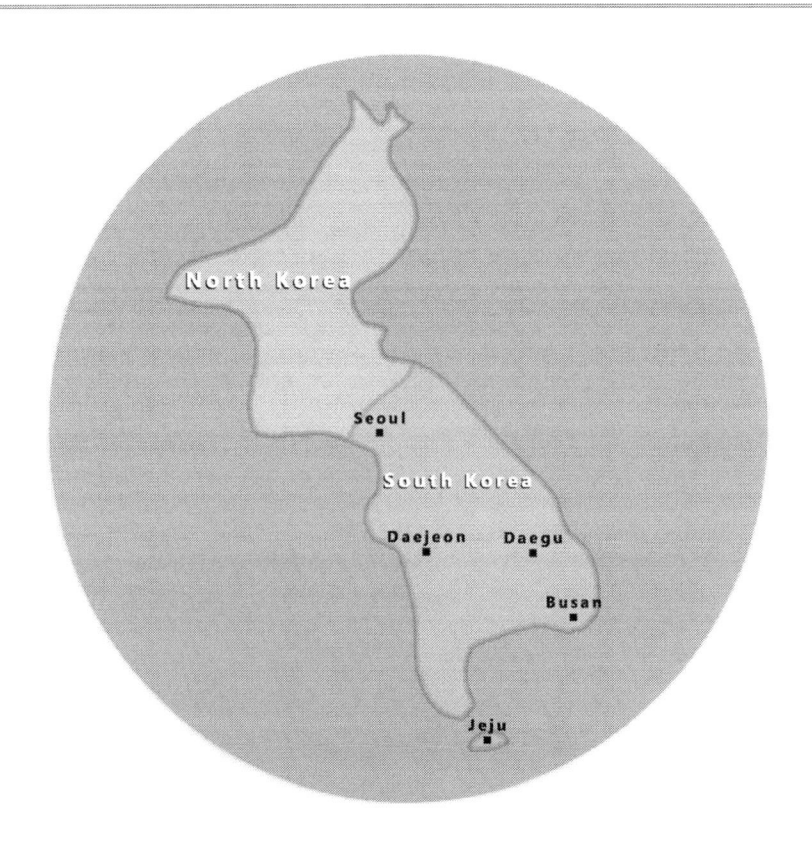

Preface

To everyone who's learning for their first time, welcome! To everyone else, welcome back! Before we dive into the language, it's important to first know a few things about the country that speaks it.

Korea is located to the west of Japan, and it shares a border with the eastern part of China.

Originally, Korea was one country, but the end of the Korean War in 1953 resulted in the two sides separating into North Korea and South Korea. "Why?" To put it simply, North Korea and South Korea had some serious disagreements that led to the Korean War starting in the first place.

Both North Koreans and South Koreans speak the same Korean language, but decades of being divided from each other caused separate dialects to emerge, and the way each country spoke the same language began to become more different. For comparison, you can think of North Korean speech to South Korean speech as being what British English is to American English; people from both countries can understand each other fine, but have their own distinct differences in pronunciation, and vocabulary.

For this book (and like most other Korean language books), we will be learning the Korean language as spoken in South Korea. But before we dive into Korean, let's start by learning a little bit about the country of South Korea.

- Full name: 대한민국 (shortened to 한국)

- Population: 50 million

- Current capital: Seoul

- Language: Korean – of course!

Korea shares a lot of its history with its neighbor, China. A large portion of the Korean vocabulary originally came from Chinese as well, although the sounds of these words were changed as they were brought into Korea. Still, although Korea has adopted much of its vocabulary from Chinese, and some of its grammar from Japanese, it is unrelated to either languages; Korean is completely unique from any other language. This makes it even more interesting.

We'll be learning to speak Korean through this book, as well as read and write it. If you can't yet read or write Korean, no worries! We'll be covering everything about the written language in the next few sections.

Preface

Approximately 80 million people speak Korean natively worldwide. Including non-native speakers, and people currently learning to speak Korean (such as yourself), that number is much larger.

Korean Sentence Structure

The Korean language works differently from other languages. For comparison, let's take a look at a simple sentence in English:

"I kicked the ball."
S V   O

The English language uses a S.V.O. sentence structure – **S**ubject, **V**erb, and **O**bject. This means that the subject comes first ("I"), followed by the verb ("kicked"), and then the object ("the ball").

↪ what the verb refers to

However, the Korean language uses a S.O.V. sentence structure – **S**ubject, **O**bject, and **V**erb.

Here's the same sentence written again, but using Korean sentence structure:

"I   ball   kicked."
저는   공을   찼습니다.
S   O   V

You'll see in future lessons how sentence structure works, and it's not that complicated once you've practiced with it. As I mentioned, there are over 80 million people speaking Korean currently, and I'm sure that you can learn it as well.

Why Korean?

But why are you learning Korean?

- Business?
- Travel? ✓
- Making friends? ✓
- Dating?
- For fun?
- "Because I can, that's why."

All of these are great reasons to study Korean. No matter your reason, you've truly chosen a fun, interesting, and useful language. I hope that this book will help you reach your own goals for learning Korean.

Preface

Note About the 니다 Form

If this is your first time learning Korean and you have never heard of the 니다 form before, you can feel free to skip this section and begin learning the Korean alphabet. I would like to discuss my usage of the 니다 form in this book.

This book has been designed to help people to learn the Korean language clearly and correctly, including proper grammar rules, and is not a phrase book. As such, I've chosen to introduce the 니다 form (a *very* polite way of speaking) first and foremost in this book, and only introduce the 요 form (used for the majority of informal speaking) toward the end, beginning with Chapter 19.

As a disclaimer, the 니다 form is not commonly used in real, regular Korean conversations. This is because it is a formal form, and is used most often for formal and business situations. I also discuss this in detail, including when to use the 니다 form, in Chapter 19. In addition, the 니다 form can sound awkward when used to friends or to people who are younger than the speaker. Regardless, I felt it was best to introduce it first for several reasons.

However, the 니다 form has several advantages over the 요 form for first time students of the Korean language.

1. It's simpler to learn, helping to ease the learner into Korean, to save mental resources for focusing on adjusting to the Korean alphabet and grammar.

2. It's better to be too polite than to be rude.

3. Students who have just begun studying Korean will likely not be able to hold a full conversation, so knowing the 요 form is unnecessary for introductory concepts.

While some students of Korean who have already passed the basics may see the 니다 form as useless, or counterproductive to learning Korean, I strongly believe that it is not, and decided to structure the book in this way after intensely comparing the options.

While studying the 요 form first can help to adjust the learner to conjugating and using it, it has its own share of problems that I feel outweighs its benefits – at least in the beginning.

1. It requires knowledge of several rules in order to conjugate. This can be intimidating to first time learners.

Preface

2. Although it is not rude in itself, when used in situations where formality is required, the 요 form can sound rude.

3. It should not be used to ask questions to people who are older. As such, the learner must also learn honorific grammar and vocabulary in order to properly speak using the 요 form.

Nevertheless, I understand the importance of knowing the 요 form in order to hold a real conversation in Korean. Although it is introduced late (Chapter 19), I have included every conversation from every chapter re-written using the 요 form in the back of this book, for practice and also for study.

My ultimate goal is for this book to give you a comprehensive introduction to the Korean language – consider it a solid stone step up a tall mountain. I hope that you can trust my methods long enough to be able to take over on your own.

Good luck in your language learning, and feel free to contact me with any questions or comments at any time (just please don't call me late at night when I'm sleeping).

Introduction to Hangul

What is Hangul?

"Hangul" is the name of the *writing system* used all throughout Korea, both in South Korea and in North Korea. Specifically, it's an *alphabet*, meaning that it's made up of *consonants* and *vowels*, just like the English language.

Before the 1500s in Korea, there was no way of writing the Korean language. Instead, wealthy and educated Koreans would simply learn Chinese if they wanted to read and write. Because the Chinese language could only be studied by those with money and prestige, the majority of Korea was unfortunately illiterate. But all of this changed with the creation of the Korean alphabet, known as *Hangul*.

Hangul was introduced to Korea in 1446 by King Sejong (세종대왕), who also happens to be one of the most famous people in all of Korean history. This event was extremely important in the development of the Korean language, and allowed even the poorest Korean to read and write due to Hangul's simplicity.

Do I Need to Learn Hangul?

The short answer is "yes." The long answer is also "yes." The only truly reliable way of writing and reading the Korean language is through Hangul. Although there are ways of using the English alphabet to spell Korean words, none of these are perfect, and all have their flaws – Hangul is the only true way of learning to correctly read and write Korean.

There are several systems available for writing the Korean language with the English alphabet, and yet none of them can correctly capture the sound, spelling, and meaning of the original word written at the same time.

Introduction to Hangul

For example, take the Korean word 독립문 ("Independence Gate"). Depending on which system you are using, it could be written as Dongnimmun, Toklipmun, or even Dog-Rib-Moon, among several others. While one system might preserve the actual sound of the word (Dongnimmun), it loses the original spelling in the process. A different system may preserve the original spelling (Toklipmun), but loses the actual sound. And while another system may preserve the original spelling and the original sound (Dog-Rib-Moon), it looks completely silly. In short, there is no substitute for learning to read and write Hangul.

Hangul is an Alphabet

Fortunately for you, Hangul is simple. As I mentioned, it's an alphabet. As such, you only need to learn the letters in order to be able to construct every sound possible in the Korean language.

Although Hangul might look like complex symbols, such as Chinese, each syllable is composed of simple consonants and vowels. There are 10 unique vowels and 14 basic consonants in Hangul, making a total of 24 letters (contrast this with English which has 26 letters). Just like in English, consonants combine with vowels to form *syllables*, and words.

Syllables are written one letter at a time, and letters are written in order from *left to right*, and *top to bottom*.

Each syllable is written as a single *block*. For example, the word 한글 ("Hangul") is made up of two separate blocks, which are actually separate syllables – 한 and 글. The first syllable, 한, is made of three letters (ㅎ, ㅏ, and ㄴ). The second syllable, 글, is also made of three letters (ㄱ, ㅡ, and ㄹ). Although we haven't learned what these letters mean yet, for now take note that letters – vowels and consonants – combine to form blocks of syllables. These syllables then combine to form words and sentences.

I'll be with you through our entire process of learning Hangul and the Korean language in this book. Take your time with these lessons, and learn each new letter as well as you can. Having a solid grasp of Hangul will greatly help you later on with the lessons, as well as with your own personal goals of mastering the Korean language.

Basic Consonants and Vowels

Before we start covering all of the different letters, let's first take a look at the basic structure of Hangul. To begin, we'll take a look at three consonants and one vowel. We'll learn how to combine consonants with vowels to create our first syllables.

Introduction to Hangul

ㄱ ㄱ

Type: Consonant
Pronunciation: This is similar to a "k" or "g." However, it is not strong like a "k" in "**k**ite," nor is it strong like a "g" in "**g**reat." It's a bit *softer*, and somewhere between a "k" and a "g." To keep things simple, let's call it a "g."

Number of Strokes: 1
Stroke Order: Starting from the top left, draw a single line to the right, and without lifting your writing instrument, curve down.

What is Stroke Order?

Before going any further, let's take a moment to talk about *stroke order*. Every letter in Korean has a certain order in which it must be drawn. Think of stroke order like following a recipe; although you know what the end result should be, you have to make sure you get there by adding ingredients in the right order. Having proper stroke order is essential to producing good, legible Korean letters. Incorrect stroke order can easily result in the letter looking like something else – take my word on this for now.

It is much easier to learn proper stroke order in the beginning than to try to fix it later. Take care to practice proper stroke order from the beginning and you will thank me later.

Since it's difficult to compare the Korean alphabet with English sounds (such as in the above letter ㄱ), all sounds in this book will be compared to *American English* as it is the most widely taught and used version of English internationally.

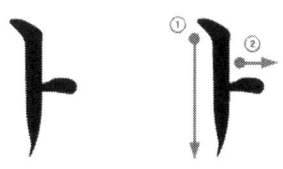

ㅏ ㅑ

Type: Vowel
Pronunciation: This is similar to an "a," as in the word "l**a**w" or "c**a**r." You can also think of it as the "ah" sound you might say when you've realized something.

Number of Strokes: 2
Stroke Order: Starting from the top, draw a single line down. Then draw a second, shorter line beginning from the middle of the first, going to the right.

Introduction to Hangul

ㄴ　ㄴ

Type: Consonant
Pronunciation: This is similar to an "n," such as in the word "**n**ow."

Number of Strokes: 1
Stroke Order: Starting from the top, draw a line down, and without lifting your writing instrument, continue drawing to the right.

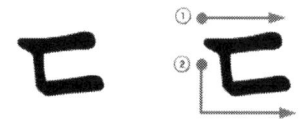

ㄷ　ㄷ

Type: Consonant
Pronunciation: This is similar to a "t" or "d." However, it is not strong like a "t" in "**t**en," nor is it strong like a "d" in "**d**og." It's a bit *softer*, and somewhere between a "t" and a "d." To keep things simple, let's call it a "d."

Number of Strokes: 2
Stroke Order: Starting from the top left, draw a single line to the right. Start a second line from the left end of the first line, moving down then right, just like you did earlier when drawing ㄴ.

Making Syllables

Now that we've got a few consonants and a vowel to work with, let's try making some syllables. Remember that a syllable, just like in English, consists of at least one vowel and at least one consonant.

Try to see what the following syllables will sound like, before reading their explanations. You can do this by covering the right side of the page as you complete each one.

ㄱ + ㅏ = ?

Answer: "ga"

ㄴ + ㅏ = ?

Answer: "na"

ㄷ + ㅏ = ?

Answer: "da"

Introduction to Hangul

Remember that ㄱ is not a strong "k" or a strong "g," and ㄷ is not a strong "t" or a strong "d." These sounds are softer, and somewhere between these two sounds.

As you can already see, many sounds in Korean do not have exact English equivalents. This is why it's best to learn Korean through Hangul, instead of through writing the language with English or another writing system. Being able to pronounce Hangul correctly will greatly improve your overall Korean pronunciation.

But syllables in Hangul aren't written like "ㄱ + ㅏ," so we need to learn the proper way to write them. Remember that Hangul uses blocks of syllables to create words. These blocks are formed in a few ways. Let's take a look at what the above examples would look like written in Hangul as real syllable blocks.

가　나　다

Each of these syllable blocks contains at least one consonant and at least one vowel. Since these are our first basic syllables, they each contain only one consonant and only one vowel. Later on we'll learn how to make more complex syllables using more letters.

Notice also how each of these is written – the consonant is on the left, and the vowel is on the right. This is due to the vowel that we used. The vowel that is used in a consonant will determine the way that a syllable block is written. For *vertical vowels*, such as ㅏ in the above examples, here's the block form used to write them.

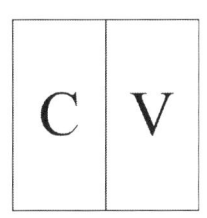

| C | V |

For block forms represented in this book, "C" represents a *consonant* and "V" represents a *vowel*.

Let's re-write our first example (ㄱ + ㅏ) as a real syllable using the above block form.

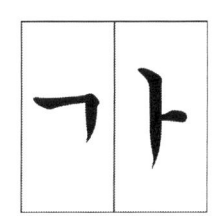

| 가 |

Introduction to Hangul

This is what we get, but it looks a bit awkward, kind of like a robot wrote it. To make it more natural, the ㄱ is stretched out longer to make it match closer to the height of the ㅏ. Here's how it will be written:

가

And just as English will have different ways of writing the alphabet (different styles or fonts), Korean will too. This is another reason why it's important to learn the right stroke order. As long as you know the correct stroke order for a letter, you will be able to read Hangul written in any possible style.

Before moving on, practice writing a few syllables on your own.

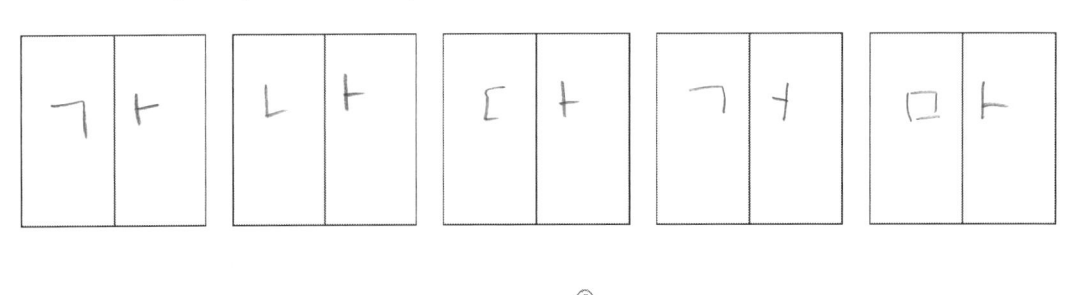

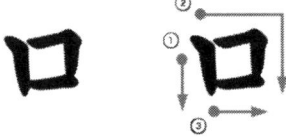

| 가 | 나 | 다 | 거 | 마 |

ㅁ

Type: Consonant
Pronunciation: This is pronounced like an "m," as in the word "**m**other."

Number of Strokes: 3
Stroke Order: Starting from the top left, draw a single line down. Start a second line from the top of the first line, going to the right and then downward like drawing a ㄱ. Start the third line from the bottom of the first line, going to the right and connecting with the second line.

Be especially careful with the stroke order on ㅁ, as drawing it the wrong order (or just drawing a square) can easily cause it to appear as a different letter (ㅇ, which we will learn soon).

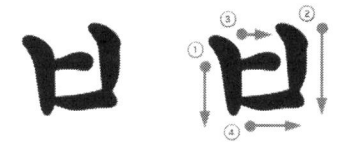

Introduction to Hangul

ㅂ

Type: Consonant
Pronunciation: This is similar to a "p" or "b." However, it is not strong like a "p" in "**p**ark," nor is it strong like a "b" in "**b**at." It's a bit *softer*, and somewhere between a "p" and a "b." To keep things simple, let's call it a "b."

Number of Strokes: 4
Stroke Order: Starting from the top left, draw a single line down. Start a second line parallel to the first, from the top, also going down. Start a third line from the middle of the first line, going to the right and connecting to the middle of the second line. Start a fourth line from the bottom of the first line, going to the right and connecting to the bottom of the second line.

ㅅ

Type: Consonant
Pronunciation: This is pronounced like "s," such as in the word "**s**nake."

Number of Strokes: 2
Stroke Order: Starting from the top, draw a slightly curved line down sideways and to the left. Start a second line, also slightly curved, from the top of the first line, going sideways and to the right. Both lines should curve inward.

ㅈ

Type: Consonant
Pronunciation: This is similar to a "ch" or "j." However, it is not strong like a "ch" in "**ch**erry," nor is it strong like a "j" in "**j**ob." It's a bit *softer*, and somewhere between a "ch" and a "j." To keep things simple, let's call it a "j."

Number of Strokes: 3

Introduction to Hangul

Stroke Order: Starting from the top left, draw a line to the right. Start a second line from the middle of the first line, going down and to the left. Start a third line again from the middle of the first line, going down and to the right. You can think of this letter as a flat line sitting on top of a ㅅ. Just like ㅅ, make sure to curve the two bottom lines inward slightly.

> **Advanced**
>
> You might also see this letter written in the above way; either way is fine. To draw it this way, start the first stroke the same way, but begin the second line from the right end of the first line. The third stroke will then instead begin from the middle of the second stroke. Here, the second stroke will curve, just like for ㅅ, but the third stroke will curve in the opposite direction. Feel free to write this letter either way you'd prefer.

Type: Consonant
Pronunciation: This is pronounced similar to an "h," as in the word "**h**all."

Number of Strokes: 3
Stroke Order: Starting from the top, draw a short line downward. Start the second stroke on the left, going to the right, and connecting with the first stroke in the middle. The third stroke is simply a circle, but you should start drawing it from the very top, going counterclockwise.

This consonant might remind you of a stick figure's head wearing a pointed hat.

> **Advanced**
>
> You might also see this letter written in the above way; either way is fine. To draw it this way, start the first stroke by going parallel to the second stroke, instead of perpendicular to it. The rest is completed the same way.

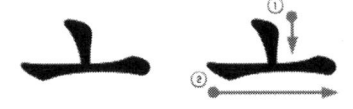

Type: Vowel
Pronunciation: This is pronounced like an "o," as in the word "**o**ld."

Introduction to Hangul

Number of Strokes: 2
Stroke Order: Starting from the top, draw a short line downward. Start the second stroke on the left, going to the right, and connecting with the first stroke in the middle. It will look like the top part of ㅎ, only larger.

When you say this vowel, your lips will round into an "o" shape.

Now that we've introduced this new vowel (ㅗ), there's an additional block form we can use to create syllables with. Previously, we learned the following method for *vertical vowels*, such as ㅏ.

C	V

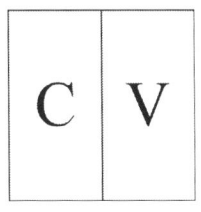

But now we can also make syllables using *horizontal vowels*, such as ㅗ. Here's what that block form would look like:

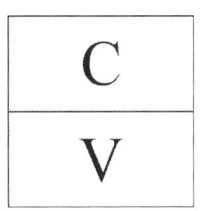

C
V

Using this format, let's take the letters ㅁ ("m") and ㅗ ("o") and combine them together. This would then be pronounced as "mo."

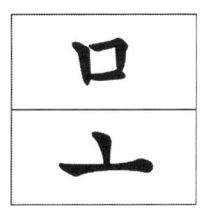

ㅁ
ㅗ

This can then be written on its own to look like:

모

23

Introduction to Hangul

Reading Practice

Using every letter that we've covered so far (ㄱ, ㅏ, ㄴ, ㄷ, ㅁ, ㅂ, ㅈ, ㅅ, ㅎ, ㅗ), let's make some new syllables. Try to read them on your own before looking at the explanations.

ㄱ + ㅗ = 고

Answer: "go"

ㄱ + ㅏ = 가

Answer: "ga"

ㄴ + ㅗ = 노

Answer: "no"

ㄴ + ㅏ = 나

Answer: "na"

ㄷ + ㅗ = 도

Answer: "do"

ㄷ + ㅏ = 다

Answer: "da"

ㅁ + ㅗ = 모

Answer: "mo"

ㅁ + ㅏ = 마

Answer: "ma"

ㅂ + ㅗ = 보

Answer: "bo"

ㅂ + ㅏ = 바

Answer: "ba"

ㅈ + ㅗ = 조

Answer: "jo"

ㅈ + ㅏ = 자

Answer: "ja"

ㅅ + ㅗ = 소

Answer: "so"

ㅅ + ㅏ = 사

Answer: "sa"

ㅎ + ㅗ = 호

Answer: "ho"

ㅎ + ㅏ = 하

Answer: "ha"

Above is every possible combination of two-letter syllables that we can make using only the letters that what we've learned so far.

Introduction to Hangul

Practice writing your own syllables below, using what we've learned so far.

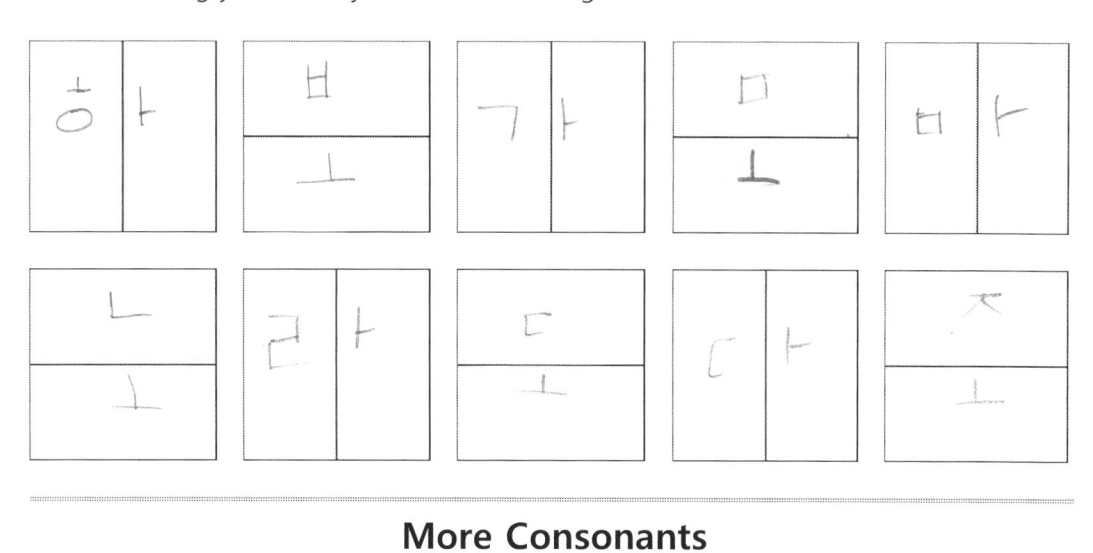

More Consonants

Believe it or not, we've almost finished learning all of the basic consonants in Hangul. There are just two more, which we'll cover now.

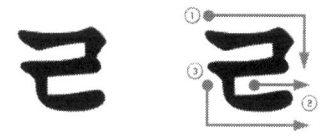

ㄹ

Type: Consonant
Pronunciation: This is pronounced like an "l" sound, such as in the word "long." However, when you say ㄹ, position your *tongue* as if you were saying a "d" (such as in "**d**og") – then say "l" instead. It will come out sounding like a cross between an "l" and an "r," and this is exactly what you will want it to sound like.

Number of Strokes: 3
Stroke Order: Starting from the top left, draw a single line to the right, and without lifting your writing instrument, curve down – just like ㄱ. Start the second line, a single straight line going from left to right and connecting at the end of the first line. The third line will start from the left side of the second line, going downward, then to the right – just like when drawing ㄴ.

Although it may be tempting, do not write this letter with one stroke. It's essential to maintain the correct stroke order. Even if the end result might appear similar to you, it will not look correct to the trained eye of a native Korean speaker.

Introduction to Hangul

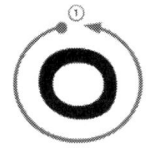

ㅇ ⓞ

Type: Consonant
Pronunciation: This is pronounced "ng," such as in the word "so**ng**" or "ha**ng**," but only when ㅇ is used at the *end* of a syllable.

Number of Strokes: 1
Stroke Order: Start from the top, and draw a circle going counterclockwise (just like you did for ㅎ).

Although ㅇ is pronounced "ng" at the end of a syllable, when it's used at the *beginning* of a syllable it has no sound. We'll go over how to use this letter in detail soon.

Vowel Sounds

So far we've learned how to combine consonants with vowels to form syllable blocks, but what if we want to have a vowel sound by itself? What if we only want to say the sound that ㅏ makes?

We learned that a syllable must have at least one consonant and one vowel. In this case, we can use ㅇ as the consonant, which has no sound when used at the *beginning* of a syllable (its "ng" sound only applies when ㅇ appears at the *end* of a syllable, which we will cover soon).

ㅇ + ㅏ = 아

Answer: "a"

ㅇ + ㅗ = 오

Answer: "o"

Remember that it would be incorrect to write ㅏ or ㅗ on their own, because every syllable in Korean must have at least one consonant and one vowel.

Quick Reading Practice

Practice reading the following syllables. Just as before, first try reading them on your own before looking at their answers.

Introduction to Hangul

ㄹ + ㅗ = 로

Answer: "lo"

ㅇ + ㅗ = 오

Answer: "o"

ㄹ + ㅏ = 라

Answer: "la"

ㅇ + ㅏ = 아

Answer: "a"

Three Letter Syllables

Up until now we've only been working with syllables using two letters – one consonant and one vowel. We need to learn how to make syllables with *two consonants* and one vowel. Let's look at the syllable blocks we can use to do this.

Like before, the type of syllable block you will choose depends on whether you're using a *vertical vowel* (such as ㅏ) or a *horizontal vowel* (such as ㅗ).

For vertical vowels, we have this syllable block:

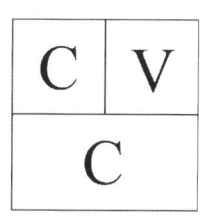

C	V
C	

(C | V on top, C on bottom spanning both)

And for horizontal vowels, we have this syllable block:

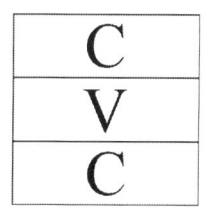

C
V
C

Let's take a look at some examples of various three letter syllables. Try to guess what they will sound like on your own first, before looking at the answers.

ㄹ + ㅏ + ㅇ = 랑

Answer: "lang"

ㄱ + ㅏ + ㄴ = 간

Answer: "gan"

27

Introduction to Hangul

ㅁ + ㅗ + ㅁ = 몸

Answer: "mom"

ㅇ + ㅏ + ㅇ = 앙

Answer: "ang"

ㅇ + ㅗ + ㅇ = 옹

Answer: "ong"

ㄴ + ㅗ + ㄹ = 놀

Answer: "nol"

ㅅ + ㅗ + ㄴ = 손

Answer: "son"

ㄴ + ㅏ + ㄱ = 낙

Answer: "nag"

ㄷ + ㅏ + ㅂ = 답

Answer: "dab"

ㅈ + ㅗ + ㄱ = 족

Answer: "jog"

More Vowels

We've done everything so far using only two vowels, ㅏ and ㅗ. Let's go over some more vowels we can use to expand our Korean.

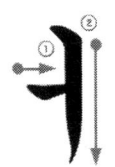

ㅓ

Type: Vowel
Pronunciation: The vowel this sound makes is similar to "uh" – as if you're thinking of something. You can also think of it as the "uh" sound at the beginning of the word "**u**p."

Number of Strokes: 2
Stroke Order: Starting from the left, draw a short line going to the right, which will touch the middle of the second line. Draw a longer second line from the top, going down.

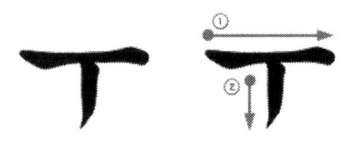

ㅜ

Type: Vowel
Pronunciation: This is pronounced like the "u" sound in the word "gl**u**e."

Introduction to Hangul

Number of Strokes: 2
Stroke Order: Starting from the left, draw a line to the right. Start a second line from the middle of the first line, going down.

Type: Vowel
Pronunciation: This is pronounced like "oo" in the word "g**oo**d."

Number of Strokes: 1
Stroke Order: Start from the left and draw a single straight line to the right.

Type: Vowel
Pronunciation: This is pronounced like "ee" in the word "tr**ee**."

Number of Strokes: 1
Stroke Order: Start from the top and draw a single straight line down.

More Practice

Try to read the following syllables on your own before reading their pronunciation.

ㅁ + ㅓ = 머

Answer: "muh"

ㄱ + ㅜ = 구

Answer: "gu"

ㅂ + ㅡ = 브

Answer: "boo" ("oo" as in "g**oo**d")

ㅎ + ㅣ = 히

Answer: "hee"

Introduction to Hangul

ㅅ + ㅣ

When you combine ㅅ with ㅣ you get a slightly different result than what you might expect. Instead of becoming "see" (like the English word) it actually becomes "shee" (like the word "she" in English).

ㅅ + ㅣ = 시

Answer: "shee"

ㅅ + ㅣ + ㄴ = 신

Answer: "sheen"

ㅅ + ㅣ + ㄹ = 실

Answer: "sheel"

ㅅ + ㅣ + ㅇ = 싱

Answer: "sheeng"

ㅅ + ㅣ + ㅁ = 심

Answer: "sheem"

ㅅ + ㅣ + ㄱ = 식

Answer: "sheeg"

ㅅ + ㅣ + ㅂ = 십

Answer: "sheeb"

Practice writing a few syllables using the following block forms.

Introduction to Hangul

Your First Korean Words

We've covered several consonants and vowels, and now it's time to start learning some real words (just a few). We'll actually be going over these words again later in the lessons (so don't stress too much about memorizing them), but take a moment to look over them here and become familiar with as many of them as you can. Just like before, try reading them on your own before looking at the answers.

한글 "Hangul" (the Korean alphabet)

Answer: "han-gool" ("oo" as in "g**oo**d")

한국 "Korea"

Answer: "han-guk" ("u" as in "gl**u**e")

저 "I" or "me"

Answer: "juh"

당신 "You"

Answer: "dang-sheen"

More Vowels

Let's continue learning the rest of the vowels in 한글.

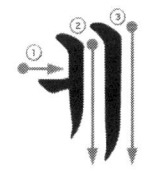

Type: Vowel
Pronunciation: This is pronounced like the "e" in the word "**e**gg." You can also think of it as an "eh" sound.

Number of Strokes: 3
Stroke Order: Start from the left, drawing a short line to the right (this will touch the middle of the second line). The second line starts from the top, going down and perpendicular to the first line. Begin the third line from the top, parallel to the second line, going down.

Introduction to Hangul

ㅐ ㅐ

Type: Vowel
Pronunciation: This is pronounced like the "e" in the word "**e**gg."

Number of Strokes: 3
Stroke Order: Start from the top left, drawing a line straight down. Draw the second line starting from the middle of the first line, going to the right (this will touch the middle of the third line, connecting the middles of the first and third line together). Draw the third line parallel to the first line, starting from the top and going down.

ㅐ is only pronounced *slightly* differently from ㅔ, with the lips a tiny bit wider apart, and actually the difference is not very important. Even many Koreans are not able to distinguish them by sound (but will be able to distinguish the spelling). Therefore, although ㅐ is slightly different from ㅔ, feel free to pronounce ㅐ the same way as ㅔ ("eh") until you are more comfortable with distinguishing it.

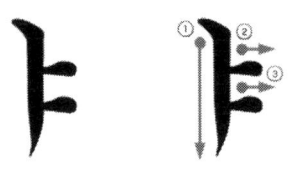

ㅑ ㅑ

Type: Vowel
Pronunciation: This is pronounced like "ya," such as in the expression "**ya**'ll."

Number of Strokes: 3
Stroke Order: Start from the top, drawing a line straight down. Draw the second line starting from 1/3 down the first line, going to the right. Draw the third line starting from 2/3 down the first line, also going to the right, and parallel to the second line.

You can also think of this vowel as being ㅣ combined with ㅏ ("ee" + "a" = "ya").

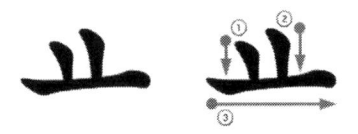

ㅛ ㅛ

Type: Vowel
Pronunciation: This is pronounced "yo," like the slang word "**yo**."

32

Introduction to Hangul

Number of Strokes: 3
Stroke Order: Start from the top and draw a line down (this will connect at the point 1/3 of the way to the right on the third line). Begin the second line parallel to the first, going down (this will connect at the point 2/3 of the way to the right on the third line). Draw the third line from left to right, connecting at the end of the first and second lines. Except for having a different stroke order, this letter is a ㅏ turned on its back.

You can also think of this vowel as being ㅣ combined with ㅗ ("ee" + "o" = "yo").

More Practice

Try to read the following syllables on your own before looking at their pronunciations.

ㅇ + ㅔ = 에

Answer: "e" ("e" in "**e**gg")

ㅇ + ㅐ = 애

Answer: "e" (the "e" sound in "**e**gg")

ㅇ + ㅑ = 야

Answer: "ya"

ㅇ + ㅛ = 요

Answer: "yo"

ㄱ + ㅔ = 게

Answer: "ge"

ㄱ + ㅑ = 갸

Answer: "gya"

ㄱ + ㅛ = 교

Answer: "gyo"

ㄹ + ㅔ = 레

Answer: "le"

ㄹ + ㅏ = 라

Answer: "la"

ㄹ + ㅛ = 료

Answer: "lyo"

ㅈ + ㅐ = 재

Answer: "je"

ㅈ + ㅑ = 쟈

Answer: "jya"

ㅈ + ㅛ = 죠

Answer: "jyo"

ㅅ + ㅑ = 샤

Answer: "shya"*

33

Introduction to Hangul

ㅅ + ㅛ = 쇼

Answer: "shyo"*

*ㅅ will actually become "sh" not only before ㅣ, but also before ㅑ and ㅛ.

Let's start taking a look at some examples that are a bit longer.

ㅇ + ㅔ + ㄹ + ㅂ + ㅣ + ㅅ + ㅡ = 엘비스

Answer: "el-bee-soo" ("oo" as in "good")

ㅎ + ㅔ + ㅇ + ㅓ + ㅁ = 헤엄

Answer: "he-uhm"

ㅇ + ㅐ + ㄱ + ㅈ + ㅔ = 액제

Answer: "eg-je"

ㅁ + ㅐ + ㄱ + ㅈ + ㅜ = 맥주

Answer: "meg-ju"

ㅅ + ㅏ + ㄴ + ㅑ + ㅇ = 사냥

Answer: "sa-nyang"

ㄴ + ㅑ + ㅁ + ㄴ + ㅑ + ㅁ = 냠냠

Answer: "nyam-nyam"

ㅇ + ㅛ + ㄱ + ㅈ + ㅗ = 욕조

Answer: "yog-jo"

ㅎ + ㅏ + ㄱ + ㄱ + ㅛ = 학교

Answer: "hag-gyo"

ㅎ + ㅛ + ㅈ + ㅓ + ㅇ = 효정

Answer: "hyo-juhng"

Goodbye Romanization

"It's not you. It's me." As you've probably noticed already, writing Korean using Romanization (using the English alphabet) is a bit messy, and as we go on it will grow even further away from the actual Korean sounds. This is why from now on, there will be no more Romanization used in this book, with the exception of teaching pronunciation of new sounds. By the start of Chapter 1, it will be completely absent from this book.

It's important to become comfortable with how 한글 actually sounds, and to steer away from writing or even reading the sounds written with the English alphabet.

It might be a bit difficult at first, but I promise you that your Korean will improve much more by learning the language exclusively through 한글.

Now let's continue learning the rest of the letters in 한글.

Introduction to Hangul

New Vocabulary

Let's go over just a few more words that we can learn using the letters we know so far. Like before, don't stress about memorizing these words, as we'll be covering them again later in this book.

네	"yes"
아니요	"no"
개	"dog"
고양이	"cat"
용	"dragon"

Vowels.... Again?

We're almost at the finish line. We can see the light at the end of the tunnel. There are only a few more vowels left in 한글 to learn.

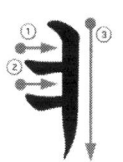

ㅋ ㅖ

Type: Vowel
Pronunciation: This is a combination of a "y" sound with ㅓ, so it is pronounced like "**yuh**."

Number of Strokes: 3
Stroke Order: Draw a short line from left to right (this line will connect 1/3 down the third line). Draw a second line below, parallel to the first, going from left to right (this line will connect 2/3 down the third line). Draw the third line starting from the top, going straight down and touching the first two lines.

Knowing how to pronounce ㅓ will make pronouncing this letter simple. You can also think of this vowel as being ㅣ combined with ㅓ ("ee" + "uh" = "yuh").

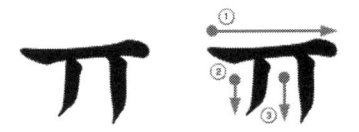

Introduction to Hangul

ㅠ

Type: Vowel
Pronunciation: This is a combination of a "y" sound with ㅜ, so it is pronounced "**yu**" (like the English word "you").

Number of Strokes: 3
Stroke Order: Start from the top left, drawing a line to the right. Begin the second line from the point 1/3 of the way to the right on the first line. Begin the third line parallel to the second from the point 2/3 of the way to the right on the first line, going down. Except for having a different stroke order, this letter is a ㅗ turned upside down.

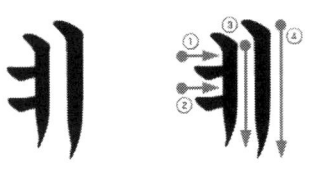

ㅖ

Type: Vowel
Pronunciation: This is a combination of a "y" sound with ㅔ, so it is pronounced "**ye**."

Number of Strokes: 4
Stroke Order: First draw a ㅕ, then draw a ㅣ parallel to the right of it.

You can also think of this vowel as being ㅣ combined with ㅔ ("ee" + "eh" = "yeh").

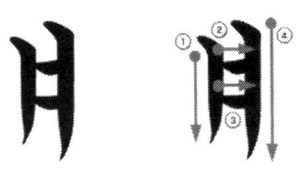

ㅒ

Type: Vowel
Pronunciation: This is a combination of a "y" sound with ㅐ, so it is pronounced "**ye**."

Number of Strokes: 4
Stroke Order: First draw a ㅑ, then draw a ㅣ parallel to the right of it.

You can also think of this vowel as being ㅣ combined with ㅐ ("ee" + "eh" = "yeh").

Introduction to Hangul

More Practice

Try reading the following syllables on your own.

여 유 예 얘 열 육 레 쟤 벼 규 계 걔

Blending Syllables Together

We learned that ㅇ has no sound when at the *beginning* of a syllable. Because of this, it essentially acts like an *empty space*. Therefore, whatever letter that comes before it will replace it, as if it never existed.

미국인 "an American"

We can read this word as **미 + 국 + 인**, right? Yes. But if you wanted to say it at a regular speed, what would happen? Try saying it yourself. Since the ㅇ in the beginning of 인 will have no sound, this allows the sound *before* it to flow through, taking its place.

미국인 would therefore be said **미구긴** when speaking at a normal speed, to make it easier to pronounce.

Let's take a look at some more examples of this happening.

Spelling	Pronunciation
백인	배긴
믿어	미더
사람이	사라미
할아버지	하라버지
만이	마니
걸어	거러
발음	바름
한옥	하녹
연어	여너
한우	하누

Before we move on, practice writing a few syllables using the block forms we've learned. You can combine any characters that you'd like. The more you practice, the faster you'll be able to write and read, and the better you'll be able to learn Korean.

Introduction to Hangul

Four Letter Syllables

So far we've seen both two letter and three letter syllables. Now let's take a look at syllables that have four letters in them. Here's what the block form will look like for vertical, or for horizontal vowels.

For *vertical vowels*, we have this syllable block:

C	V
C	C

And for *horizontal vowels*, we have this syllable block:

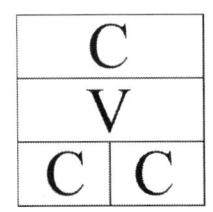

C
V
C C

Three consonants and *one vowel* will come together to form a four letter syllable. Here are some examples using four letter syllables, along with their pronunciations:

38

Introduction to Hangul

Spelling	Pronunciation
앉아	안자
읽은	일근
밝은	발근
삶이	살미
맑은	말근
흙을	흘글
값이	갑시
긁어	글거

For syllables that have two consonants on the bottom, one of them being ㄹ, and which are not followed by any other letter which might affect the pronunciation (such as being followed by ㅇ, allowing the sound to simply pass through), most of the time the consonant which is not ㄹ will be pronounced.

Some combinations you will see often are ㄺ, ㄻ, ㄼ, and ㅀ.

Spelling	Pronunciation
옮기다	옴기다
삶	삼
흙	흑
여덟*	여덜*

*Note that I said *most of the time*. The above example is a common exception to the rule.

New Vocabulary

Let's learn some more words. As before, don't worry about memorizing these words as we'll be going over them in later chapters.

안녕하세요.	"Hello."
미국인	"an American"
한국인	"a Korean"
삶	"life"

39

Introduction to Hangul

Let's take moment to practice writing some more syllables, using each of the possible forms. Try to make unique characters each time. As this is only practice, feel free to create any combination you'd like, provided it follows the rules for the block forms.

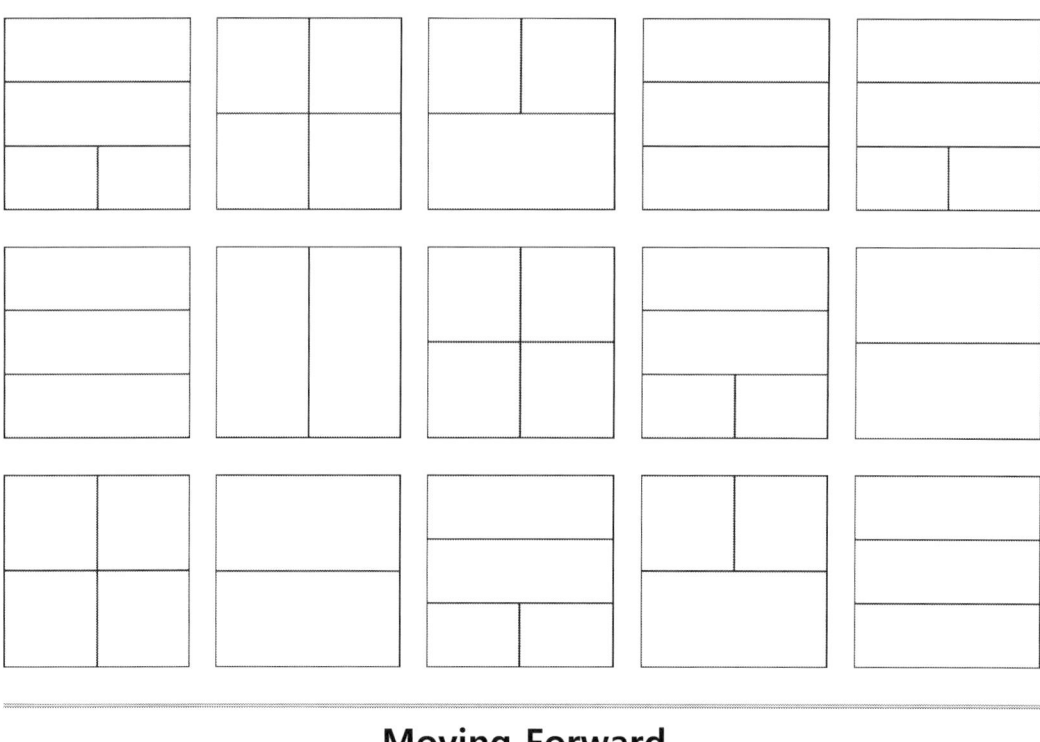

Moving Forward

Congratulations on learning all of the individual vowels and consonants in Korean. But wait, there's more! We still need to cover *double consonants* (when two copies of the same consonant combine together), *strong consonants* (when a consonant is pronounced with more force) and *diphthongs* (when more than one vowel combines together). But if you know the vowels and consonants we've learned so far, these should all be a piece of cake. I'll guide you through the next lesson as soon as you're ready to tackle it.

More Hangul

Take your time on these introductory lessons, and go through them slowly. 한글 can be difficult because it's an alphabet and there are numerous letters and rules to cover, but you'll be using it everywhere once we start learning Korean and it will become second nature. Once you're ready to move on, let's get started and finish learning everything you will need to know about 한글.

Double Consonants

A double consonant is simply two of the same consonant combined together. There are five of them to learn, but they shouldn't be a problem to remember. Let's learn them all at the same time.

ㄲ ㄸ ㅃ ㅆ ㅉ

Notice how each double consonant is composed of *two* of the same consonant – ㄱ, ㄷ, ㅂ, ㅅ, and ㅈ. In addition, they're drawn in the same space that one single consonant would normally take up.

Pronunciation: Each of these is pronounced the same way as their singular versions, but is spoken by *tensing* your mouth before saying them.

Before pronouncing a double consonant, take a *short, quick pause*. This will naturally cause the sound after the pause to come out *tensed*.

Stroke Order: Each of these is drawn the same way as their singular versions. Draw the left half first, then draw the right half.

For comparison, take a look at the following two syllables:

가 까

The left one is somewhere between a "ka" or "ga." Think of ㄲ as the "k" in the English word "s**k**a" – notice that while saying "ska" the "k" becomes tense because of its position in the word (coming after an "s"). This is what a double consonant sounds like.

다 따

Think of ㄸ as the "t" in the English word "s**t**op."

More Hangul

바 빠

Think of ㅃ as the "p" in the English word "s**p**a."

사 싸

Think of ㅆ as either of the "s" sounds in the English word "**sees**aw," or "**p**sycho." It's more of a hissing "s" sound than simply saying "**s**nake."

자 짜

Think of ㅉ as the "ch" sound in "got'**ch**a" ("got you").

Double Consonant Practice

Practice by reading the following sounds.

가 까 다 따 바 빠 사 싸 자 짜 고 꼬 도 또 보 뽀 소 쏘 조 쪼

New Vocabulary

Let's take a look at a few examples of words that use double consonants.

딸	"daughter"
빵	"bread"
쌀	"(uncooked) rice"
꼭	"surely," "certainly"
뿔	"horn(s)"
똥	"poop"
말씀	"words"
꿀	"honey"

More Hangul

Strong Consonants

A *strong consonant* is similar to a normal consonant, but pronounced with more force. Imagine saying 가, but putting more force into your voice when saying the consonant – it would come out sounding more like a strong "k," like the word "**k**ite." This is what a strong consonant is. There are only *four* to learn. Let's take a look at all of them before we go over them individually.

ㅋ ㅌ ㅍ ㅊ

Three of these four should be simple to learn, as they look similar to their normal versions.

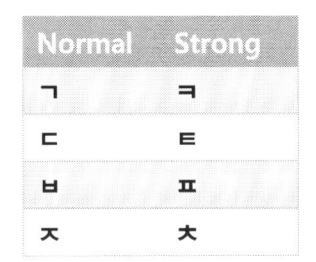

Normal	Strong
ㄱ	ㅋ
ㄷ	ㅌ
ㅂ	ㅍ
ㅈ	ㅊ

> **Adv** Another word for strong consonant is "aspirated consonant." Depending on what additional sources you use for studying Korean, you might see them referred to in this way.

ㅋ

Pronunciation: This is pronounced more strongly than a ㄱ, so you can think of it as a hard "k."

Number of Strokes: 2
Stroke Order: First draw a ㄱ. Start the second stroke from the left, going right, connecting with the middle of the first stroke.

43

More Hangul

ㅌ

Pronunciation: This is pronounced more strongly than a ㄷ, so you can think of it as a hard "t."

Number of Strokes: 3
Stroke Order: Draw the first line, on top, going from left to right. Start a second line parallel to the first and below it. Begin the third line from the left side of the first stroke, going down and touching the left side of the second stroke, and continuing a bit further. Without starting a fourth stroke, draw a straight line to the right.

> **Advanced** 
>
> You might also see this letter written in the above way; either way is fine. To draw it this way, simply draw the third line beginning from the left side of the second stroke. The rest is drawn in the same way.

ㅍ

Pronunciation: This is pronounced more strongly than a ㅂ, so you can think of it as a hard "p."

Number of Strokes: 4
Stroke Order: First draw a line on top, going to the right. Begin the second stroke from the first line, a bit to the right from the far-left side, going down. Start the third stroke also from the first line, parallel to the second, a bit to the left from the far-right side, going down. Draw the fourth line on the bottom, from left to right, touching the second and third strokes.

ㅊ

Pronunciation: This is pronounced more strongly than a ㅈ, so you can think of it as a hard "ch."

More Hangul

Number of Strokes: 4
Stroke Order: First draw a short line from the top middle, going down. Then draw a ㅈ attached to it.

A d v a n c e d

ㅊ ㅊ

You might also see this letter written in the above way; either way is fine. To draw it this way, simply draw the first stroke horizontally instead of vertically, going from left to right. The rest is drawn in the same way as normal.

Normal Consonants, Double Consonants, and Strong Consonants

Here's a useful trick. You can *see* the difference between a normal consonant, a double consonant, and a strong consonant by using a *piece of paper*.

Hold a single sheet of paper out in front of your mouth, and try saying the following three sounds one at a time.

가　까　카

The 카 should cause the piece of paper to *shake*. In comparison, the 가 will only cause the piece of paper to wobble *slightly*. However, the 까 should *not* cause the piece of paper to move noticeably at all.

This is because strong consonants require more energy to say, and therefore more air to say them. Double consonants, however, are made by taking a short, quick pause before saying them. As a result most of the air released when pronouncing a double consonant is *dissipated* – the air isn't leaving the mouth in a concentrated burst like it is for normal consonants or strong consonants.

Pay close attention to the different sounds made from normal consonants, double consonants, and strong consonants. Knowing the difference is *extremely* important, and words can easily be misunderstood if pronounced using the wrong one.

Although 불 means "fire," 뿔 means "horns," and 풀 can mean "grass" or "glue." Koreans can easily hear the differences between these sounds because they're accustomed to using them on a regular basis, and with practice so can you.

More Hangul

More Consonant Practice

Practice reading these syllables on your own.

가 까 카 다 따 타 바 빠 파 자 짜 차 고 꼬 코 도 또 토 보 뽀 포 조 쪼 초

Practice writing just a few more syllables, using double consonants and strong consonants.

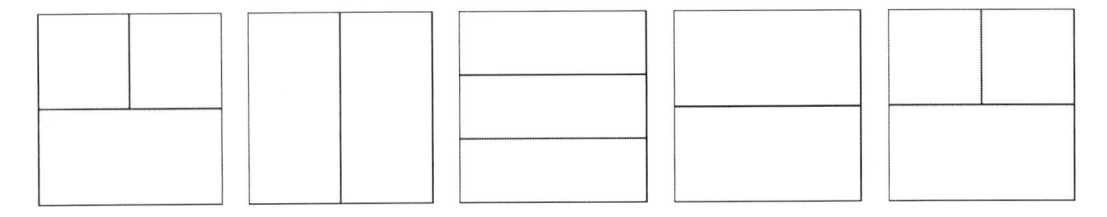

New Vocabulary

Here are a few new words to read over and practice. Notice how words using normal consonants, double consonants, and strong consonants can each have separate, unrelated meanings.

코	"nose"
털	"hair," "fur" (not on the head)
핸드폰	"cell phone" (literally, "hand phone")
검	"sword"
껌	"gum"
춤	"a dance"
컴퓨터	"computer"
덕	"moral"
떡	"rice cake"
턱	"chin"
베다	"to cut (into)"
빼다	"to remove"
패다	"to beat," "to bash"
자다	"to sleep"
짜다	"to be salty"
차다	"to kick"

More Hangul

Diphthongs

What is a *diphthong*? Well, it's nothing to be afraid of. A diphthong is a combination of more than one vowel into a single *new* vowel. Imagine taking a 오 sound (ㅗ) and mixing it with a 아 sound (ㅏ) – you'd get a "wa" sound, right? Right! And in Korean, there's an easy way to combine two vowels together into a new vowel. These combinations are called *diphthongs*.

Let's go over each of them. There are *seven* in total.

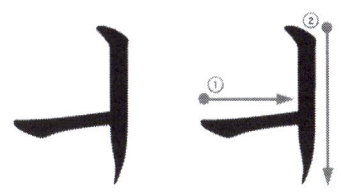

ㅢ

Pronunciation: This is a combination of ㅡ and ㅣ. It is pronounced the same way as saying 으 immediately followed by 이, quickly – as in "uh-ee."

Number of Strokes: 2
Stroke Order: First draw a ㅡ. Next, draw a ㅣ.

Although this diphthong is pronounced "uh-ee" when written as 의, when used with any other consonant besides ㅇ it becomes pronounced the same as ㅣ. For example, 희 is simply pronounced 히.

> **Adv** There's also one more situation where 의 is pronounced differently, and that's when it's used as the *Possessive Marker*. We'll learn about the Possessive Marker in Chapter 11.

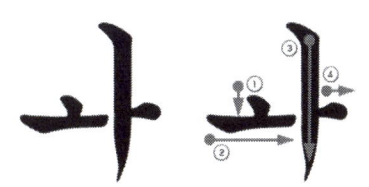

ㅘ

Pronunciation: This is a combination of ㅗ and ㅏ. It is pronounced the same way as saying 오 immediately followed by 아, quickly – as in "wa."

Number of Strokes: 4
Stroke Order: First draw a ㅗ. Next, draw a ㅏ.

More Hangul

Pronunciation: This is a combination of ㅜ and ㅓ. It is pronounced the same way as saying 우 immediately followed by 어, quickly – as in "u-uh" or the English word "whoa."

Number of Strokes: 4
Stroke Order: First draw a ㅜ. Next, draw a ㅓ.

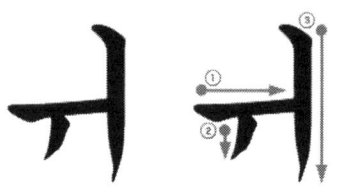

Pronunciation: This is a combination of ㅜ and ㅣ. It is pronounced the same way as saying 우 immediately followed by 이, quickly – as in "u-ee" or the French word "oui."

Number of Strokes: 3
Stroke Order: First draw a ㅜ. Next, draw a ㅣ.

Pronunciation: This is a combination of ㅗ and ㅐ. It is pronounced the same way as saying 오 immediately followed by 애, quickly – as in "o-e" or the English word "way."

Number of Strokes: 5
Stroke Order: First draw a ㅗ. Next, draw a ㅐ.

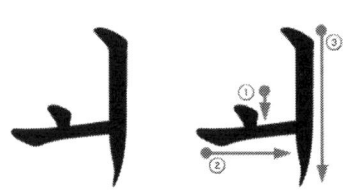

Pronunciation: This is a combination of ㅗ and ㅣ. However, it is pronounced differently than it may look. It is actually pronounced the same way as saying 오 immediately followed by ㅔ, quickly – as in "o-e" or the English word "way." Just like how ㅔ and ㅐ are pronounced similarly, ㅙ and ㅚ are similar as well; feel free to pronounce ㅚ the same way as ㅙ.

More Hangul

Number of Strokes: 3
Stroke Order: First draw a ㅗ. Next, draw a ㅣ.

> **Adv** You will never see a diphthong that is written combining ㅗ and ㅔ. It can't even be typed on a Korean keyboard. Instead, remember to use either ㅙ or ㅚ when writing.

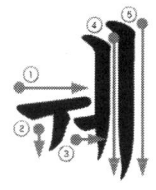

Pronunciation: This is a combination of ㅜ and ㅔ. It is pronounced the same way as saying 우 immediately followed by 에, quickly – as in "u-e."

Number of Strokes: 5
Stroke Order: First draw a ㅜ. Next, draw a ㅔ.

Practicing Diphthongs

Now that wasn't so bad, right? Practice reading these syllables on your own.

의	와	워	위	왜	외	웨
희	과	궈	귀	괘	괴	궤
긔	봐	줘	뒤	돼	뇌	쉐
흰	찰	꿩	원	괜	뵙	웬

New Vocabulary and Final Practice

Here are a few new words you can learn using diphthongs.

의사	"doctor"
희망	"hope"
과일	"fruit"
원	"Won" (the Korean currency)
귀	"ear"
왜	"why"
열쇠	"key"
웰빙	"healthy" (literally, "well being")

More Hangul

For a final exercise, before moving onto sound changes, practice writing 한글 using the following block forms. Try to use different letters for each syllable as much as possible, and incorporate diphthongs in several of them; to keep things simple it might be best at first to practice using diphthongs in syllable blocks with fewer letters (2 or 3).

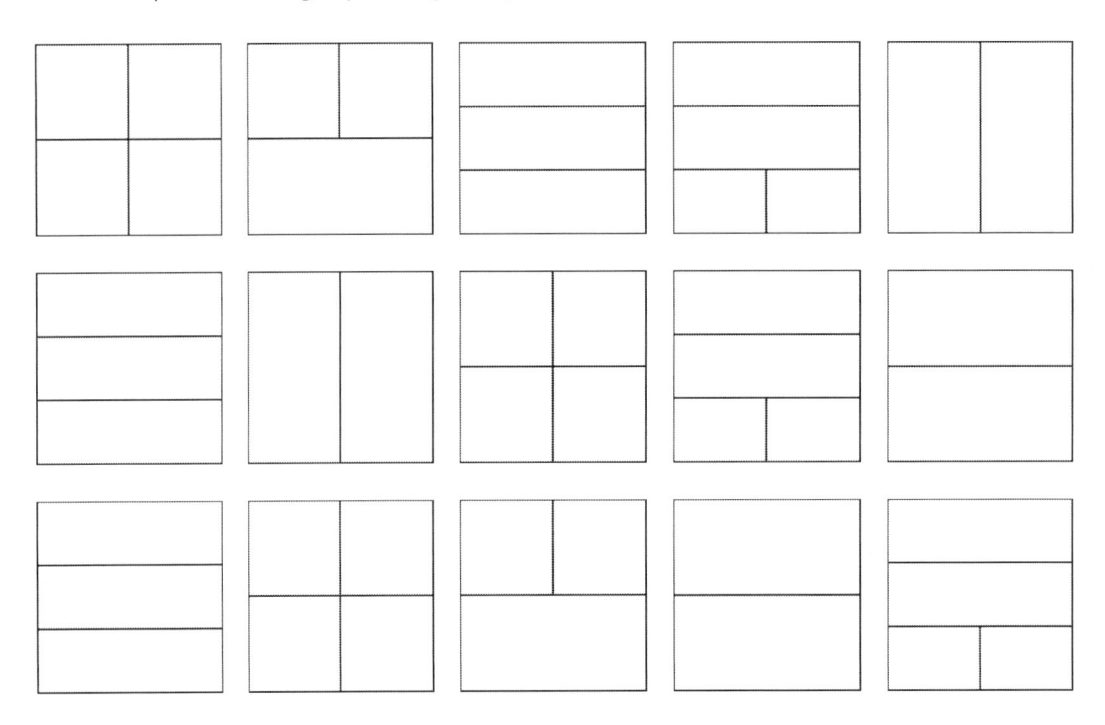

Of course, don't limit your 한글 practice to solely these exercises. Also don't limit yourself to using block forms when writing – they're only for helping you to adjust to the way that 한글 syllables are written. Practice writing in a notebook, on your own, as much as possible. If you have time, I'd also recommend copying down as much as you can from this book as you move through it, such as conversations and example sentences, in order to improve your writing even more.

Introduction to Sound Changes

Congratulations! We've now finished learning every basic consonant and vowel, every double consonant and strong consonant, and now every diphthong. In fact, there are no more letters left to learn in 한글. What remains are rules regarding how sounds are pronounced. Let me explain what that means.

Take this English sentence: "Nice to meet you."

First say it slowly: "Nice to meet you."

Next, say it at a normal speed: "Nice **t' mee'chu**."

The individual words haven't changed, but their sounds do because of their relationship to other sounds (for example, the 't' in "meet" coming before the 'y' in "you"). A similar thing happens in Korean. Of course, these changes occurred only to make the words easier to pronounce, just like in English. Imagine having to say "Nice to meet you," while pronouncing each individual word accurately, every time you wanted to say it. Although there are many rules for sound changes in Korean, they are for the good of everyone. Learning the rules for sound changes as thoroughly as possible will greatly improve your speaking and understanding.

This section will introduce only *basic* sound change rules that are necessary to say individual syllables. For a complete explanation of sound change rules, please read through Appendix C after completing this section (before beginning Chapter 1).

As you learn sound change rules, I recommend reading each example out loud as practice. Don't worry about memorizing any of the words, as they're only to demonstrate the rules when pronouncing 한글.

Let's go over the rules for sound changes in Korean.

Bottom Consonants

We've actually already been working with syllables that have *bottom consonants*. Any syllable with three or more letters contains one or two bottom consonants.

Introduction to Sound Changes

A bottom consonant is simply a consonant on the bottom of a syllable. For the syllable 강, it's ㅇ. And for the syllable 삶, they are ㄹ and ㅁ.

Korean has a special word for these bottom consonants – 받침, which literally means "support." Knowing what a syllable's 받침 is will help you know how to pronounce it in a sentence.

You might be thinking, "But I already know how to pronounce 강 and 삶. We learned that ㅇ is pronounced like "ng" at the end of a syllable, so 강 is just 강. And 삶 is pronounced 삼. Well, you're right. 강 is just 강, and 삶 is pronounced 삼." Most rules for sound changes only apply when syllables are combined together with others in a sentence, just like the individual words in "Nice to meet you" do not change when pronounced individually.

But sometimes even on their own, we need sound change rules to pronounce certain syllables – specifically, syllables with bottom consonants.

낮

This is the word for "day." But how would you pronounce it? You couldn't say it like "나즈" because that would be adding in an additional vowel, and there is no vowel at the end – its 받침 is simply ㅈ, which has no sound on its own without a vowel. We need rules to dictate how to pronounce words like these.

Let's take a look at our first rule for pronouncing 받침.

1. ㅅ, ㅆ, ㅈ, ㅊ, ㄷ, ㅌ, ㅎ

This rule applies to syllables ending in any of the consonants ㅅ, ㅆ, ㅈ, ㅊ, ㄷ, ㅌ, and ㅎ.

Whenever a syllable's 받침 is one of the above consonants, and the syllable is at the end of a word or phrase (or said on its own), it will be pronounced as if it were a ㄷ.

Spelling	Pronunciation
낮	낟
갖	갇
핫	핟
멧	멛
못	몯
있	읻

Introduction to Sound Changes

갔	갇
낮	낟
갗	갇
밭	받
맡	맏
히웅	히은

You'll often find ㅅ at the end of words that were imported into Korean from other languages, especially English. One example is the word 인터넷 for "internet." When writing English words that end in 't' into Korean, remember to use ㅅ at the end to represent the final sound, instead of another letter such as ㄷ.

> **Adv**
> ㅉ and ㄸ are absent from this rule because there are no syllables in Korean that end with these letters at the bottom.

2. ㄱ, ㄲ, ㅋ

Any of these three consonants (ㄱ, ㄲ, and ㅋ) are simply pronounced as ㄱ at the end of a syllable.

Spelling	Pronunciation
박	박
각	각
싹	싹
부엌	부억
닭*	닥*
깎	깍
볶	복
묶	묵

*Review how to pronounce syllables ending in ㄺ.

> **Adv**
> Syllables ending in ㅋ are quite rare (although 부엌 is a common word), while syllables ending in ㄱ are the most common.

53

Introduction to Sound Changes

3. ㅂ and ㅍ

Both of these two consonants (ㅂ and ㅍ) are pronounced as ㅂ at the end of a syllable.

Spelling	Pronunciation
갑	갑
합	합
업	업
잎	입
값	갑
숲	숩

Adv: ㅃ is absent from this list because there are no syllables in the Korean language that end with it on the bottom.

4. ㅁ, ㄴ, ㅇ, ㄹ

This is an easy rule. These four consonants are all pronounced like normal at the end of a syllable.

Spelling	Pronunciation
감	감
움	움
혼	혼
난	난
멍	멍
옹	옹
쌀	쌀
말	말

Introduction to Sound Changes

However, remember that 받침 sounds will still *flow through* the consonant ㅇ as we learned previously.

Spelling	Pronunciation
낫	낟
낫이	나시
낮	낟
낮에	나제
있	읻
있어	이써
낯	낟
낯이	나치
믿	믿
믿어	미더
맡	맏
맡아	마타

Make sure you feel comfortable with each of these rules before moving on to our first Korean lesson. To see all of the letters we've learned in one place, look at the chart in Appendix B in the back of this book. Also, make sure to check out the expanded sound change rules in Appendix C.

It's much easier, and will save you a lot of time, to learn how to read 한글 properly now than to have to go back and fix your own pronunciation later. If possible, study these rules with flashcards and have them memorized, and then move onto the next section. I'll wait here patiently until you're ready to move on.

Introduction to Sound Changes

Saying Hello

Chapter 1

Like acquiring any skill, Korean can be learned through dedication and study. I'm here to help make your work a bit easier by guiding you along this process.

Before we go into anything else, the most important thing you'll need to know in Korean is how to introduce yourself to others. Let's start with a few of the most commonly used greetings.

Read the conversation below on your own first, and then we'll break it up and learn what each part means.

Conversation 1

A:	안녕하세요.
B:	안녕하세요.
A:	안녕히 가세요.
B:	안녕히 계세요.

It might not look like much, but this is our very first Korean conversation, and it's certainly important. Let's go over each part one at a time.

"Hello." – 안녕하세요.

This means "hello," and you can say it to anyone you'd like. It also happens to be an appropriate reply to anyone saying "hello."

Chapter 1: Saying Hello

"Goodbye." (to a person *leaving*) – 안녕히 가세요.

Although the first two syllables look the same as "hello," this phrase means "goodbye." However, Korean has two ways of saying "goodbye." This is how to say "goodbye" to a person who is leaving. It literally means "*Go* in peace."

"Goodbye." (to a person *staying*) – 안녕히 계세요.

Here is the second way to say "goodbye" in Korean. This is how to say "goodbye" to a person who is staying. It literally means "*Stay* in peace."

Notice how the two ways of saying "goodbye" differ in only one syllable – 안녕히 **가**세요 and 안녕히 **계**세요. Remembering this difference will help you save time memorizing them both individually.

When meeting someone for the first time, it's best to start off by saying "hello." Let's look at another conversation, this time between 철수 and 영희, and then go over what each of its parts mean.

Culture Notes

Koreans will bow slightly when greeting others, and the amount that they bow will depend on the *status* of the other person. For example, it would be acceptable to greet someone younger than you by just lowering your head as if nodding, while greeting a company's boss would require a formal bow – if you want specifics, the maximum angle for a more formal bow will be *around* 45 degrees... but I didn't do any scientific studies so don't quote me on that number (I'm a Korean teacher, not a mathematician). Your greetings will vary between lowering your head and a formal bow, depending on how much respect you wish to show them. **When in doubt, choose the formal bow**.

You may also *shake hands* while bowing. This is common as well in any situation.

If you want to be extra polite and formal (usually for business transactions), use *both hands* when shaking hands. Or, use your right hand to shake hands, while holding your right forearm with your left hand (you read that right). However, save these kind of handshakes for only the most heartfelt and formal situations, such as the day you get to meet your favorite actor or actress in Korea.

Saying Hello

Chapter 1

Conversation 2

철수:	안녕하세요.
영희:	안녕하세요.
철수:	저는 철수입니다.
영희:	저는 영희입니다.
철수:	만나서 반갑습니다.
영희:	네, 반갑습니다.

Let's break apart the conversation to understand what it means.

철수: 안녕하세요.

"Hello."

This line and the next are straightforward. 철수 is saying "hello."

Culture Notes

The names 철수 and 영희 are to Koreans what "Bob" and Sally" are to English speakers, and are standard names used frequently in Korean textbooks. In fact, they were used so frequently that everyone in Korea associates these names with textbooks.

Chapter 1

Saying Hello

영희: 안녕하세요.

"Hello."

철수: 저는 철수입니다.

"I am Chul-soo."

Here we have 저는 followed by a name, 철수, and then 입니다 (we'll talk about 입니다 in just a moment).

What is 저는?

저 means "I" or "me." The 는 that comes after it is called a *Topic Marker*, and basically means "this is what we're going to be talking about now." 저는 can therefore translate to "we're going to be talking about me now."

I'll go over the Topic Marker in detail later on, but for now, feel free to simply remember that you can use 저는 at the start of sentences when you're talking about yourself.

Using 입니다

입니다 means "am" or "is" or "are" – as in "I am," or "he/she is," or "you are." Here, since we used 저는 at the beginning, it means "I *am*."

You can also think of 입니다 as meaning "equals."

저는 철수입니다.
"I am Chul-soo," or "I *equal* Chul-soo."

In English, even a verb as simple as "to be" can have several ways to say it depending on the subject – I **am**, you **are**, he/she **is**, they **are**, et cetera. Korean has no such thing. 입니다 can be used in all of these cases.

Attach 입니다 directly after a noun (here, after a name).

입니다 will only appear at the *end* of a sentence.

Remember that due to sound change rules, 입니다 is pronounced 임니다.

Saying Hello

Chapter 1

영희: 저는 영희입니다.

"I am Yung-hee."

철수: 만나서 반갑습니다.

"It's nice to meet you."

철수 says 만나서 반갑습니다, which means "It's nice to meet you."

영희: 네, 반갑습니다.

"Yes, nice to meet you."

"Nice to meet you."

영희 replies with a "yes" (네), followed by 반갑습니다. Notice how even though 영희 did not use 만나서 in her reply, the translation is still "It's nice to meet you." This is because "만나서" is optional in this phrase; it's fine to use it, and it's fine to leave it off.

If you look in another textbook for learning Korean, you might find "nice to meet you" taught as 처음 뵙겠습니다. This is actually the most standard and formal way of saying "nice to meet you," but is much less commonly used. However, feel free to learn it and you might hear it a few times. I would recommend (만나서) 반갑습니다 in most normal situations besides formal business meetings.

> Advanced
>
> 만나서 comes from the verb 만나다, which means "to meet." However, 반갑습니다 comes from the verb 반갑다, which means "to be glad," and implies that you're glad because you're meeting someone.
>
> Adding 만나서 onto 반갑습니다 simply lengthens the phrase, and can make it sound a bit more polite. Its meaning stays the same.

Chapter 1: Saying Hello

Practice

Complete the conversation:

1. 안녕하세요.
   - "Hello."

2. 안녕하세요. 저는 철수 입니다.
   - "Hello. I am Chul-soo."

3. 저는 영희 입니다. 만나서 반갑습니다.
   - "I am Yung-hee. Nice to meet you."

4. 네, 반갑습니다.
   - "Yes, nice to meet you."

5. 안녕히 가사요.
   - "Goodbye." (to someone leaving)

6. 안녕히 계세요.
   - "Goodbye." (to someone staying)

Translate to English:

7. 안녕하세요. 저는 철수입니다. 만나서 반갑습니다. 안녕히 가세요.

Hello. I am Chul-soo. Nice to meet you. Goodbye.

Saying Hello

Chapter 1

Translate to Korean:

8. "Hello. Nice to meet you. I am [your name]. Goodbye (you are leaving)."

안녕하세요, 저는 가이 입니다. 안녕히 세요

New Phrases

안녕하세요.	"Hello."
안녕히 가세요.	"Goodbye." ("Go in peace.")
안녕히 계세요.	"Goodbye." ("Stay in peace.")
저는 ___ 입니다.	"I am ___."
(만나서) 반갑습니다.	"Nice to meet you."
처음 뵙겠습니다.	"Nice to meet you."
네	"yes"
아니요	"no"

New Vocabulary

저	"I," "me"
입니다	"am," "is," "are," "equals"

Chapter 1

Saying Hello

Likes and Dislikes

Chapter 2

Once you're able to introduce yourself, you'll need to learn how to express your feelings and emotions to other people in order to communicate freely. Because after all, expression is the heart of any language. In this chapter we'll go over how to express a few emotions related to *likes* and *dislikes*.

As this is a shorter chapter, take your time to make sure that you feel comfortable with each expression and grammar form before moving on.

Conversation

A:	저는 스포츠를 좋아합니다.
B:	저는 음악을 좋아합니다. 스포츠를 싫어합니다.

formal; used in presentation when speaking to someone older or in a higher position

This lesson brings us a short conversation, but it should be enough for what we need to cover. Let's go over each part.

> A: 저는 스포츠를 좋아합니다.
> "I like sports."

You'll notice right away that "I like" comes *after* "sports." This is a bit backwards from the way we do things in English. I'll explain how this works in the next chapter, but for now simply remember that what you like comes *before* the word "like."

Chapter 2: Likes and Dislikes

What is that 을 or 를?

This is called an *Object Marker*. Its purpose is to point out, "hey, there's an *object* right before me!"

"What is an object?" Let's look at the sentence "I eat food." Here, the *verb* is "eat," and the *object* of that verb is "food." An object is what receives the action of a verb.

An Object Marker is placed directly *after* the object, and never before. Use 를 when it comes after a *vowel*, and use 을 when it comes after a *consonant*.

Vowel: 스포츠를
Consonant: 음악을

> B: 저는 음악을 좋아합니다. 스포츠를 싫어합니다.
> "I like music. I dislike sports."

Here, the sentence works the same as above. We put "music" before "like" because that's how Korean does things.

Pronouns

You may have noticed that although we translated the second sentence as "I dislike sports," there is no word for "I" in the sentence anywhere. Korean is a bit unique, in that as long as the pronoun can be easily *guessed* from the sentence, you don't need to include it. Pronouns in Korean are only used when necessary.

In addition, once it's already clear who you are talking about, there is no need to repeat 저는 every sentence.

> 저는 수영을 좋아합니다. 축구를 싫어합니다.
> "I like swimming. I dislike football." → soccer

In this sentence it is not necessary to use 저는 in the second sentence, because it is already clear who you are talking about.

> 댄스를 싫어합니다.
> "I dislike dance."

Here, unless it would be vague *who* dislikes dance, it's not necessary to include 저는 at the beginning.

Likes and Dislikes

Chapter 2

저는 수영을 좋아합니다.
"I like swimming."

For this sentence, perhaps someone else was talking about his or her opinions before, and now you want to add your thoughts.

Culture Notes

김 철 수
Last Name · First Name

Most Korean names are 3 syllables; one syllable for the family name, or last name, and two syllables for the first name. For example, in the name 김철수, 김 is the last name and 철수 is the first name.

Practice

Practice making your own sentences using a noun, the Object Marker, and one of each of our phrases in the spaces below. Choose the correct Object Marker for each sentence.

1. 저는 <u>음악</u> (을)/를 좋아합니다.   *I like*

2. 저는 <u>댄스</u> 을/(를) 사랑합니다.   *I love*

3. 저는 <u>스보츠</u> 을/(를) 싫어합니다.   *I dislike*

Translate to English:

4. 안녕하세요. 저는 철수입니다. 음악을 좋아합니다. 댄스를 싫어합니다.

   Hello. I'm Cholsu. I like music. I don't like dance

Translate to Korean:

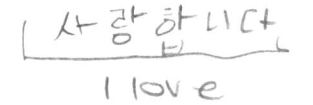

5. I love sports. I like American football. I dislike swimming.

   저는 스포츠를 사랑합니다. 저는 미식축구를 좋아합니다. 저는 수영을 싫어합니다.

   사랑합니다
   I love

Chapter 2

Likes and Dislikes

New Phrases

좋아합니다.	"I like."
사랑합니다.	"I love."
싫어합니다.	"I dislike."

New Vocabulary

을/를	Object Marker
스포츠	"sports"
야구	"baseball"
축구	"football"
미식축구	"American football"
농구	"basketball"
배구	"volleyball"
테니스	"tennis"
탁구	"table tennis," "ping-pong"
피구	"dodge ball"
하키	"hockey"
수영	"swimming"
골프	"golf"
등산	"mountain climbing," "hiking"
음악	"music"
시	"poetry"
댄스	"dance"
역사	"history"
음식	"food"

Simple Sentences

Chapter 3

In this lesson we'll learn how to make simple sentences using what we've learned so far. We'll also learn about basic sentence structure in Korean. Let's go over the conversation, and then break it down a bit to understand it. Try reading each part on your own first.

Conversation

철수:	저는 고양이를 좋아합니다.
영희:	저는 고양이를 싫어합니다. 개를 좋아합니다.
철수:	저는 김치를 좋아합니다.
영희:	저는 삼겹살을 더 좋아합니다.

[handwritten note: pork belly]

Let's take a look at each sentence in the conversation one at a time.

[handwritten note: 고양이 – cat]

철수: 저는 고양이를 좋아합니다.

"I like cats."

Korean Sentence Structure

English is an "SVO" language. "SVO" means that the language uses sentences structured with a *subject*, followed by a *verb*, and then an *object*. Let's take the sentence "I eat food." "I" is the *subject*, "eat" is the *verb*, and "food" is the *object* that is being eaten.

Chapter 3

Simple Sentences

Korean is an "SOV" language. This means that the object will always come *before* the verb, so the sentence "I eat food" would be structured "I food eat" in Korean – the subject, followed by the object, and then the verb. Become comfortable with this structure as soon as you're able to, as it's what all of Korean grammar is based upon. It's quite important!

We learned previously that 저 is used to say "I" or "me," and that 는 (the Topic Marker) is added onto the end to *mark* that we're talking about "me." 고양이 means cat, and it's followed by the *Object Marker*, here 를.

> 영희: 저는 고양이를 싫어합니다. 개를 좋아합니다.
> "I dislike cats. I like dogs."

Notice that the second sentence, "I like dogs," doesn't begin with 저는 like the first one does. This is because we already said that we're going to be talking about "me" in the first sentence, so there's no need to repeat 저는 in the second sentence, assuming we're still referring to "me."

Remember that anytime it's clear what the topic is, feel free to omit it.

> 철수: 저는 김치를 좋아합니다.
> "I like kimchi."

What is 김치?

A long time ago before there were refrigerators, people had to get creative to find ways to make their food last longer. Often, adding some type of preservative (salt) to food allowed it to stay edible for a long time. Koreans began adding salt to cabbage, then storing it underground where it was cooler in large clay pots. It would ferment (get old with the help of bacteria), but remain safe to eat. This allowed people to eat cabbage all year round, which was a good source of vitamins and fiber. More recently, Koreans added red peppers to the recipe, and led us to what 김치 is today – spicy, fermented (and delicious) cabbage.

Simple Sentences

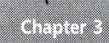

Chapter 3

There are more varieties of 김치 than could ever fit in this book. I encourage you to experiment and try some if you're able to get your hands on any. There's a saying that language learners who love to eat 김치 speak the best Korean.

영희: 저는 삼겹살을 더 좋아합니다.

"I like pork belly more."

더 - more

What is 삼겹살?

삼겹살 is sliced pork belly, which resembles thick bacon, but has not been cured or salted. It's fried directly at tables in restaurants, cut into bite-sized pieces, and eaten with a combination of vegetables, side dishes, and 김치. I'm not going to talk about 삼겹살 anymore because it's making me hungry.

Adverbs in Korean

In Korean, adverbs are most often placed *directly before* a verb.

저는 티파니를 사랑합니다.
"I love Tiffany."

저는 제시카를 **더** 사랑합니다.
"I love Jessica more."

더 is an adverb which means "more." Its opposite is 덜, which means "less."

저는 수지를 **덜** 좋아합니다.
"I like Suzy less."

덜 - less

Adv | Although using adverbs after a verb can sometimes be acceptable in casual conversation, it is not the norm. For better-sounding and clearer Korean, only use adverbs directly before verbs.

71

| Chapter 3 | # Simple Sentences |

Plurals

Let's take one more look at the first sentence in the example conversation.

철수: 저는 고양이를 좋아합니다.
"I like cats."

고양이 means "cat," but notice how the English translation is "I like cats" and not "I like cat."

In Korean, using plurals is optional. It's only necessary to use a plural when you need to emphasize that something is plural.

고양이 therefore can mean either "cat" or "cats," depending on what fits better in the sentence.

But sometimes you might need to emphasize that something is plural. If you do, here's how you do it.

Noun + 들

Take any noun you want to make plural, and attach 들.

고양이 "cat"
→ 고양이들 "cats"

원숭이 "monkey"
→ 원숭이들 "monkeys"

However, remember that most of the time, you won't need to use 들.

저는 원숭이를 좋아합니다.
"I like monkeys."

But you wouldn't say, 저는 원숭이들을 좋아합니다.

It would be unnecessary, and strange, to add 들 since it is already clear that we mean "monkeys" and not "monkey." And the same applies to any sort of thing.

However, there is an exception when talking about "people." It's more common to use 사람들 to refer to "people" in general.

[handwritten: 친구들 - friends]

Simple Sentences

Chapter 3

Articles

English uses articles such as "a," "an," and "the" to indicate several things, such as quantity ("a car" can mean "*one* car"), or to be specific about a certain thing ("the car" refers to a car that the speaker has already previously referred to). There's good news – Korean has no such thing to worry about.

In the future, we will cover how to indicate quantity simply using numbers (Chapter 13), and how to be specific about a certain thing by pointing out "this" or "that" (Chapter 11).

Practice

Translate to English:

1. 저는 고양이를 더 좋아합니다.

    I like cats more

2. 저는 개를 더 좋아합니다.

    I like dogs more.

Translate to Korean:

3. I like movies.

    저는 영화를 좋아합니다

4. I like books more.

    저는 책을 더 좋아합니다

5. I dislike bugs.

    저는 벌레를 싫어합니다

6. I dislike spiders more.

    저는 거미를 더 싫어합니다

Chapter 3: Simple Sentences

New Vocabulary

고양이	"cat"
개	"dog"
원숭이	"monkey"
벌레	"bug," "insect"
거미	"spider"
책	"book"
작가	"author"
사전	"dictionary"
전자 사전	"electronic dictionary"
영화	"movie"
김치	"kimchi"
삼겹살	"pork belly"
더	"more" (adverb)
덜	"less" (adverb)

Wanting and Not Wanting

Chapter 4

In this chapter we'll cover how to express our wants, as well as what we don't want. We'll also learn how to ask for things politely with "please," and a few essential Korean *particles*.

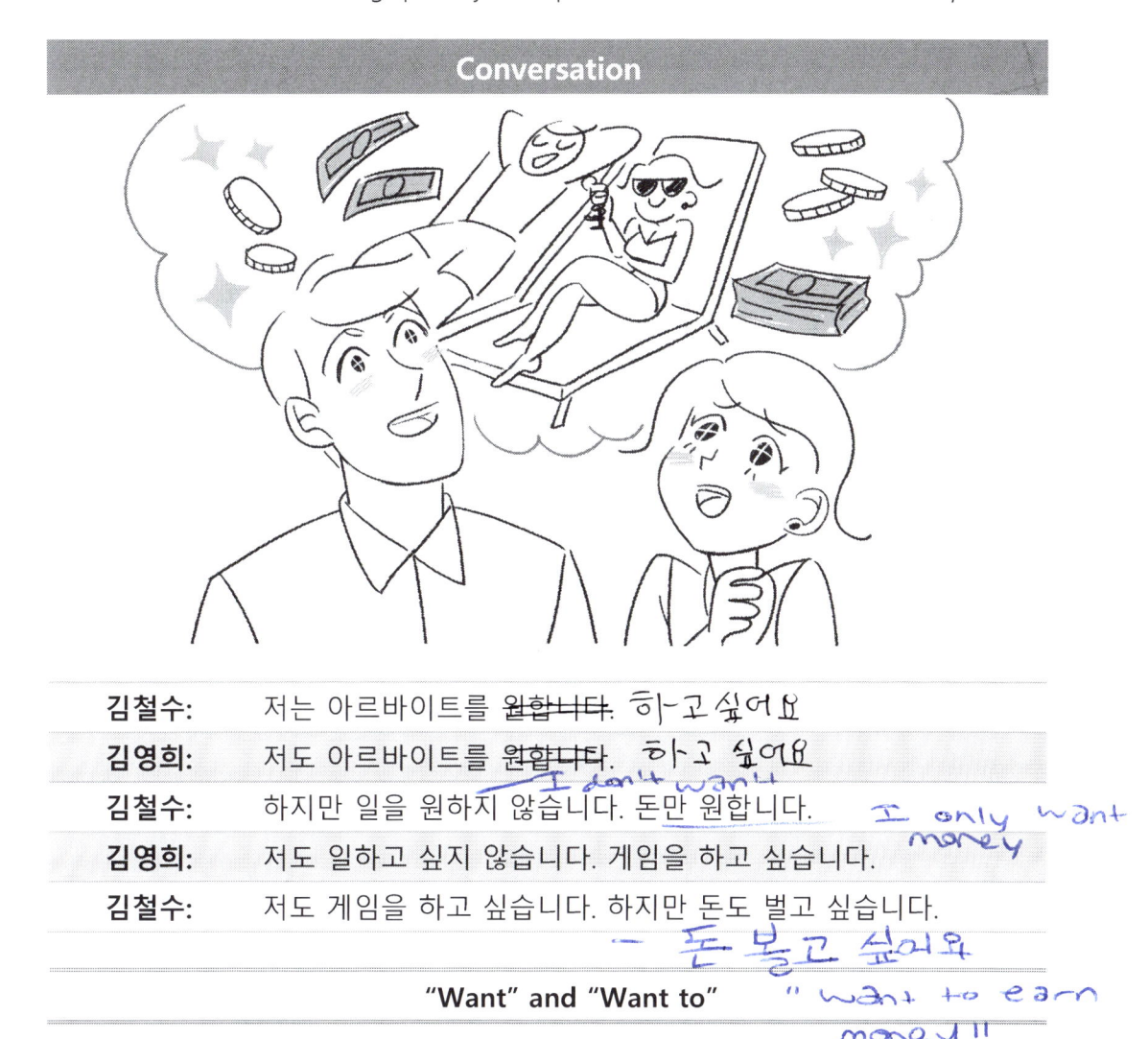

Conversation

김철수:	저는 아르바이트를 ~~원합니다~~. 하고싶어요
김영희:	저도 아르바이트를 ~~원합니다~~. 하고 싶어요
김철수:	하지만 일을 원하지 않습니다. 돈만 원합니다. *(I don't want / I only want money)*
김영희:	저도 일하고 싶지 않습니다. 게임을 하고 싶습니다.
김철수:	저도 게임을 하고 싶습니다. 하지만 돈도 벌고 싶습니다.

돈 벌고 싶어요 — "want to earn money"

"Want" and "Want to"

Korean has two ways to say "want" – which one you use will depend on whether you're using a *verb* or a *noun*.

저는 핸드폰을 원합니다.
"I *want* a cell phone."

저는 핸드폰을 받고 싶습니다.
"I *want to* get a cell phone."

The difference between the two above sentences is the first one uses only a *noun* – "cell phone." The second sentence uses a *verb* – "to get."

Chapter 4: Wanting and Not Wanting

Let's go over both of these:

"Want" – Noun + (을/를) 원합니다.

"Don't want" – Noun + (을/를) 원하지 않습니다.

When you want to express that you want something, take the noun and attach the *Object Marker*. Then add 원합니다.

저는 음식을 원합니다.
"I want food."

저는 연필을 원합니다.
"I want a pencil."

The opposite can be expressed by using 원하지 않습니다 instead.

저는 채소를 원하지 않습니다. *[vegetable]*
"I don't want vegetables."

저는 돈을 원하지 않습니다. 사랑을 원합니다.
"I don't want money. I want love."

"Want to" – Verb Stem + 고 싶습니다.

"Don't want to" – Verb Stem + 고 싶지 않습니다.

When you want to express that you want *to do an action*, take the **verb stem** and attach 고. Then add 싶습니다.

What is the Verb Stem?

Getting the *verb stem* of a verb is simple. Just take a verb and remove the 다 at the end, and that's it! You're going to see verb stems used everywhere in Korean grammar.

하다
→ 하 *싶습니다*

벌다
→ 벌 *싶습니다*

먹다
→ 먹 *싶습니다*

Wanting and Not Wanting

> 저는 과일을 먹고 싶습니다.
> "I want to eat fruits."

> 저는 돈을 벌고 싶습니다.
> "I want to earn money."

The opposite would be made by using 고 싶지 않습니다.

> 저는 채소를 먹고 싶지 않습니다.
> "I don't want to eat vegetables."

> 저는 죽고 싶지 않습니다.
> "I don't want to die."

> 저는 웃고 싶지 않습니다.
> "I don't want to *laugh*."

Note that the verb 웃다 can mean both "to smile" or "to laugh." Which one it translates to depends on the context of the sentence. If either seem to fit, feel free to translate it as either.

> 저는 웃고 싶지 않습니다.
> "I don't want to *smile*."

> *Advanced*
>
> *However!* This form (verb stem + 고 싶습니다) can only be used for "I" or "you," and it *cannot* be used to mean "he" or "she" – it cannot be used to mean "he/she wants to." This is because in Korean, you cannot talk about the desires of another person directly.
>
> Although you can say "I want to go" or "you want to go," in Korean it is not acceptable to say "he wants to go" or "she wants to go" with this same form. You can use this form only when talking about yourself or someone else who you are directly speaking to.

Remember that if you're expressing that you want *to do* something, use 고 싶습니다, and if you're expressing that you want *something*, use 원합니다.

Chapter 4: Wanting and Not Wanting

"Please give me..."
Noun + (을/를) 주세요

In order to ask for something politely, say *what you want* followed by the Object Marker, and then add 주세요.

돈을 주세요.
"Please give me money."

힌트를 주세요.
"Please give me a hint."

책을 주세요.
"Please give me a book."

Culture Notes

Approximately 5% of all Korean vocabulary comes from foreign words, most of those from the English language. This includes words such as 힌트, and 오렌지.

Words such as these are sometimes referred to as *Konglish* – a combination of *Korean* and *English*. So if you hear a word in Korean that sounds a lot like an English word, chances are it originally was.

Now that we've learned some important grammar, let's read over the conversation.

김철수: 저는 아르바이트를 원합니다.
"I want a part time job."

The word "아르바이트" comes from the German word "Arbeit" (which means "job"). In slang, this word is commonly shortened to 알바.

Wanting and Not Wanting

> 김영희: 저도 아르바이트를 원합니다.
> "I want a part time job too."

Here in the conversation we have the word 저, meaning "I" or "me," followed by 도. Together, 저도 means "I also" or "me too."

The Particle 도

Notice how 도 is taking the place of 는 in the above sentence. Saying 저는도 would be incorrect. The particle 도 replaces whatever particle was there (but not all as we'll learn later).

도 is placed *directly* after a word. The meaning of 도 is "also," "even," or "too."

> 저**도** 김치를 좋아합니다.
> "I also like kimchi." (Other people also might like kimchi)

> 저는 김치**도** 좋아합니다.
> "I like kimchi too." (I might also like other things)

Notice how the meaning changes by placing the 도 in a different location. 도 emphasizes "also," "even," or "too" only for the noun or pronoun that it directly follows.

> 저**도** 자동차를 원합니다.
> "I also want a car." (Other people also might want a car)

> 저는 자동차**도** 원합니다.
> "I want a car too." (I might also want other things)

Because the 도 in this sentence is placed after "car," it means "I want a car, *in addition to* whatever else I may want," and not "I *also* want a car, just like you do."

The word car can be shortened simply to 차, but know that 차 can also mean "tea." Only shorten 자동차 to 차 when the meaning is clear from the context.

Let's continue with the conversation.

> 김철수: 하지만 일을 원하지 않습니다. 돈만 원합니다.
> "But I don't want work. I only want money."

하지만 means "but" or "however," and can only be used at the *beginning* of a sentence.

Chapter 4: Wanting and Not Wanting

The Particle 만

만 works grammatically similar to 도, in that it comes after a noun. It replaces whatever particle was previously there (but not all as we'll learn later), except for the Object Marker, which you *may* replace if you want.

저**만** 좋아합니다.
"Only I like it."

저는 참치**만** 원합니다.
"I only want tuna."

Here, without 만, the sentence would be 저는 참치를 원합니다. Because it would normally use an Object Marker, you could have also written the above sentence like this:

저는 참치**만**을 원합니다.
"I only want tuna."

To keep things simple, feel free to remove whatever particle was previously there every time, and you'll be just fine.

> 김영희: 저도 일하고 싶지 않습니다. 게임을 하고 싶습니다.
> "I also don't want to work. I want to play games."

> 김철수: 저도 게임을 하고 싶습니다. 하지만 돈도 벌고 싶습니다.
> "I also want to play games. But I want to earn money too."

Practice

Translate to English:

1. 저는 토마토도 먹고 싶습니다.

    I also want to eat tomato also

2. 저는 토마토만 먹고 싶습니다.

    I only want to eat tomato

Wanting and Not Wanting

Chapter 4

3. 저도 돈을 벌고 싶습니다.

   I also want to earn money.

4. 저만 돈을 벌고 싶습니다.

   I only want to earn money.

Translate to Korean:

5. "Only I like kimchi."

   저만 김치를 좋아합니다.

6. "I like only kimchi."

   저는 김치만 좋아합니다.

7. "I also want to eat vegetables."

   저도 채소를 먹고 싶습니다.

8. "I want to eat vegetables also."

   저는 채소도 먹고 싶습니다.

New Phrases

원합니다.	"I want…"
원하지 않습니다.	"I don't want…"
Verb Stem + 고 싶습니다.	"I want to…"
Verb Stem + 고 싶지 않습니다.	"I don't want to…"
주세요.	"Please give me…"

New Vocabulary

하다	"to do"

Chapter 4: Wanting and Not Wanting

먹다	"to eat"
죽다	"to die"
태어나다	"to be born"
받다	"to get," "to receive"
벌다	"to earn (money)"
울다	"to cry"
웃다	"to smile," "to laugh"
게임(을) 하다	"to play games"
게임	"game"
하지만	"but," "however"
아르바이트 (or 알바)	"part time job"
돈	"money"
일	"work," "job"
일(을) 하다	"to work"
연필	"pencil"
(자동)차	"car"
배	"boat"
핸드폰	"cell phone" (literally, "hand phone")
사랑	"love"
채소	"vegetables"
과일	"fruit"
바나나	"banana"
포도	"grape"
토마토	"tomato"
레몬	"lemon"
오렌지	"orange"
아이스크림	"ice cream"
차	"tea"
참치	"tuna"
힌트	"a hint"
도	"also," "even," "too" (particle)
만	"only" (particle)

Verbs

Chapter 5

This chapter is all about using verbs. We'll learn how to use verbs to make our own sentences and conversations, as well as how to refer to other people.

Conversation

김철수:	영희 씨, 안녕하세요.
김영희:	안녕하세요. 저는 학교에 갑니다.
김철수:	저는 집에 갑니다.
김영희:	저는 공부합니다.
김철수:	저는 놉니다.

Let's read over the conversation together.

김철수: 영희 씨, 안녕하세요.

"Hello Yung-hee."

Using 씨

In Korean, 씨 takes the place of "Mr.," "Mrs.," or "Miss." 씨 is placed after a person's name. If you don't know a person's first name, it is fine to simply place 씨 after their *last name*.

김 씨
"Mr./Mrs./Miss Kim"

83

Chapter 5

Verbs

박 씨
"Mr./Mrs./Miss Park"

But a more common, recommended usage of 씨 is with *first names*.

영희 씨
"Yung-hee"

철수 씨
"Chul-soo"

Although it is a bit formal and impersonal, it is also acceptable to refer to someone by their full name with 씨 attached.

김영희 씨
"Mr./Mrs./Miss Kim Yung-hee"

In Korean, calling someone by *only* their first name (without 씨) is only acceptable in casual situations with close friends; it would be *impolite* at other times. This is different from other English speaking countries, where calling someone by their first name is considered friendly.

Also notice in the conversation how the person's name comes before the greeting. In English we would say "Hello Yung-hee," but in Korean it's proper to place the name of the person you are talking to at the *beginning* of the sentence.

철수 씨, 안녕하세요.
"Hello Chul-soo."

Also remember that 씨 is used when referring to *other* people – you should not add 씨 when saying your own name.

김영희: 안녕하세요. 저는 학교에 갑니다.
"Hello. I go to school."

The 니다 Verb Form
Verb Stem + ㅂ니다/습니다

It's time we started looking at how verbs work. Let's take a moment and go over how to *conjugate* – change the form of – a verb in *present tense*.

Verbs

Chapter 5

An example of a *present tense* sentence in English would be "I *watch* a movie." Present tense means the sentence is happening in the *present*. This is different from past tense ("I *watched* a movie yesterday.") which we will cover later, or future tense ("I *will watch* a movie tomorrow.")

In the last chapter we learned a few of our first verbs such as 하다 ("to do"), 먹다 ("to eat"), and 받다 ("to get," "to receive"). To make it easier to learn verbs, we'll teach them first in this book in their standard un-conjugated form. But we can't simply use them in a sentence without *conjugating* them first. Verbs will *conjugate* differently depending on how they're being used.

To conjugate a verb to the present tense, take the verb stem (review how from the last chapter) and attach ㅂ니다 if it ends in a vowel, or attach 습니다 if it ends in a consonant. Here are a few examples: *used after vowel* ... *after consonant*

가다 → 가 + ㅂ니다
→ 갑니다

하다 → 하 + ㅂ니다
→ 합니다

먹다 → 먹 + 습니다
→ 먹습니다

받다 → 받 + 습니다
→ 받습니다

오다 → 오 + ㅂ니다
→ 옵니다

죽다 → 죽 + 습니다
→ 죽습니다

놀다 → 놀 + ?

Verb stems that end in ㄹ are an exception. For verbs in the present tense with this form, *remove* the ㄹ after you get the verb stem.

놀다 → 놀 – ㄹ → 노 + ㅂ니다
→ 놉니다 *irregular*

벌다 → 벌 – ㄹ → 버 + ㅂ니다
→ 법니다 – *to earn*

85

Chapter 5 — Verbs

Here are some more examples.

저는 갑니다.
"I go."

저는 옵니다.
"I come."

저는 치즈를 먹습니다.
"I eat cheese."

저는 게임을 합니다.
"I play games."

The Particle 에

에 is a particle that can have a few different meanings depending on how it's used. It can mean "to," such as in the above dialogue, "I go to school" (going *to* somewhere). It can also mean "at" (located *at* somewhere), or "in" (located *in* somewhere). However, for this chapter we will focus on its meaning of "*to*" a location.

저는 병원에 갑니다.
"I go to the hospital."

저는 영화관에 갑니다.
"I go to the movie theater."

Let's go back to the conversation.

김철수: 저는 집에 갑니다.

"I go home."

More on 에

The above sentence, "I go home," might sound a bit strange – almost robotic, or like a caveman – when read in English. However in Korean, speaking in the present tense is perfectly normal, and does not sound strange.

But to make a more natural translation, feel free to translate the present tense to the *ing* form in English.

Verbs

저는 집에 갑니다.
"I'm going (to) home."

저는 학교에 갑니다.
"I'm going to school."

김영희: 저는 공부합니다.

"I study."

Here we have a new verb, 공부(를) 하다. This verb is a combination of 공부, which means "study" and is a noun, with the verb 하다 ("to do"). Together it literally means "to do study." In this book and through your own studying you will learn many verbs in Korean which are a combination of a noun and the verb 하다.

김철수: 저는 놉니다.

"I play."

The Verb 놀다

놀다 can translate as either "to play" or "to hang out." This is because although it means "to play," it is the standard word you would use when meeting up with a friend to do something. In English, "to play" is a word reserved for certain things such as games or for *children* meeting together. However in Korean, it's normal to keep using the verb 놀다 into adulthood.

In the above example as well, to make a more natural sounding translation, feel free to translate this sentence as "I'm playing."

Chapter 5

Verbs

Practice

Translate to Korean:

1. "I go to the hospital."

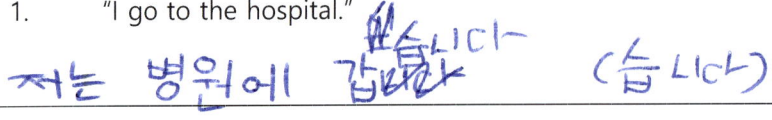

   저는 병원에 갑~~니다~~ 습니다   (습니다)

2. "I come to the hospital."

   저는 병원에 옵~~니다~~ ㅆ니다   (옵니다)

3. "I want to go to school."

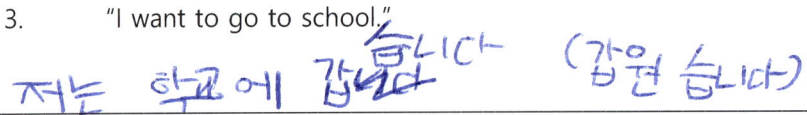

   저는 학교에 갑~~니다~~ 습니다   (가고 싶습니다)

4. "I want to hang out."

   저는 늘습니다

Translate to English:

5. 저는 게임을 합니다.

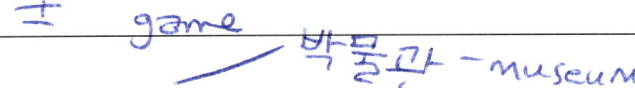

   I game

   박물관 – museum

6. 저는 박물관에 갑니다.

   I go to the museum

   beach
   seaside

7. 저는 ~~바닷가~~에 갑니다.

   I go to the seaside/beach

8. 저는 치즈도 먹고 싶습니다.

   I ~~also~~ want to eat

88

Verbs

Chapter 5

New Vocabulary

가다	"to go"
오다	"to come"
놀다	"to play," "to hang out"
살다	"to live"
공부(를) 하다	"to study"
좋아하다	"to like"
싫어하다	"to dislike" (person/thing)
미워하다	"to hate" (person)
사랑(을) 하다	"to love"
환전(을) 하다	"to exchange money"
원하다	"to want"
공부	"study"
학교	"school"
집	"home," "house"
병원	"hospital"
치과	"dentist"
수영장	"swimming pool"
도서관	"library"
사무실	"office"
카페	"café"
은행	"bank"
슈퍼(마켓)	"supermarket"
영화관	"movie theater"
박물관	"museum"
바다	"ocean"
바닷가	"beach"
해변	"seaside," "seashore"
주소	"an address"
집 주소	"home address"
고향	"hometown"
도시	"city"
지역	"an area," "a region"

Chapter 5 — Verbs

길	"a street," "a road," "a way"
부분	"part," "portion"
역할	"(acting) role"
연극	"performance," "play"
방송	"a broadcast"
프로그램	"a program"
치즈	"cheese"
에	"to," "at," "in" (particle)
씨	"Mr," "Ms./Mrs."

More Verbs

Chapter 6

This chapter contains a more in-depth explanation of Korean verbs, as well as introduces a few more important verbs that you'll need to know. Also, you'll be introduced to the Subject Marker, and another way of working with verbs – to connect two sentences using "but" ("I am an American, *but* I love Korea.").

Conversation

A:	저는 한국 사람입니다. 한국에 아파트가 있습니다.
B:	저는 미국 사람입니다. 미국에 집이 있습니다.
A:	저는 미국에 가고 싶습니다.
B:	저는 한국에 가고 싶지만 지금 미국에 있습니다.

Let's go over each line in the conversation one at a time.

A: 저는 한국 사람입니다. 한국에 아파트가 있습니다.
"I am a Korean. I have an apartment in Korea."

More About 입니다

입니다 is actually the verb 이다 conjugated to the *present tense*.

The verb 이다 (here, 입니다) attaches *directly* to the word before it, with no spaces.

저는 일본 사람입니다.
"I am Japanese."

91

Chapter 6

More Verbs

저는 영국 사람입니다.
"I am English."

저는 독일 사람입니다.
"I am German."

The Verb 있다

The verb 있다 literally means "to exist." However, it can be used in two ways.

First, you can use the verb 있다 to say that something or someone exists – there *is* something or someone. Use a *noun*, followed by the *Subject Marker* (we'll go over this next), and then conjugate the verb 있다.

집**이** 있습니다.
"There is a house."

Literally this sentence means, "a house exists."

And second, you can use 있다 to say that you *have* something.

저는 돈**이** 있습니다.
"I have money."

Literally this sentence means "I, money exists," but you can use 있다 in this way to say that you *have* something. Use the *Subject Marker* after what it is that you have.

저는 자동차**가** 있습니다.
"I have a car."

저는 펜**이** 있습니다.
"I have a pen."

> **Advanced**
>
> As you discover more about Korean markers in this book in later chapters, you will learn that other markers can also be used instead of only the *Subject Marker*.
>
> 저는 자동차도 있습니다.
> "I also have a car."
>
> 자동차는 있습니다.
> "As for a car, I have one."
>
> The *Object Marker*, however, cannot be used in this way.
>
> The sentence 저는 자동차를 있습니다 would therefore be incorrect. This is because the verb 있다 does not have an object – it merely means that something or someone *exists*.

More Verbs

Chapter 6

Introducing the Subject Markers – 이 and 가

In the sentences above you'll notice either 이 or 가 after a noun. These are *Subject Markers*.

A Subject Marker in Korean marks a *subject* of a verb. This is different from the *Topic Marker*, which I'll go over in a later chapter. For now, you don't need to know exactly how to use a Subject Marker yet; we'll cover it more in detail later on as we use it. Simply know that a Subject Marker is used together with 있다 to say that you *have* something, or to say that something or someone *exists*.

The Subject Marker is 이 when it comes after a *consonant*, or 가 when it comes after a *vowel*.

집**이**
자동차**가**
한국**이**
아파트**가**

Let's look at some examples with the Subject Marker and the verb 있다.

저는 일이 있습니다.
"I have work."

저는 자동차가 있습니다.
"I have a car."

자동차가 있습니다.
"There is a car," or "I have a car."

집이 있습니다.
"There is a house," or "I have a house."

The context of a sentence will always make it clear whether someone is talking about something they *have* or something that simply *exists*.

More About 에

In the last chapter we focused on how 에 can mean "to" (*to* somewhere). In this chapter we'll learn how it can also mean "at" (located *at* somewhere) and "in" (located *in* somewhere).

Chapter 6

More Verbs

(저는) 한국에 집이 있습니다.
"I have a house in Korea."

This sentence literally can mean "I, a house exists in Korea," but here in context 있다 is being used to mean "have."

What you *have*, or what *exists*, will most often come right before the verb 있다 in a sentence.

저는 집에 티비가 있습니다.
"I have a TV at my house."

> **Adv** It is also accurate to say (저는) 집이 한국에 있습니다. Switching 집이 around with 한국에 is still grammatically accurate, and *adds emphasis* to the location. Although the English translation would be similar, you can think of it meaning "I have a house in *Korea*" (emphasis added).

병원에 환자가 있습니다.
"There are patients at the hospital."

한국에 한국 사람이 있습니다.
"There are Koreans in Korea."

저는 미국에 여자 친구가 있습니다.
"I have a girlfriend in America."

저는 한국에 남자 친구가 있습니다.
"I have a boyfriend in Korea."

Additional Notes on "Have"

While the verb 있다 is used to say that someone "exists" for people and things, it cannot be used to say that you "have" an *animal*. For animals, the verb 키우다 ("to raise") must be used.

More Verbs   *키우다*   Chapter 6

저는 고양이를 키웁니다.
"I have a cat (as a pet)."

저는 개를 키우고 싶습니다.
"I want to have a dog (as a pet)."

However, you will still use the verb 있다 when stating that an animal simply exists.

학교에 고양이가 있습니다.
"There is a cat in the school."

B: 저는 미국 사람입니다. 미국에 집이 있습니다.
"I am an American. I have a house in America."

It's not required to state 저는 at the beginning of every single sentence, once it's already clear that you're talking about yourself.

An alternate word for 미국 사람 is 미국인. Both have the same meaning, but 미국인 is a bit more formal sounding. 인 means "person," but can't be used by itself. Feel free to use either word. The same thing applies to 일본인 and 한국인, among others.

A: 저는 미국에 가고 싶습니다.
"I want to go to America."

있다 can also be used for saying that a *person* is "in" or "at" a location.

저는 집에 있습니다.
"I am at home."

Literally this means, "I exist at home."

저는 한국에 있습니다.
"I am in Korea."

Remember that 에 can mean both "in" or "at" (as we used it with 있다), or "to" (as we used it last chapter). Also remember that the location you are going "to" will come *before* the verb.

저는 유럽에 가고 싶습니다.
"I want to go to Europe."

95

Chapter 6

More Verbs

B: 저는 한국에 가고 싶지만 지금 미국에 있습니다.
"I want to go to Korea, but now I'm in America."

Verb Stem + 지만

In Chapter 4 we learned about how to use 하지만 at the *beginning* of a sentence to mean "but" or "however." This time, let's learn how to say "but" or "however" when it's in the *middle* of a sentence.

Take the verb stem and attach 지만, then finish the sentence with whatever you want to say. That's all there is to it.

저는 미국 사람이지만 한국을 사랑합니다.
"I am an American, but I love Korea."

이지만 comes from the verb 이다. However, the verb stem of 이다 changes when used after words ending in a *vowel*.

First, here is what 이다 looks like with 지만 when used after a *consonant*:

미국 사람**이지만**

And here is what it looks like after a *vowel*:

남자**지만**

Notice how after a vowel, the verb stem of 이다 changes to become nothing.

> **Adv**
> Although I said that the verb stem of 이다 changes after a vowel, it's actually not completely wrong to say 남자**이지만**. But this sounds lengthy and looks more like something you might find in an old textbook than in modern spoken Korean.

저는 우유를 싫어하지만 마십니다.
"I dislike milk, but I drink it."

저는 한국 사람이지만 한국말을 공부합니다.
"I am a Korean, but I study Korean."

The Adverbs 지금 and 이제

지금 is an *adverb*, meaning it describes a verb (similar to how an adjective describes a noun); it means "now" or "right now," and comes *before* the verb in a sentence.

More Verbs

Chapter 6

저는 지금 가고 싶습니다.
"I want to go now."

저는 지금 한국에 있습니다.
"I am in Korea now."

Notice how it comes before the verb – in the first sentence before 가다, and in the second sentence before 있다. It will never appear at the end of the sentence.

Another similar word is 이제, which also means "now." While 지금 emphasizes "*right* now," 이제 emphasizes "*from* now." However, both will translate simply as "now."

저는 지금 가고 싶습니다.
"I want to go (right) now."

저는 이제 가고 싶습니다.
"I want to go (from) now."

Both have similar meanings, so feel free to use either one.

Practice

Translate to English:

1. 저는 지금 유럽에 갑니다.

   Now ~~I want~~ to go to Europe

2. 저는 핸드폰이 있습니다.

   I have a cell phone

3. 저는 미국에 자동차가 있습니다.

   I have a car in the U.S.

4. 저는 한국에 가고 싶지만 미국에도 가고 싶습니다.

   I want to Korea but I also want to go to the U.S.

Chapter 6 — More Verbs

Translate to Korean:

5. "I'm going to Korea."

   저는 한국에 갑니다.

6. "I'm going to America now."

   저는 지금 미국에 있습니다.

7. "I have a car."

   저는 자녕자가 있습니다.

8. "There is kimchi in Korea."

   한국에 김치가 있습니다.

9. "There are Americans in America."

   미국에 미국 사람 있습니다.

10. "I want to go to England, but I want to go to Korea also."

    저는 영국에 가고 싶지만 한국에도 가고 싶습니다.

New Vocabulary

말(을) 하다	"to speak," "to say"
거짓말(을) 하다	"to lie"
이다	"to be"
있다	"to exist"
키우다	"to raise"
진실(을) 말하다	"to tell the truth"
고백(을) 하다	"to confess"
한국말	"Korean (language)"
영어	"English (language)"

More Verbs

Chapter 6

중국말	"Chinese (language)"
일본말	"Japanese (language)"
독일어	"German (language)"
프랑스어	"French (language)"
스페인어	"Spanish (language)"
말	"word"
거짓말	"lie"
진실	"truth"
의미	"meaning"
의견	"opinion"
성격	"personality"
차이	"difference"
사이다	"(lemon-lime) soda"
아파트	"apartment"
환자	"a patient"
여자	"girl," "woman"
남자	"boy," "man"
친구	"friend"
여자 친구	"girlfriend"
남자 친구	"boyfriend"
외국	"foreign country"
외국어	"foreign language"
섬	"island"
정원	"garden"
호수	"lake"
강	"river"
한국	"(South) Korea"
한국 사람	"a Korean (person)"
한국인	"a Korean (person)"
미국	"America"
미국 사람	"an American (person)"
미국인	"an American (person)"
일본	"Japan"
일본 사람	"a Japanese (person)"

Chapter 6

More Verbs

일본인	"a Japanese (person)"
영국	"England"
영국 사람	"English (person)"
독일	"Germany"
독일 사람	"a German (person)"
중국	"China"
중국 사람	"a Chinese (person)"
유럽	"Europe"
북한	"North Korea"
지금	"(right) now"
이제	"(from) now"
사람	"person"
인간	"human"
괴물	"monster"
귀신	"ghost"
신	"god"
텔레비전	"television"
티비	"television" (abbreviation)
펜	"pen"
우유	"milk"
물	"water"
마시다	"to drink"
보다	"to see"
읽다	"to read"
듣다	"to listen"
믿다	"to believe"
신문	"newspaper"
뉴스	"news"
지도	"map"
사진	"photo"
카메라	"camera"
사진(을) 찍다	"to take a photo"
그림	"drawing"
그리다	"to draw"

More Verbs

그림(을) 그리다	"to draw (a drawing)"
출발(을) 하다	"to depart"
도착(을) 하다	"to arrive"
떨어지다	"to fall"
떨어뜨리다	"to drop (something)"
열다	"to open (something)"
닫다	"to close (something)"
만들다	"to make"

Chapter 6 More Verbs

Asking Questions — Chapter 7

So far we've only been able to make statements in Korean. This chapter will explain how to ask questions, as well as how to respond. We'll also learn an additional way of referring to other people. Then, we'll learn how to connect two *nouns* together using "and" – "pizza *and* cola."

Conversation

김철수:	선생님, 안녕하세요. 잘 지내세요?
김영희:	아, 네. 김철수 씨도 잘 지내세요?
김철수:	네. 요즘 무엇을 합니까?
김영희:	저는 학생들을 가르칩니다.
김철수:	무엇을 가르칩니까?
김영희:	저는 수학과 과학을 가르칩니다.
김철수:	저도 수학과 과학을 배우고 싶습니다.
김영희:	정말 배우고 싶습니까?
김철수:	네. 하지만 숙제와 시험을 싫어합니다. 선생님은요?
김영희:	하하. 저도 숙제와 시험을 싫어합니다.

Try reading the conversation on your own before we start dissecting it. Got it? Okay, let's start.

Actually, before we go over the conversation, let's learn how to ask questions in Korean.

103

Chapter 7

Asking Questions

Verb Stem + ㅂ니까/습니까

Just like when we conjugated the present tense (ㅂ니다/습니다), making questions is done in the same way. Take the verb stem (review Chapter 5 if you're not sure) and add ㅂ니까 if it ends in a *vowel*, or add 습니까 if it ends in a *consonant*. Add a question mark to the end just like in English.

가다 → 가 + ㅂ니까
→ 갑니까?

받다 → 받 + 습니까
→ 받습니까?

하다 → 하 + ㅂ니까
→ 합니까?

먹다 → 먹 + 습니까
→ 먹습니까?

김치를 좋아합니까?
"Do you like kimchi?"

네, 김치를 좋아합니다.
"Yes, I like kimchi."

김치를 먹습니까?
"Do you eat kimchi?"

네, 김치를 먹습니다.
"Yes, I eat kimchi."

Now let's look over the conversation.

김철수: 선생님, 안녕하세요. 잘 지내세요?
"Hello teacher. Are you doing well?"

What is a 선생님?

In Chapter 5 we learned about 씨, and how it can be used to mean "Mr.," "Mrs.," or "Miss" when attached to the end of a person's full name or last name.

Asking Questions

Chapter 7

선생님 can mean "Mr." when attached to a male's full name or last name, or it can also mean "Sir" when used on its own. Using 선생님 can be even more polite than using 씨, so use it when you're able to with older males.

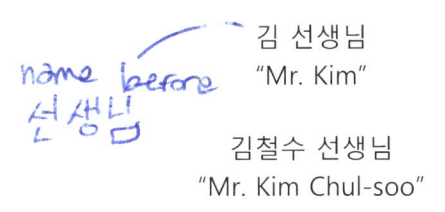

김 선생님
"Mr. Kim"

(handwritten note: name before 선생님)

김철수 선생님
"Mr. Kim Chul-soo"

선생님
"Sir"

However, 선생님 can also be used as a polite way to refer to someone who is a *teacher*. When used to mean "teacher," it can be used for both males *and* females.

선생님
"Teacher"

김 선생님
"Mr./Mrs./Miss Kim" (who is a teacher)

Note that although 선생님 can mean "teacher," it is not necessary that they be *your* teacher.

잘 지내세요 is a common and polite way to ask someone if they are doing well. 잘 is an adverb which means "well."

김영희: 아, 네. 김철수 씨도 잘 지내세요?

"Ah, yes. Are you doing well too, Mr. Kim Chul-soo?"

Remember that 도 ("also," "even," "too") is attached directly to whatever it's used with – in this case 씨, since 씨 is a title and counts as part of the person's full name. It would be incorrect to say 김철수도 씨.

김철수: 네. 요즘 무엇을 합니까?

"Yes. What do you do these days?"

요즘 means "lately," "nowadays," or "these days."

무엇 means "what" (it even kind of sounds like "what"). Here, since we're using the verb 하다 after it, 무엇 is acting as an *object*, and therefore is followed by the Object Marker.

105

Chapter 7: Asking Questions

무엇 can be used in many situations.

무엇을 먹고 싶습니까?
"What do you want to eat?"

무엇을 좋아합니까?
"What do you like?"

무엇이 있습니까?
"What do you have?"

Notice how there's no pronoun (here, "you") at the start of the sentence above. This is because pronouns in Korean are not necessary unless it is not clear who you are referring to. Here, it's clear that the speaker is talking about the other person, so it's not necessary to add the pronoun "you."

김영희: 저는 학생들을 가르칩니다.

"I teach students."

Here, 들 is used after 학생 to *emphasize* that she teaches multiple students. Without 들, it could be vague whether the teacher is teaching only one student, or more. However, in situations where it's not vague, remember that 들 is not necessary. When in doubt, don't add 들.

김철수: 무엇을 가르칩니까?

"What do you teach?"

This is another example of 무엇 being used as an *object*.

김영희: 저는 수학과 과학을 가르칩니다.

"I teach math and science."

과 and 와

You can use 과 and 와 to connect two *nouns* together in a sentence, just like "and." Attach it directly to the first noun it's placed after. Use 와 when following a *vowel*, and use 과 when following a *consonant*.

피자와 콜라
"pizza and cola"

Asking Questions

Chapter 7

그릇**과** 젓가락
"bowl and chopsticks"

개**와** 고양이
"dog and cat"

사람**과** 동물
"person and animal"

You will still use an Object Marker after listing two or more nouns connected in this manner, but remember to only use one Object Marker after the *last* noun.

저는 스테이크**와** 감자를 먹고 싶습니다.
"I want to eat steak and potatoes."

저는 미국 사람**과** 한국 사람을 좋아합니다.
"I like Americans and Koreans."

김철수: 저도 수학과 과학을 배우고 싶습니다.
"I also want to learn math and science."

There are no new concepts in this sentence, but it combines together several things that we've learned. Make sure you're able to understand this sentence, as well as the whole conversation, before moving on.

김영희: 정말 배우고 싶습니까?
"You really want to learn?"

정말(로) is an adverb that means "really." The 로 is optional.

햄버거를 정말 먹고 싶습니다.
"I really want to eat a hamburger."

저는 정말 프랑스에 갑니다.
"I'm really going to France."

정말 돈이 있습니까?
"Do you really have money?"

정말 can be used almost anywhere in a sentence, just like "really" can be placed anywhere in an English sentence. However, typically 정말 will come *before* the verb in a sentence.

Chapter 7

Asking Questions

김철수: 네. 하지만 숙제와 시험을 싫어합니다. 선생님은요?

"Yes. But I dislike homework and tests. What about you, teacher?"

은요 and 는요

은요 or 는요 is a combination of the Topic Marker (which we haven't yet gone over in detail) and 요. It can be used after a noun to *end* a question, when there is no other verb to end it.

It would not be polite in Korean to end a sentence with a noun and nothing else. Adding 은요 or 는요 after a noun at the end of your sentence is polite, and gives the meaning of "*how about...?*" or "*what about...?*" when you're asking for *more information* about something.

Use 은요 when following a *consonant*, and 는요 when following a *vowel*.

김철수 씨는요?
"How about Mr. Kim Chul-soo?"

미국 사람은요?
"How about Americans?"

고양이는요?
"What about the cat?"

삼겹살은요?
"How about pork belly?"

학교는요?
"What about school?"

"숙제는요?"
"How about homework?"

> **Adv**: Just adding a question mark to the end of a noun (or person), instead of attaching 은요 or 는요, would be the equivalent of *repeating* what a person said, as if you didn't hear correctly. However, speaking this way is impolite, and should be avoided.

Asking Questions

> 김영희: 하하. 저도 숙제와 시험을 싫어합니다.
> "Haha. I also dislike homework and tests."

In this chapter we learned both 아 ("Ah") and 하하 ("Haha"). In addition to these two, there's also 헉 ("My gosh"), 휴 ("Phew"), 음 ("Hm"), and many more.

Culture Notes

돼지꿈 꾸세요!
"Dream of pigs!"

돼지 means "pig," and "꿈" means "a dream," so together 돼지꿈 means "a dream about pigs."

You might find gold colored ceramic pigs in street-side stores while shopping in any city in Korea. This is because in Korea, pigs are considered to be a sign of good luck (they certainly taste delicious).

Although it would be rude to call a person 돼지, just as it would be in English, it is acceptable, and humorous, to tell someone to "dream of pigs" before going to bed. This can be done with the phrase 돼지꿈 꾸세요, which literally means "dream a dream about pigs."

Chapter 7

Asking Questions

Practice

Translate to English:

1. 김철수 선생님과 김영희 선생님이 한국 사람입니다.

   Mr. Kim Chol Su and Mr. Kim Yong Hui are Korean

2. 저는 김치와 삼겹살을 좋아합니다. ― pork belly

   I like kimchi and

3. 저는 수학을 정말 좋아합니다. ― 저는 수학을 정말 좋아요

   I really like math

4. 김철수 선생님은요?

   How about Mr. Kim Chul-Soo?

5. 무엇을 먹고 싶습니까?

   what do you want to eat

6. 요즘 무엇을 합니까?

   these days what have you been up to?

Translate to Korean:

7. "Hello. Are you doing well?"

   안녕하세요. 잘 지내세요?

8. "I am also an American."

   저도 미국 사람입니다

Asking Questions

Chapter 7

9. "Mr. Kim Chul-soo is really a Korean."

   김철수 선생님 정말 한국 사람입니다.

10. "I dislike homework but I like math and science."

    숙제를 싫어하지만 수학과 과학 좋아합니다

11. "What do you want to do?"

    뭐 무엇이 하고 싶습니까?

12. "How about pizza?"

    피자를 먹고 습습니까?

13. "Do you love monkeys?"

    원성이 사랑합니까?

New Phrases

잘 지내세요?	"Are you doing well?"
안녕히 주무세요.	"Goodnight." ("Sleep well.")
돼지꿈 꾸세요.	"Dream of pigs."

New Vocabulary

소개(를) 하다	"to introduce"
아	"Ah"
하하	"Haha"
헉	"My gosh"
휴	"Phew"
음	"Hm"
저	"Uh..."
그	"Uh..."
선생님	"Sir," "Mr.," "teacher"

111

Chapter 7: Asking Questions

학생	"student"
잘	"well" (adverb)
요즘	"lately," "nowadays," "these days"
정말(로)	"really" (adverb)
파스타	"pasta"
피자	"pizza"
콜라	"cola"
초밥	"sushi" (vinegared rice with fish, etc.)
회	"sashimi" (raw fish)
수학	"math"
과학	"science"
미술	"art"
지리	"geography"
숙제	"homework"
숙제(를) 하다	"to do homework"
시험	"test"
결과	"result"
무엇	"what" (noun)
가르치다	"to teach"
배우다	"to learn"
기다리다	"to wait"
앉다	"to sit"
서다	"to stand"
눕다	"to lie down"
차다	"to kick"
치다	"to hit"
싸우다	"to fight"
이기다	"to win"
지다	"to lose"
그릇	"bowl"
젓가락	"chopsticks"
포크	"fork"
가위	"scissors"
풀	"glue"

Asking Questions

Chapter 7

스테이크	"steak"
감자	"potato"
양파	"onion"
파	"green onion"
햄버거	"hamburger"
소시지	"sausage"
프랑스	"France"
힘	"strength," "power"
자리	"a seat," "space (for something)"
동물	"animal"
돼지	"pig"
꿈	"a dream"
꿈(을) 꾸다	"to dream"
춤(을) 추다	"to dance"
과/와	"and"

Chapter 7

Asking Questions

More Questions

Chapter 8

This chapter builds upon the last, and we'll learn how to make more natural sentences using a few new grammatical forms. Specifically, we'll learn how to ask questions about certain individual people or things, instead of only general questions about another person.

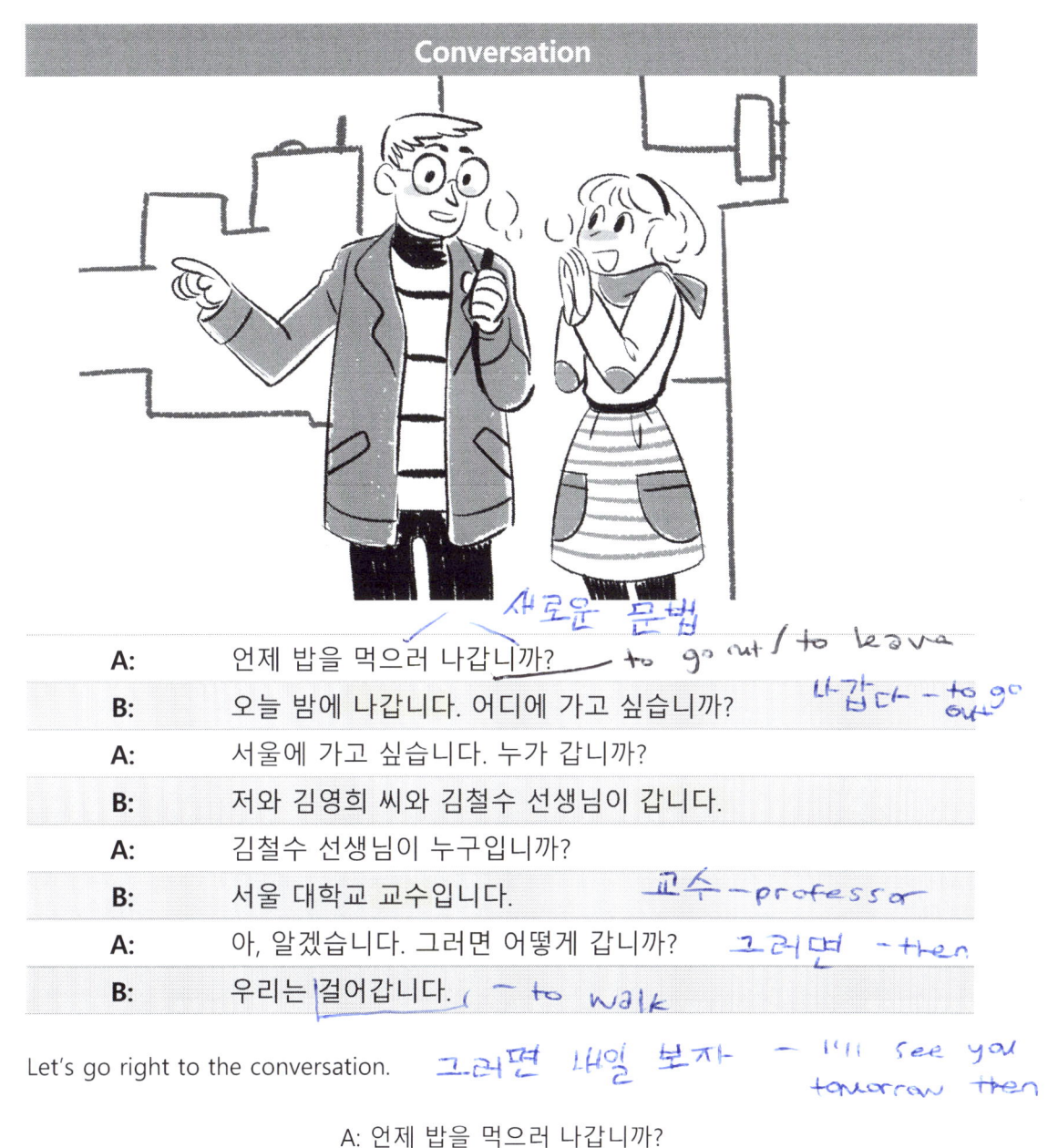

Conversation

A:	언제 밥을 먹으러 나갑니까? — to go out / to leave
B:	오늘 밤에 나갑니다. 어디에 가고 싶습니까? 나갑다 – to go out
A:	서울에 가고 싶습니다. 누가 갑니까?
B:	저와 김영희 씨와 김철수 선생님이 갑니다.
A:	김철수 선생님이 누구입니까?
B:	서울 대학교 교수입니다. 교수 – professor
A:	아, 알겠습니다. 그러면 어떻게 갑니까? 그러면 – then
B:	우리는 걸어갑니다. — to walk

새로운 문법

그러면 내일 보자 – I'll see you tomorrow then

Let's go right to the conversation.

A: 언제 밥을 먹으러 나갑니까?

"When will you leave to eat?"

115

Chapter 8

More Questions

Verb Stem + (으)러

When you want to say "to go *to* do something" or "to come *to* do something," such as "to go *to* eat" or "to come *to* watch a movie," use this form. Take the verb stem of the verb you are going to do, then add 으러 if it ends in a *consonant*, or add 러 if it ends in a *vowel*.

The verb following this form will always be a verb that shows movement, such as *going* or *coming*, among others.

먹으러 가다
"to go to eat"

먹으러 오다
"to come to eat"

일을 하러 가다
"to go to work"

일을 하러 오다
"to come to work"

영화를 보러 가다
"to go to see a movie"

영화를 보러 오다
"to come to see a movie"

자러 가다
"to go to sleep," "to go to bed"

자러 오다
"to come to sleep," "to come to bed"

Verb stems ending in ㄹ will add 러 to the end.

놀러 가다
"to go to play"

놀러 오다
"to come to play"

More Questions

Chapter 8

This chapter's conversation uses the verb 나가다, which means "to leave" (literally, it means "to go out from where you are and go somewhere else"). The opposite of this word is 나오다, which means "to come out" (or literally, "to go out from where you are and come here").

영화를 보러 나가다
"to go out to see a movie" or "to leave to see a movie"

> **Adv** Most commonly, you'll see words such as "who," "what," "where," "when," "why," and "how" used at the *beginning* of a sentence. But they can also come directly *before* a verb, just like an *adverb*.

Eating 밥

밥 means *cooked* rice, and when used together with 먹다 means "to eat cooked rice." However, because 밥 is so commonly used in Korea, this word has gained a more common meaning as simply "a meal."

Unless it is already clear, it's important to specify what is being eaten by saying it before using the verb 먹다.

저는 먹습니다.
"I eat."

The above sentence, while grammatically correct, would only be acceptable if the person you are speaking to already knows what you are referring to eating. The following sentence would be clearer.

저는 밥을 먹고 싶습니다.
"I want to eat (a meal)."

Note that the Object Marker 을 in 밥을 먹다 is *optional*. However, I recommend using it at first until you feel more comfortable with how the Object Marker functions.

In fact, any time you see parentheses around a word or a syllable it means that it is *optional* and can be removed – or you can leave it as is.

Chapter 8 — More Questions

This applies to every verb with 하다 and the Object Marker in parenthesis. For example, 공부(를) 하다 can be said as 공부를 하다 or 공부하다. Both are correct.

B: 오늘 밤에 나갑니다. 어디에 가고 싶습니까?
"I leave tonight. Where do you want to go?"

오늘 means "today," and 밤 means "night," so used together they mean "tonight." You can also use them separately.

오늘 나갑니다.
"I'm leaving today."

밤에 먹습니다.
"I'm eating at night."

오늘 밤에 숙제를 합니다.
"I'm doing homework tonight."

The word 어디 by itself means "where," but you'll often see 에 added onto the end to add emphasis – "where *to*" or "where *at*." It should be noted though that this 에 is *optional* with 어디, just as it would be in English.

어디**에** 가고 싶습니까?
"Where do you want to go *to*?"

어디 가고 싶습니까?
"Where do you want to go?"

어디**에** 있습니까?
"Where is it *at*?"

어디 있습니까?
"Where is it?"

어디 can also be used with the verb 이다 (입니까) when asking where something is – instead of using 어디(에) 있다. This works in the same way as above.

집이 어디입니까?
"Where is the house?"

우리가 지금 어디입니까?
"Where are we now?"

More Questions

Chapter 8

A: 서울에 가고 싶습니다. 누가 갑니까?
"I want to go to Seoul. Who is going?"

More About Subject Markers

Before going over the above sentence, we need to talk a little bit more about *Subject Markers*. A Subject Marker is a particle in Korean which marks a *subject* – a subject is something in a sentence that does something. Let's take a look at an example.

김 씨가 김치를 먹습니까?
"Does Mr. Kim eat kimchi?"

Here, the question is specifically asking about 김 씨. Because of that, 김 씨 is the *subject* of this sentence, and any subjects in a sentence need to be marked with a Subject Marker.

Although I'll go over the Subject Marker in more detail in a later chapter, for this chapter you should know that when you are asking a question, mark the subject of that sentence (whoever or whatever it is that you are asking about specifically) with the Subject Marker.

김영희 씨가 갑니까?
"Will Mrs. Kim Yung-hee go?"

고양이가 개를 좋아합니까?
"Do cats like dogs?"

Remember that the Subject Marker is 이 when after a *consonant*, and 가 when after a *vowel*. They attach *directly* to the end of the word that they mark.

펜**이**
자동차**가**

Also note that the Subject Marker (이 or 가) is different from the Topic Marker (은 or 는), which we will cover in a later lesson.

Let's finish the rest of the dialogue.

The word for "who" is 누구, but when 누구 is combined with a Subject Marker (누구 + 가), it changes to become 누가. Here "who" is being used as a *subject* in the sentence, since the speaker is specifically asking *who* will go.

Chapter 8: More Questions

> B: 저와 김영희 씨와 김철수 선생님이 갑니다.
> "Me and Mrs. Kim Yung-hee and Mr. Kim Chul-soo are going."

This sentence makes 3 people the *subject* of the action – 저, 김영희 씨, and 김철수 선생님 are the ones who are going.

> A: 김철수 선생님이 누구입니까?
> "Who is Mr. Kim Chul-soo?"

The Subject Marker is placed after 김철수 선생님, showing that he is the *subject* of this sentence. You'll find that Subject Markers commonly appear in sentences with questions.

We did not use 누가 here because the subject is not "who" but "Mr. Kim Chul-soo" that the speaker is asking about. For comparison, here is the sentence with 누가 as the subject.

> 누가 김철수 선생님입니까?
> "Who is Mr. Kim Chul-soo?"

In this sentence there is a stronger emphasis on "who," since "who" is the *subject*, while the original sentence emphasizes Mr. Kim Chul-soo. As the speaker, you can choose which words to emphasize in a sentence, changing the way it sounds. We will talk more about emphasis later.

> B: 서울 대학교 교수입니다.
> "He is a Seoul University professor."

Notice how the words combine together – 서울 대학교 교수 – "Seoul University professor." Nouns can combine together in the same order as they do in English.

> A: 아, 알겠습니다. 그러면 어떻게 갑니까?
> "Ah, I see. Well then how will you go?"

알겠습니다 is used to express "I see," or "Understood." It comes from the verb 알겠다 ("to know," "to understand"), which is another form of the verb 알다 ("to know").

그러면 means "well then," and can only be used at the *beginning* of a sentence.

More Questions

Chapter 8

B: 우리는 걸어갑니다.

"We are walking."

우리 means "we" or "us." 우리는 can be used in the same way as 저는.

Adv

걸어가다 comes from a combination of the verbs 걷다 ("to walk") and 가다 ("to go"). Together, it means "to walk (in order to get somewhere)," or simply "to walk (somewhere)."

Its opposite is therefore 걸어오다, which is a combination of 걷다 ("to walk") and 오다 ("to come"), and means "to walk (in order to come here)," or simply "to walk (here)."

Culture Notes

The largest city in South Korea is 서울 by far, with a population of over 10 million people (and a metropolitan population of 20 million). Within 서울 there are several top universities, the most famous and prestigious being 서울대 (서울 대학교), 고려대 (고려 대학교), and 연세대 (연세 대학교). Korean students will spend their entire academic lives competing with each other for a spot at one of these exclusive universities, for graduating from a top university in Korea helps to secure a bright financial future. Not going to college is seen by others as a failure, and the pressures of college acceptance are a constant source of stress and depression for students in Korea.

Other major cities in South Korea include 부산 in the South, 대구 in the East, and 대전 in the West. Of course there are other cities as well, but these are the biggest of the big.

Practice

Translate to English:

1. 저는 밥을 먹으러 갑니다.

   I am going to eat 밥

2. 오늘 김 씨가 어디에 갑니까?

   Today where did Mr. Kim go?

3. 우리는 학교에 걸어갑니다.

   Our school I walked to

Chapter 8 — More Questions

4. 저는 일을 하러 갑니다.

   I am going to go to work

5. 화장실이 어디에 있습니까?

   Where is the bathroom at?

Translate to Korean:

6. "Who is Mr. Park?"

   박 씨 누구예요? / 박씨가 누구입니까?

7. "Who do you love?"

   누가 사랑하니까? → 누구를 사랑합니까?

8. "We want to go."

   우리 원한 갑니다 → 우리는 가고 싶습니다

9. "When do you want to eat (a meal)?"

   언제는 식샹을 먹습니까? 언제 밥을 먹고 싶습니까?

10. "Where is the house?"

    집이 어디에 있습니까?

New Phrases

알겠습니다.	"I see.," "Understood."

New Vocabulary

이/가	Subject Marker
언제	"when"

More Questions

Chapter 8

어디	"where"
누구/누가	"who"
왜	"why"
어떻게	"how"
잠	"sleep"
(잠[을]) 자다	"to sleep"
일어나다	"to wake up," "to get up"
가방	"bag"
우리	"we," "us"
나라	"country"
우리나라	"Korea" (literally, "our country")
그러면	"well then"
오늘	"today"
내일	"tomorrow"
어제	"yesterday"
밤	"night"
교수	"professor"
박사	"doctor" (someone holding a PhD)
의사	"(medical) doctor"
가수	"singer"
대학교	"university"
고등학교	"high school"
중학교	"middle school"
초등학교	"elementary school"
교실	"classroom"
교육	"education"
화장실	"bathroom"
냉장고	"refrigerator"
냉동실	"freezer"
침대	"bed"
침실	"bedroom"
천장	"ceiling"
지붕	"roof"
거실	"living room"

123

Chapter 8: More Questions

방	"room"
문	"door"
열쇠	"key"
다니다	"to attend (school)," "to commute (to work)"
서울	"Seoul"
나가다	"to leave," "to go out"
나오다	"to come out"
걷다	"to walk"
걸어가다	"to walk (somewhere)"
달리다	"to run"
뛰다	"to fly," "to jump," "to run"
밥(을) 먹다	"to eat (a meal)"
밥	"(cooked) rice," "a meal"
쌀	"(uncooked) rice"
살	"flesh," "fat"
빵	"bread"
떡	"rice cake"
버터	"butter"
캔디	"candy"
과자	"snacks"
사탕	"sweets"
설탕	"sugar"
꿀	"honey"
소금	"salt"
후추	"pepper"
식초	"vinegar"
후식	"dessert"
아침 (식사)	"breakfast" (literally, "morning meal")
점심 (식사)	"lunch" (literally, "afternoon meal")
저녁 (식사)	"dinner" (literally, "evening meal")
알겠다	"to know," "to understand"

Adjectives

Chapter 9

Adjectives make sentences more interesting, and allow us to express ourselves in more detail. We'll learn in this chapter how to describe people and things using adjectives – specifically, *descriptive verbs* in Korean.

Conversation

웨이터:	맛이 괜찮습니까?
김철수:	김치가 아주 맛이 있습니다. 감사합니다.
웨이터:	아, 좋습니다.
김철수:	하지만 복음밥이 조금 차갑습니다.
웨이터:	죄송합니다.
김철수:	그리고 식당도 조금 춥습니다.
웨이터:	많이 춥습니까?
김철수:	네. 그리고 음식이 많이 비쌉니다.

Before we go over today's conversation, let's learn a little bit about adjectives.

In Korean, many *adjectives* actually come from *verbs*.

Specifically, adjectives in Korean are called *descriptive verbs*, meaning they're verbs that are used to describe things – it's okay to just call them adjectives if that's easier.

125

Chapter 9

Adjectives

So far in this book, every verb we learned before this chapter has been an *action verb* (action verbs are all verbs which involve doing something, such as "to eat," "to go," "to see," etc.). From now on, we will be learning both *descriptive verbs* and *action verbs*.

In order to use a descriptive verb in a sentence, we must first *conjugate* it. Conjugating a descriptive verb in the *present tense* is similar to conjugating an action verb.

Let's learn how to conjugate a *descriptive verb* in the *present tense*.

Descriptive Verb Stem + ㅂ니다/습니다

Look familiar? That's because conjugating a descriptive verb in the present tense – with the 니다 form – is the *same* as conjugating an action verb in the present tense.

Take the verb stem and add ㅂ니다 if it ends in a *vowel*, or add 습니다 if it ends in a *consonant*.

춥다 → 춥 + 습니다
→ 춥습니다

예쁘다 → 예쁘 + ㅂ니다
→ 예쁩니다

> **Adv**: Although 예쁘다 is the correct spelling, you might also come across 이쁘다 which is a popular variation. They are the same thing.

> 웨이터: 맛이 괜찮습니까?
> "Is the flavor okay?"

The waiter is asking whether or not the *flavor* is okay. Therefore, 맛 is the *subject* and needs to be marked with the Subject Marker.

Another way to translate this sentence could be, "Does it *taste* okay?"

> 김철수: 김치가 아주 맛이 있습니다. 감사합니다.
> "The kimchi is very delicious. Thank you."

아주 is an adverb which means "very." It is used directly *before* a verb.

> 아주 작습니다.
> "It is very small."

Adjectives

Chapter 9

아주 예쁩니다.
"It is very pretty."

맛이 있다 can also be said as 맛있다. Remember that any time you see parentheses around a word or syllable in a chapter's New Vocabulary section, it means it is *optional* and can be removed – or you can use it as is.

감사합니다 is going to be one of the most important Korean phrases we will learn in this book. Memorize it and use it often whenever appropriate.

> **Adv** Another way to say "thank you" is with the verb 고맙다 – 고맙습니다. They both mean the same thing, but using the verb 감사하다 is a bit more polite than using 고맙다.

웨이터: 아, 좋습니다.
"Ah, good."

김철수: 하지만 볶음밥이 조금 차갑습니다.
"But the fried rice is a little cold."

조금 is an adverb that means "a little," as in "I eat a little" or "I study a little."

저는 조금 먹습니다.
"I eat a little."

저는 조금 공부합니다.
"I study a little."

조금 can be also combined with the particle 만 to mean "*only* a little."

저는 정말 조금만 먹습니다.
"I really eat only a little."

춥다 and 차갑다

Chapter 9

Adjectives

Both 춥다 and 차갑다 mean "to be cold," but are each used differently. 춥다 is used when you're talking about the weather, or the temperature of the air in a room; if you feel cold, 춥다 is the word to use. If you're talking about something being "cold to the touch," such as a beverage, or an item, or another person's skin, then 차갑다 is the word to use.

의자가 차갑습니다!
"The chair is cold!"

오늘 아주 춥습니다!
"Today is very cold!"

커피가 차갑습니다.
"The coffee is cold."

한국도 춥습니까?
"Is Korea cold too?"

웨이터: 죄송합니다.
"I'm sorry."

죄송합니다 is another important phrase to learn, and means "I'm sorry." Hopefully, you won't have to say this too often.

> **Adv** Another way to say "sorry" is using the verb 미안하다 – 미안합니다. They both mean the same thing, but using 죄송하다 sounds a bit more polite than 미안하다.

김철수: 그리고 식당도 조금 춥습니다.
"And the restaurant is also a little cold."

그리고 means "and" or "also," and is used at the *beginning* of a sentence.

그리고 저는 친절합니다!
"And, I am nice!"

그리고 김 씨도 먹으러 갑니다.
"Also, Mr. Kim is going to eat too."

웨이터: 많이 춥습니까?
"Is it cold a lot?"

Adjectives

Chapter 9

Although the translation "a lot" seems a bit awkward in English, the adverb 많이 is the opposite of 조금, and means "a lot." For a more natural sounding sentence, it might be better to translate this sentence to English as "Is it really cold?"

저는 많이 먹습니다.
"I eat a lot."

저는 커피를 많이 마십니다.
"I drink a lot of coffee."

저는 영화를 많이 좋아합니다.
"I like movies a lot."

저는 영화를 많이 봅니다.
"I watch a lot of movies."

As an adverb, 많이 will go directly *before* a verb.

김철수: 네. 그리고 음식이 많이 비쌉니다.
"Yes. And the food is very expensive."

Practice

Identify the following verbs as descriptive verbs or action verbs:

1. 크다 — *descriptive*
2. 먹다 — *action*
3. 작다 — *descriptive*
4. 수영(을) 하다 — *action*
5. 내다 — *action verb (to make, to build)*
6. 덥다 — *descriptive*

Translate to English:

7. 김 씨가 술을 정말 많이 마십니다.

   Mr. Kim really drank a lot of alcohol.

129

Chapter 9

Adjectives

8. 오늘 저는 조금 춥습니다.

   Today I'm a little bit cold.

9. 물이 차갑습니까?

   Is the alcohol cold? (to the touch)

Translate to Korean:

10. "The soup is a little cold."

    수프가 ~~많이 춥습니다~~ 차갑습니다

11. "Today is very cold."

    오늘 ~~너무~~ 아주 춥습니다

12. "I really like Korea."

    한국이 정말 좋습니다

New Phrases

감사합니다.	"Thank you."
죄송합니다.	"I'm sorry."

New Vocabulary

감사하다	"to be grateful"
죄송하다	"to be sorry"
웨이터	"waiter"
식당	"restaurant"
그리고	"and," "also"
그래서	"so," "therefore"
볶음밥	"fried rice"
아주	"very" (adverb)

130

Adjectives

Chapter 9

조금	"a little"
조금만	"only a little"
많이	"a lot" (adverb)
많다	"to be a lot"
맛	"flavor"
춥다	"to be cold" (weather)
차갑다	"to be cold" (to the touch)
덥다	"to be hot" (weather)
뜨겁다	"to be hot" (to the touch)
따뜻하다	"to be warm" (weather, or to the touch)
시원하다	"to be cool" (weather, or to the touch)
맑다	"to be bright and clear" (weather)
괜찮다	"to be okay," "to be alright"
악하다	"to be evil"
맛(이) 있다	"to be delicious"
멋(이) 있다	"to be cool," "to be stylish"
좋다	"to be good"
나쁘다	"to be bad"
예쁘다	"to be pretty"
아름답다	"to be beautiful"
크다	"to be big"
배(가) 고프다	"to be hungry"
목(이) 마르다	"to be thirsty"
흔하다	"to be common"
드물다	"to be rare"
내다	"to pay (money)"
작다	"to be small"
수영(을) 하다	"to swim"
의자	"chair"
비싸다	"to be expensive"
맵다	"to be spicy"
커피	"coffee"
수프	"soup"
날씨	"weather"

Chapter 9

Adjectives

비(가) 오다	"to rain"
눈(이) 오다	"to snow"
술	"alcohol"
담배	"tobacco," "cigarettes"
친절하다	"to be nice"
강하다	"to be strong"
약하다	"to be weak"

More Adjectives

Chapter 10

Now that we've learned about *descriptive verbs* in the previous chapter, let's go over how to use them to directly describe people and things – "This is a cold soda," as opposed to "The soda is cold."

Conversation 1

한승규:	김 선생님이 어떤 사람입니까?
이선주:	아주 좋은 사람입니다.
한승규:	재미있는 사람입니까?
이선주:	네, 재미있고 밝은 사람입니다.

Conjugating Descriptive Verbs

We've learned how to conjugate descriptive verbs in the present tense already in the last chapter. Here we'll learn how to conjugate a descriptive verb so it can be used directly *before* the noun, just like an *adjective* in English.

Take a look at the following two sentences:

김 씨가 좋습니다.
"Mr. Kim is good."

This is the type of sentence we learned in the last chapter. But what if you want to say "Mr. Kim is a good *person*" instead?

Chapter 10: More Adjectives

김 씨가 좋은 사람입니다.
"Mr. Kim is a good person."

Notice that the adjective "good" (the descriptive verb) comes directly before the noun "person," just like in English; 좋은 is therefore the *adjective form* (to be used directly before a noun) of the descriptive verb 좋다.

Descriptive verbs can be used at the end of a sentence, such as in the first example, "Mr. Kim is good." Or, descriptive verbs can be used just like an adjective in English – that is, directly before a noun they are describing.

Depending on the verb stem, there can be a few different rules for how to conjugate a descriptive verb to behave like an English *adjective*.

Descriptive Verb Stem + ㄴ/은

This is how to conjugate most descriptive verbs. Korean has some verbs which are exceptions and do not follow this rule, but I'll point them out as we go along.

To use a descriptive verb before a noun, take the verb stem and attach ㄴ if it ends in a *vowel*, or attach 은 if it ends in a *consonant*. Here are some examples using this general form.

친절하다 → 친절하 + ㄴ
→ 친절한
친절한 사람 "a nice person"

좋다 → 좋 + 은
→ 좋은
좋은 생각 "a good idea"

Note that 좋은 is actually an exception. Normally, verb stems ending with ㅎ will conjugate a bit differently. This will be shown and explained later in this chapter and the next.

예쁘다 → 예쁘 + ㄴ
→ 예쁜
예쁜 여자 "a pretty girl"

낮다 → 낮 + 은
→ 낮은
낮은 성적 "a low grade"

More Adjectives

Chapter 10

Descriptive Verbs Ending in ㅂ

This is only for verb stems which end in a single ㅂ at the bottom. These verbs conjugate differently.

Take the verb stem, remove the ㅂ, add 우, then conjugate as normal by adding ㄴ.

쉽다 → 쉽 – ㅂ → 쉬 + 우 → 쉬우 + ㄴ
→ 쉬운
쉬운 숙제 "easy homework"

어렵다 → 어렵 – ㅂ → 어려 + 우 → 어려우 + ㄴ
→ 어려운
어려운 일 "difficult work"

무겁다 → 무겁 – ㅂ → 무거 + 우 → 무거우 + ㄴ
→ 무거운
무거운 가방 "heavy bag"

새롭다 → 새롭 – ㅂ → 새로 + 우 → 새로우 + ㄴ
→ 새로운
새로운 주방 "new kitchen"

Both 주방 and 부엌 mean "kitchen." Feel free to use either one.

This rule does not include verbs which have anything more than a single ㅂ at the bottom. The descriptive verb 짧다 (pronounced 짤따) has both a ㄹ and a ㅂ on the bottom, so it would simply conjugate as normal.

짧다 → 짧 + 은
→ 짧은 (pronounced 짤븐)
짧은 시간 "a short time"

For verbs ending in ㅂ in the *present tense*, you will *always* add 운 after removing the ㅂ. Just keep in mind the actual steps involved, as they will come in handy later on when we learn different verb tenses.

More Adjectives

Descriptive Verbs Ending in ㄹ

This is only for verb stems which end in a single ㄹ at the bottom. These verbs also conjugate differently.

Take the verb stem, remove the ㄹ, then conjugate as normal by adding ㄴ.

길다 → 길 – ㄹ → 기 + ㄴ
→ 긴
긴 머리 "long hair"

머리 can mean either "head" or "hair" (on one's head) depending on the context. An alternative is to use 머리카락, which only means "(head) hair."

멀다 → 멀 – ㄹ → 머 + ㄴ
→ 먼
먼 집 "a far house"

달다 → 달 – ㄹ → 다 + ㄴ
→ 단
단 사과 "a sweet apple"

> **Advanced**
>
> There are a few verbs that don't follow these rules, such as verb stems ending with ㅎ. This includes 어떻다, 그렇다, 이렇다, as well as all of the color verbs which are taught in the next chapter. For these verbs, first remove the ㅎ from the verb stem, then conjugate as normal by adding ㄴ.
>
> 어떻다 → 어떻 – ㅎ → 어떠 + ㄴ
> → 어떤
> 어떤 사람 "what kind of person"
>
> 그렇다 → 그렇 – ㅎ → 그러 + ㄴ
> → 그런
> 그런 일 "that kind of work"
>
> 이렇다 → 이렇 – ㅎ → 이러 + ㄴ
> → 이런
> 이런 음식 "this kind of food"
>
> It is not yet necessary to memorize the above verbs 어떻다 ("to be how"), 그렇다 ("to be so"), and 이렇다 ("to be this way"). However, it would help to be able to understand how these verbs are the origin of the adjectives 어떤 ("what kind of"), 그런 ("that kind of"), and 이런 ("this kind of").

Conjugating 있다

More Adjectives

Chapter 10

The exception to the above rules is the verb 있다, which means "to exist." 있다 conjugates in a special way.

> **Adv** Actually, 있다 ("to exist") is not a descriptive verb, but an *action verb*. However, because 있다 appears in many descriptive verbs, such as 재미(가) 있다 and others, I've included it in this chapter.

있다 becomes 있는 when used to describe things as an adjective.

있다 → 있 + 는
→ 있는

재미있다 → 재미있 + 는
→ 재미있는
재미있는 사람 "a fun person"

맛이 있다 → 맛이 있 + 는
→ 맛이 있는
맛이 있는 음식 "delicious food"

Remember that all of these rules only apply when you're using descriptive verbs directly *before* nouns. At the end of a sentence, everything goes back to normal.

저는 **매운** 음식을 좋아합니다.
"I like spicy food."

한국 음식이 아주 **맵습니다**.
"Korean food is very spicy."

김 씨가 **재미있는** 사람입니다.
"Mr. Kim is a fun person."

김 씨가 **재미있습니다**.
"Mr. Kim is fun."

Make sure to review each of these rules and understand them before continuing. Now let's go over the first conversation for this chapter.

한승규: 김 선생님이 어떤 사람입니까?

"What kind of person is Mr. Kim?"

137

Chapter 10

More Adjectives

Since we're asking specifically about 김 선생님, we used the Subject Marker (here, 이) to mark him as the *subject* of this sentence.

어떤 is *already* an adjective, and can be attached to a noun. Above it is attached before 사람.

> 이선주: 아주 좋은 사람입니다.
> "He is a very good person."

Although we've covered it before, I'd like to point out again how 입니다 is used to mean "he is" in this sentence. Since it's already established what the other person is asking ("What kind of person is Mr. Kim?"), there's no need to restate 김 선생님 in this reply. However, it would not be wrong to reply with the following sentence instead:

> 김 선생님이 아주 좋은 사람입니다.
> "Mr. Kim is a very good person."

Although this would not be incorrect, it would simply be a bit repetitive.

Avoid Repetitive Korean

~~I~~ like kimchi.

In Korean, pronouns such as "he," "she," and "it" are simply not necessary as long as it's already clear who or what you are talking about.

In the same way, it's unnecessary to repeat any *noun* if it's clear what you're talking about. We've already seen this in action in previous chapters, but let's take a look at some more examples.

> **Q:** 김치를 좋아합니까?
> "Do you like kimchi?"

> **A:** 네, 김치를 좋아합니다.
> "Yes, I like kimchi."

More Adjectives

Chapter 10

The previous sentences are an example of a simple exchange between two people. However, it would be perfectly acceptable (and in fact, more natural sounding) to reply in this way instead:

A: 네, 좋아합니다.
"Yes, I like it."

Just as we didn't need to repeat 김 선생님 in the first conversation, it's not necessary to repeat 김치 either, assuming it's clear to the listener what we are talking about. In English, we might replace these words with "it," "he," "she," or "they," but in Korean such words are usually not needed.

Let's continue going over the conversation.

한승규: 재미있는 사람입니까?

"Is he a fun person?"

Again, here it is also not necessary to repeat "Mr. Kim," as it's already been established who they're talking about.

이선주: 네, 재미있고 밝은 사람입니다.

"Yes, he is a fun and bright person."

In Chapter 7 we learned how to connect *nouns* together in a sentence using 와 and 과. Here is how to connect two (or more) separate *sentences* together.

As you listen to native Korean speakers talk, you may notice that 사람 ("person") and 것 ("thing") are used quite frequently in Korean after adjectives, as shown in this chapter, when describing people or things.

Verb Stem + 고

Take the verb stem and add 고. Then, attach a second connecting sentence.

저는 먹**고** 갑니다.
"I eat and leave."

김 선생님이 재미있**고** 밝은 사람입니다.
"Mr. Kim is a fun and bright person."

저는 공부하**고** 시험을 봅니다.
"I study and take a test."

139

Chapter 10

More Adjectives

저는 미국 사람이**고** 한국을 좋아합니다.
"I am an American and I like Korea."

These are each two separate sentences connected by their verbs to become one new sentence.

고 is versatile, and can also be used to connect descriptive verbs together, even outside of a complete sentence. Let's look at a few more examples.

크**고** 맛이 있는 케이크
"a big and delicious cake"

저는 크**고** 맛이 있는 케이크를 먹고 싶습니다.
"I want to eat a big and delicious cake."

빠르**고** 싼 컴퓨터
"a fast and cheap computer"

저는 빠르**고** 싼 컴퓨터를 원합니다.
"I want a fast and cheap computer."

쉽**고** 재미있는 방법
"an easy and fun method"

저는 쉽**고** 재미있는 방법을 찾습니다.
"I'm looking for an easy and fun method."

찾다 can mean both "to look for" and "to find" depending on the context of the sentence. In the above sentence, it means "to look for," but in the following sentence it means "to find."

저는 쉽**고** 재미있는 방법을 찾고 싶습니다.
"I want to find an easy and fun method."

140

More Adjectives

Chapter 10

Conversation 2

김영희:	저는 잘생긴 남자를 좋아합니다. 철수 씨는요? 어떤 여자를 좋아합니까?
김철수:	저는 예쁜 여자를 좋아합니다.
김영희:	제가 예쁜 여자입니까?
김철수:	글쎄요. 제가 잘생긴 남자입니까?

김영희: 저는 잘생긴 남자를 좋아합니다. 철수 씨는요? 어떤 여자를 좋아합니까?

"I like handsome men. What about you, Chul-soo? What kind of girls do you like?"

For the time being, only use 잘생기다 as an *adjective* – 잘생긴. Don't conjugate it at the end of a sentence (잘생깁니다 would be incorrect). We'll learn more about this verb in Chapter 20.

김철수: 저는 예쁜 여자를 좋아합니다.

"I like pretty girls."

Just like in English, 예쁘다 ("to be pretty") is used exclusively for females, and 잘생기다 ("to be handsome") is used exclusively for males.

김영희: 제가 예쁜 여자입니까?

"Am I a pretty girl?"

141

Chapter 10: More Adjectives

Here we have a word that looks new – 제가. However, 제가 is simply 저 ("I" or "me") combined with the Subject Marker (here, 가). Remember from Chapter 8 how 누구 becomes 누가 when combined with the Subject Marker? Here in the same way, 저 becomes 제가 when combined with the Subject Marker.

We use the Subject Marker here because 김영희 is asking about herself *specifically*, so she is the *subject* of her own question.

김철수: 글쎄요. 제가 잘생긴 남자입니까?
"Well... am I a handsome man?"

글쎄요 means "Well..." and is used only at the *beginning* of a sentence to show that you're considering something.

Practice

Translate to English:

1. 김철수 씨가 어떤 사람입니까?

    _____.

2. 어떤 영화를 좋아합니까?

    _____.

3. 저는 재미있는 영화를 좋아합니다.

    _____.

4. 매운 음식을 먹고 싶습니까?

    _____.

5. 짧은 영화를 좋아합니까?

    _____.

More Adjectives

6. 저는 그런 영화를 싫어합니다.

   _____.

7. 오늘 저는 학교에 가고 숙제를 합니다.

   _____.

Translate to Korean:

8. "What kind of person am I?"

   _____.

9. "I dislike that kind of food."

   _____.

10. "I am a good person."

    _____.

11. "Where is the pretty girl?"

    _____.

12. "Mrs. Kim Yung-hee is very pretty."

    _____.

13. "Do you like long movies?"

    _____.

14. "No. I like short and entertaining movies."

    _____.

Chapter 10: More Adjectives

New Phrases

글쎄요.	"Well…"

New Vocabulary

케이크	"cake"
것	"a thing"
머리	"head," "hair"
머리카락	"hair"
털	"hair (not on head)," "fur"
뿔	"horn(s)"
몸	"body"
눈	"eye"
입	"mouth"
입술	"lips"
심장	"heart"
어깨	"shoulder"
배	"belly"
위	"stomach"
허리	"waist"
이(빨)	"tooth," "teeth"
혀	"tongue"
코	"nose"
귀	"ear"
발	"foot"
발가락	"toe"
다리	"leg"
팔	"arm"
목	"neck," "throat"
소리	"sound," "noise"
목소리	"voice"
가슴	"chest"
등	"back (of body)"

More Adjectives

손	"hand"
손가락	"finger"
건강하다	"to be healthy"
건강	"health"
아프다	"to be in pain," "to be painful," "to be sick"
피곤하다	"to be tired," "to be exhausted"
졸리다	"to be sleepy"
쉬다	"to rest"
바쁘다	"to be busy"
부엌	"kitchen"
주방	"kitchen"
한국 음식	"Korean food"
한식	"Korean food" (abbreviation)
일본 음식	"Japanese food"
일식	"Japanese food" (abbreviation)
미국 음식	"American food"
미식	"American food" (abbreviation)
중국 음식	"Chinese food"
중식	"Chinese food" (abbreviation)
낮다	"to be low"
높다	"to be high"
성적	"(school) grade"
쉽다	"to be easy"
단순하다	"to be simple"
어렵다	"to be difficult"
길다	"to be long"
멀다	"to be far"
달다	"to be (sugary) sweet"
달콤하다	"to be (deliciously) sweet"
쓰다	"to be bitter"
시다	"to be sour"
어둡다	"to be dark"
밝다	"to be bright"

Chapter 10: More Adjectives

어떻다	"to be how"
그렇다	"to be so"
이렇다	"to be this way"
어떤	"what kind of" (adjective)
그런	"that kind of" (adjective)
이런	"this kind of" (adjective)
짧다	"to be short (in length)"
생각	"an idea," "a thought"
생각(을) 하다	"to think"
잘생기다	"to be handsome"
잘생긴	"handsome" (adjective)
재미(가) 있다	"to be fun," "to be entertaining"
빠르다	"to be fast"
느리다	"to be slow"
싸다	"to be cheap"
저렴하다	"to be inexpensive"
무겁다	"to be heavy"
가볍다	"to be light"
중요하다	"to be important"
새롭다	"to be new"
귀엽다	"to be cute"
추하다	"to be ugly"
깨끗하다	"to be clean"
더럽다	"to be dirty"
시험(을) 보다	"to take a test"
방법	"method," "way"
잡다	"to grab," "to catch"
찾다	"to look for," "to find"
컴퓨터	"computer"
사과	"apple"
딸기	"strawberry"

Colors

Chapter 11

Colors are another unique topic in Korean, as they also work similarly to adjectives. We'll also learn several new important vocabulary words, such as "this" and "that," as well as "here" and "there."

Conversation

A:	그것이 무엇입니까?
B:	무슨 말입니까?
A:	거기에 그 하얀 것입니다.
B:	아, 이것은 일본 국기입니다.
A:	아, 네. 그럼, 저기에 저것은 무엇입니까?
B:	저것은 태극기입니다.
A:	동그란 것은 무슨 색입니까?
B:	빨간색과 파란색입니다.
A:	저의 옷과 같은 색입니다.

Take a look at the vocabulary section for this chapter before continuing. You'll notice several different words for each color. Some of them are *descriptive verbs*, some are *adjectives* (descriptive verbs that have already been conjugated so they can be used directly before a noun), and some are *nouns* themselves.

"How can a color be a verb?"

In English, all colors can act as *nouns* or as *adjectives*.

Chapter 11: Colors

"I like *blue*." (noun)
"I like the *blue* car." (adjective)

In Korean, colors can also come from *descriptive verbs*.

파랗다 "to be blue"

> 하늘이 파랗습니다.
> "The sky is blue."

노랗다 "to be yellow"

> 연필이 노랗습니다.
> "The pencil is yellow."

These *descriptive verbs* can also be conjugated into *adjectives*.

파란 "blue"

> 파란 새
> "blue bird"

노란 "yellow"

> 노란 우산
> "yellow umbrella"

Color *adjectives* can then be conjugated into *nouns* by adding 색 *directly* to the end, which means "color."

파란색 "blue" (literally, "blue color")

> 하늘이 파란색입니다.
> "The sky is blue."

노란색 "yellow" (literally, "yellow color")

> 연필이 노란색입니다.
> "The pencil is yellow."

I've included the original *descriptive verbs* of the colors in this lesson for your reference, but feel free to only learn the *noun* and *adjective* forms for now, as they are much more common.

Colors

Chapter 11

However, some Korean colors do not come from a descriptive verb, and therefore work more simply.

초록색 "green" (noun/adjective)

초록색 can be used as a noun, or as an adjective, just like colors in English.

초록색을 좋아합니다.
"I like green." (noun)

초록색 펜
"a green pen" (adjective)

And finally, sometimes there can be more than one word for the same color, such as for *black* and for *white*. Feel free to use either one.

까만 or 검정 (adjective)

까만 고양이
"a black cat"

검정 모니터
"a black monitor"

까만색 or 검정색 (noun)

까만색을 좋아합니다.
"I like black."

검정색이 예쁩니다.
"Black is pretty."

As colors are used frequently in conversation, with a bit of practice you'll easily become able to identify them and use them for yourself.

> **Advanced**
>
> In addition to 초록색 which I mentioned above, *all* colors ending in 색 can actually be used as *adjectives* as well. The meaning is the same.
>
> 노란 뱀 "yellow snake"
>
> 노란색 뱀 "yellow(-colored) snake"

Now let's go over the conversation together.

Chapter 11: Colors

A: 그것이 무엇입니까?

"What is that?"

이, 그, and 저

Let's go over what these three *adjectives* mean, and how to use them.

이 "this"

이 is used for things which are *close to the speaker*, just like "this" in English.

이것
"this thing"

이 펜
"this pen"

이 맛이 있는 요리
"this delicious cooking"

그 "that"

그 is used for things which are *close to the listener*, but *far from the speaker*.

그것
"that thing"

그 공
"that ball"

Colors

그 빨간 드레스
"that red dress"

저 "that" (farther)

저 is used for things which are *far from both the speaker and the listener*.

저것
"that thing"

저 건물
"that building"

저 크고 무서운 집
"that big and scary house"

Going back to the conversation, in this sentence 그것 is something that is far from the speaker, but close to the listener.

Note that the words 이것, 그것, and 저것 are written as one word without any spaces. These are the most common words for saying "this thing," "that thing," and "that (farther) thing."

In addition, since 이, 그, and 저 are *adjectives*, they cannot be used by themselves, and therefore must be used before another word.

B: 무슨 말입니까?

"What?"

무슨 말 literally means "what words." The expression above can be used for asking what someone else is talking about, when you really have no idea.

We'll cover 무슨 in more detail in just a moment.

A: 거기에 그 하얀 것입니다.

"That white thing there."

여기, 거기, and 저기

Let's go over what these *nouns* mean, and how to use them.

Chapter 11

Colors

여기 "here"

Like 이, 여기 is used for places that are *close to the speaker*.

여기에 옵니까?
"Are you coming here?"

여기가 정말 좋습니다.
"Here is really good."

거기 "there"

Like 그, 거기 is used for places that are *close to the listener*, but *far from the speaker*.

저는 거기에 갑니다.
"I am going there (to you)."

거기가 어떤 곳입니까?
"What kind of place is there?"

저기 "there" (farther)

Like 저, 저기 is used for places that are *far from both the speaker and the listener*.

저기가 아주 멉니다.
"There is very far."

저기에 무엇이 있습니까?
"What is (over) there?"

여기, 거기, and 저기 will often appear *early* in a sentence; if there is no pronoun (such as 저는) then they will often appear at the *very beginning* of a sentence.

Going back to the conversation again, 거기에 is simply 거기 combined with 에 ("to," "at," or "in") to mean "*at* there." When stating that something *exists* somewhere, it's proper to include 에 to show *where* that thing exists at.

여기에 선물이 있습니다.
"There is a present (at) here."

Colors

Chapter 11

Notice that the above sentence uses the verb 있다 ("to exist") and *not* the verb 이다 ("to be"). This is because what we are actually saying is "There exists a present here" and not "This here equals a present." It's important to realize that 이다 only means "to be" in the sense of being equal to something else.

여기에 선물입니다.
"This (in) here is a present."

This sentence, while also grammatically correct, has an entirely different meaning than the previous one using 있다.

Also, notice how in the conversation 하얀 comes directly before the noun, and 그 goes before it. Words like 이, 그, and 저 will always allow other adjectives to go in front, because other adjectives are more important in describing the noun.

그 초록색 산
"that green mountain"

B: 아, 이것은 일본 국기입니다.

"Ah, this is a Japanese flag."

A: 아, 네. 그럼, 저기에 저것은 무엇입니까?

"Ah, okay. Well then, what is that thing there?"

Although 네 means "yes," it can also be used as a way to confirm that you've heard or understood something, much like "okay" is said in English.

저는 지금 먹으러 갑니다.
"I'm going to eat now."

네. 저도 먹으러 갑니다.
"Okay. I'm going to eat too."

B: 저것은 태극기입니다.

"That is the Korean national flag."

A Note on the Topic Marker

Notice how sometimes a speaker may switch from using the *Subject Marker* (for example, 그것이) to the *Topic Marker* (for example, 저것은), or vice versa.

Chapter 11

Colors

You can think of the Topic Marker (은/는) as meaning "*as for*" (as opposed to something or someone else) when used anywhere in a sentence.

The Topic Marker is 은 when following a *consonant*, or 는 when following a *vowel*. It attaches *directly* after the word it applies to.

저것은 거울입니다.
"As for that thing, it's a mirror."

김 씨는 친절한 사람입니다.
"As for Mr. Kim, he is a nice person."

저는 미국 사람입니다.
"As for me, I am American."

We'll learn about the Topic Marker and Subject Marker in more detail in Chapter 15, but keep this in mind whenever you see the Topic Marker from now on.

Culture Notes

태극기 is the Korean national flag. The circle in the center represents *yin* (blue – negative force) and *yang* (red – positive force) – the balancing forces in the universe. The white background represents *purity*, and the black lines represent *harmony* between the sky, sun, earth, and moon.

A: 동그란 것은 무슨 색입니까?

"What color is the round thing?"

Previously we learned that 무엇 is the *noun* for "what." 무슨 is the *adjective* for "what." It is used directly before a noun.

무엇을 좋아합니까?
"What do you like?"

무슨 색을 좋아합니까?
"What color do you like?"

Colors

Chapter 11

이것이 무엇입니까?
"What is this?"

무슨 책입니까?
"What book is it?"

무엇을 먹고 싶습니까?
"What do you want to eat?"

무슨 음식을 좋아합니까?
"What food do you like?"

B: 빨간색과 파란색입니다.

"It is red and blue."

A: 저의 옷과 같은 색입니다.

"It is the same color as my clothes."

Possessive Marker 의

Up until now, we haven't had any way to say that something belonged to anyone. In Korean, saying that something is "mine" or "his" is done by simply attaching 의 *after* the person who owns it, followed by *what* it is that they own. You can think of it as meaning *'s*, as in "Mr. Kim**'s** laptop."

Whenever the Possessive Marker is used, it is most commonly pronounced the same as 에. This rule only applies to when 의 is used as the Possessive Marker; if 의 appears in other situations, such as in part of another word, it cannot be pronounced 에.

김 씨의 노트북
"Mr. Kim's laptop"

저의 자동차
"my car"

저의 방
"my room"

As expected, 의 *replaces* the Topic Marker (은/는), Subject Marker (이/가), or Object Marker (을/를) when used in this way.

155

Chapter 11

Colors

의 can also be used after *things*, and not only after people. In this way, it can also translate as "*of*," such as in "the walls *of* the building"

건물의 벽
"the walls of the building," or "the building's walls"

신뢰의 문제
"a problem of trust," or "a trust problem"

And here's another useful phrase you can say with 의:

저의 이름은 ____입니다.
"My name is ____."

When 저 combines with 의, you can have two outcomes; one is 저의, and the other is simply 제. Both ways are acceptable, though more often in conversation 제 will be preferred because it's shorter.

저의 친구
"my friend"

제 친구
"my friend"

제 이름은 김철수입니다.
"My name is Kim Chul-soo."

"Like"

같다 is a descriptive verb that means "to be the same" or "to be like." When combined with 와/과, it means "to be the same *as.*"

이것이 그것과 같습니다.
"This is the same as that."

The item you are describing will come first (이것) followed by the item it is similar to (그것).

이 셔츠가 저 셔츠와 같습니다.
"This shirt is the same as that shirt."

저와 같은 사람
"a person like me"

Colors

Chapter 11

Here, 같다 is conjugated as an *adjective* to become 같은.

To emphasize that something or someone is *exactly* like something or someone else, use the descriptive verb 똑같다 which means "to be exactly the same."

제 이름과 똑같습니다.
"It's exactly the same as my name."

The verb 비슷하다 can also be used in the same way; it means "to be similar," so it's not as strong as using 같다.

이것이 그것과 조금 비슷합니다.
"This is a little similar to that."

In contrast, the verb 다르다 ("to be different") can be used to express that someone or something is *different* from someone or something else.

이것이 그것과 조금 다릅니다.
"This is a little different from that."

Culture Notes

One more color you should know about is 살구색, the color of Asian skin. Koreans, when referring to their skin color or the skin color of Japanese and Chinese people, will use 살구색 – this means "apricot color."

Practice

Translate to English:

1. 저는 검정 가방을 원합니다.

_____.

2. 저 집이 큽니다.

_____.

3. 저의 얼굴이 빨간색입니다.

_____.

157

Chapter 11 — Colors

4. 저 먼 산은 초록색입니다.

_____.

5. 저의 집이 여기에 있습니다.

_____.

6. 이것이 그것과 같습니다.

_____.

7. 김철수 씨가 저 남자와 같은 사람입니까?

_____.

Translate to Korean:

8. "I want to eat a green apple."

_____.

9. "My clothes are red."

_____.

10. "As for cats, they are cute."

_____.

11. "I want to go there."

_____.

12. "This movie is fun."

_____.

Colors

Chapter 11

13. "This hat is the same as that hat."

_____.

14. "That shirt is exactly the same as my shirt."

_____.

New Phrases

저의 이름은 ____ 입니다.	"My name is ____."
예(를) 들면...	"For example..."

New Vocabulary

색(깔)	"color"
예	"an example (of something)"
살구	"apricot"
살구색	"apricot color"
시간	"time"
시대	"a period," "an age," "a generation"
셔츠	"shirt"
티셔츠 (or T 셔츠)	"T-shirt"
이름	"name"
얼굴	"face"
턱	"chin"
뺨	"cheek"
여드름	"pimple," "acne"
주름	"wrinkle(s)"
옷	"clothing," "clothes"
속옷	"underwear"
모자	"hat"
의	Possessive Marker
같다	"to be the same," "to be like"
똑같다	"to be exactly the same"

Chapter 11: Colors

비슷하다	"to be similar"
다르다	"to be different"
빼다	"to remove"
추가(를) 하다	"to add (to something)"
패다	"to beat," "to bash"
동그랗다	"to be round"
희망	"hope"
태극기	"the Korean national flag"
국기	"flag"
무슨	"what" (adjective)
빨갛다	"to be red"
빨간	"red" (adjective)
빨간색	"red" (noun)
노랗다	"to be yellow"
노란	"yellow" (adjective)
노란색	"yellow" (noun)
파랗다	"to be blue"
파란	"blue" (adjective)
파란색	"blue" (noun)
초록색	"green" (noun/adjective)
하얗다	"to be white"
하얀	"white" (adjective)
하얀색	"white" (noun)
흰	"white" (adjective)
흰색	"white" (noun)
까맣다	"to be black"
까만	"black" (adjective)
까만색	"black" (noun)
검정	"black" (adjective)
검정색	"black" (noun)
뱀	"snake"
개구리	"frog"
이	"this" (adjective)
그	"that" (adjective)

Colors

저	"that (farther)" (adjective)
이것	"this thing"
그것	"that thing"
저것	"that thing (farther)"
여기	"here"
거기	"there"
저기	"there (farther)"
요리	"cooking"
요리(를) 하다	"to cook"
섞다	"to mix"
공	"ball"
드레스	"dress"
건물	"building"
다리	"bridge"
단계	"a step"
계단	"stairs"
무섭다	"to be scary," "to be afraid"
곳	"place" (noun)
선물	"present"
산	"mountain"
새	"bird"
말	"horse"
양	"sheep"
우산	"umbrella"
거울	"mirror"
벽	"wall"
창(문)	"window"
노트북	"laptop" (literally, "notebook")
신뢰	"trust"
모니터	"monitor"
문제	"problem"
질문	"question"
질문(을) 하다	"to ask a question"
자르다	"to cut (off)," "to sever"

Chapter 11: Colors

| 베다 | "to cut (into)" |
| 그럼 | "well then" |

Numbers

Chapter 12

Did you know Korean has two different number systems? Each one is used in different situations. This chapter will focus on the first number system, Sino-Korean numbers, as well as when and how to use it. We'll learn more about these two number systems in the next chapter.

Conversation 1

김영희:	이것이 얼마입니까?
직원:	그것은 삼만오천백원입니다.
김영희:	여기 사만원입니다.
직원:	네, 여기 사천구백원입니다.
김영희:	감사합니다. 안녕히 계세요.

Counting in Korean

Counting in Korean works differently than in English; in some ways it's more difficult (we'll get to this later), but in many ways it's much simpler. The best way to learn is to jump right in.

So let's go ahead and learn how to count from 1 to 99,999,999 in Korean.

Chapter 12: Numbers

For numbers 1 through 10, simply count them as normal.

1	일
2	이
3	삼
4	사
5	오
6	육
7	칠
8	팔
9	구
10	십

After 10, Korean numbers are made by breaking apart each of the digits, like simple math, then saying them in order one at a time.

11 = 10 & 1	십일
12 = 10 & 2	십이
19 = 10 & 9	십구
20 = 2 & 10	이십
21 = 2 & 10 & 1	이십일
50 = 5 & 10	오십
55 = 5 & 10 & 5	오십오
99 = 9 & 10 & 9	구십구

Once you've hit the next amount for which there is a separate number (here being 100), switch to that in order to count higher. Continue in the same method as before.

100	백
101 = 100 & 1	백일
111 = 100 & 10 & 1	백십일
202 = 2 & 100 & 2	이백이
550 = 5 & 100 & 5 & 10	오백오십
1,000	천
1,999 = 1000 & 9 & 100 & 9 & 10 & 9	천구백구십구
9,876 = 9 & 1,000 & 8 & 100 & 7 & 10 & 6	구천팔백칠십육

Numbers

Chapter 12

You can continue using this method to count as high as you would like.

10,000	만
10,011 = 10,000 & 10 & 1	만십일
10,555 = 10,000 & 5 & 100 & 5 & 10 & 5	만오백오십오

You can express numbers beyond 10,000 by adding 10, 100, or 1,000 before it to reach 10,000,000.

100,000 = 10 & 10,000	십만
1,000,000 = 100 & 10,000	백만
10,000,000 = 1,000 & 10,000	천만

Here are some more examples of counting with high numbers.

100,090 = 10 & 10,000 & 9 & 10	십만구십
1,900,900 = 100 & 9 & 10 & 10,000 & 9 & 100	백구십만구백
99,999,999 = 9 & 1,000 & 9 & 100 & 9 & 10 & 9 & 10,000 & 9 & 1,000 & 9 & 100 & 9 & 10 & 9	구천구백구십구만구천구백구십구

Numbers this large might be difficult to say in any language, so including them here is more to illustrate how numbers work (so don't feel bad if you're not able to calculate large numbers yet). Don't worry about memorizing any specific numbers besides the major milestones – 1 to 10, 100, 1,000, and 10,000. Knowing how these numbers come together to form larger numbers will allow you to create any number you wish from this small set of numbers.

Here are some more examples of counting in Korean.

0	영	50	오십
1	일	60	육십
10	십	70	칠십
11	십일	80	팔십
16*	십육*	90	구십
20	이십	100	백
25	이십오	101	백일
30	삼십	200	이백
40	사십	999	구백구십구

Chapter 12

Numbers

1,001	천일	5,555	오천오백오십오
1,010	천십	7,777	칠천칠백칠십칠
1,100	천백	8,099	팔천구십구
2,000	이천	9,100	구천백

Note that 십육 is pronounced as 심뉵.

> **Adv**
> Not only is 16 (십육) pronounced as 심뉵, but any combination of a ten and six will be pronounced the same way. 26 will be pronounced 이심뉵, 36 will be 삼심뉵, 186 will be 백팔심뉵, and so on.

Notice how whenever the first digit is a 1, there is no 일 added to the beginning.

100	백
500 = 5 & 100	오백
1,000	천
2,000 = 2 & 1,000	이천
10,000	만
30,000 = 3 & 10,000	삼만

This chapter, as well as the next chapter, present numbers written *phonetically* in 한글. This is only to help explain how numbers work, and how they sound. In real Korean, numbers are *written* using Arabic numerals, like in English. However, I recommend writing out the numbers phonetically in this way for this chapter and the next chapter as practice.

> **Advanced**
> The largest single number unit we covered in this chapter is 10,000, but you can count higher than 99,999,999 in Korean. The next increment beyond 만 is a hundred million (100,000,000), and is called 억. This works in the same way as our previous units. Using this next unit enables us to count up to 999,999,999,999.
>
> 100,000,000 = **억**
>
> Although numbers these high may seem useless, 억 is actually used quite frequently. This is mainly due to how South Korea's currency works, as we'll learn next.

Numbers

Chapter 12

원 – the currency of Korea

The official currency of South Korea is the "Won" – 원.

In order to count 원 ("Won"), simply attach 원 to the end of a number.

10 Won	십원
100 Won	백원
500 Won	오백원
1,000 Won	천원
10,000 Won	만원
99,999 Won	구만구천구백구십구원

Culture Notes

Exchange rates for Won can vary depending on the economy, so check with a bank before traveling to Korea to see how much money you will get when exchanging. At the time of writing this book, one US dollar is equivalent to around 1,000 Won. Be aware of the value of Won in order to budget well and avoid overpaying for things while in South Korea.

Now that we've learned how to count, let's go over the first conversation.

김영희: 이것이 얼마입니까?

"How much is this?"

얼마 means "how much," so 얼마입니까? means "how much is it?" Combining this with 이것이 makes it more specific that you are referring to "this thing."

You can use this same construction to ask the price of anything you'd like.

Chapter 12

Numbers

얼마입니까?
"How much is it?"

비행기표가 얼마입니까?
"How much is a plane ticket?"

감자튀김이 얼마입니까?
"How much are French fries?"

직원: 그것은 삼만오천백원입니다.

"That is 35,100 Won."

In the last chapter, we learned that the Topic Marker (은/는) can be used after a word to mean "as for." In this case, 그것은 means "as for that (thing)."

Another way to translate this sentence would therefore be "As for that, it's 35,100 Won."

김영희: 여기 사만원입니다.

"Here is 40,000 Won."

직원: 네, 여기 사천구백원입니다.

"Okay, here is 4,900 Won."

김영희: 감사합니다. 안녕히 계세요.

"Thank you. Goodbye."

Remember that saying 안녕히 계세요 to the employee means that the employee is staying, and the speaker is leaving.

Numbers

Chapter 12

Conversation 2

김영희:	아, 저는 오늘 기쁩니다.
김철수:	왜 기쁩니까? 무엇 때문에 그렇게 기쁩니까?
김영희:	저는 일이 있기 때문에 기쁩니다. 그것 때문에 돈도 있습니다.
김철수:	저는 슬픕니다.
김영희:	왜 슬픕니까?
김철수:	저의 일을 싫어하기 때문입니다.

Let's continue by covering this second conversation.

> 김영희: 아, 저는 오늘 기쁩니다.
> "Ah, I am happy today."

Although we'll go over the Topic Marker (은/는) in more detail later, I'd like to emphasize again that its meaning is similar to "as for."

Another way to translate this sentence would be "Ah, as for me, I am happy today."

> 김철수: 왜 기쁩니까? 무엇 때문에 그렇게 기쁩니까?
> "Why are you happy? What are you so happy because of?"

Chapter 12

Numbers

"Because"
Noun + 때문에/때문입니다

If you want to say "because of" in the *middle* of a sentence, take a *noun* and attach 때문에 after it.

저의 일 때문에 슬픕니다.
"I am sad because of my work."

숙제 때문에 학교에 갑니다.
"I am going to school because of homework."

Notice how the order of the sentence is *reversed* from how we would say the same thing in English – "Because of homework, I am going to school." In Korean, the *cause* comes before the *reason*.

If you want to say "it is because of" at the *end* of a sentence, take a noun and attach 때문, followed by 입니다 (which comes from the verb 이다).

저의 일 때문에 돈이 있습니다.
"I have money because of my work."

저의 일 때문입니다.
"It is because of my work."

This form has a *negative meaning* if used after a *person*. Saying 때문에 after a person is a rude way to say he or she made a mistake.

김 씨 때문입니다!
"It's because of Mr. Kim!"

This sentence would also feel like you are accusing Mr. Kim of something being his *fault*. Avoid using 때문 after a person.

> **Advanced**
>
> To express "because of" a person in a *positive way*, use 덕분 instead of 때문 – "thanks to."
>
> 김 씨 **덕분**에 돈이 있습니다.
> "I have money thanks to Mr. Kim."
>
> 김 씨 **덕분**입니다!
> "It is thanks to Mr. Kim!"

Numbers

Chapter 12

The Adverb 그렇게

그렇게 is an adverb which means "so" (or "in that way"), and is attached before a verb. It's most often used this way in *questions*.

그렇게 재미있습니까?
"Is it so fun?"

저도 그렇게 생각합니다.
"I think so too."

왜 그렇게 행복합니까?
"Why are you so happy?"

그렇게 맛있습니까?
"Is it so delicious?"

그렇게 comes from the verb 그렇다, which means "to be so."

A common usage of the verb 그렇다 is for requesting *confirmation* – "is that so?"

그렇습니까?
"Is that so?"

Although the literal meaning of 그렇다 is "to be so," a more natural sounding translation of the above sentence would be this:

그렇습니까?
"Really?"

그렇다 can also be used for confirming things to others – "that is so."

그렇습니다.
"That is so."

This would also be more naturally translated as "really."

그렇습니다.
"Really."

This chapter introduces two verbs which mean "to be happy" – 기쁘다 and 행복하다. Both are common and share the same meaning, so feel free to use either one.

171

Chapter 12

Numbers

김영희: 저는 일이 있기 때문에 기쁩니다. 그것 때문에 돈도 있습니다.

"I am happy because I have a job. Because of that I have money too."

"Because"
Verb Stem + 기 때문에/기 때문입니다

This same "because of" form also works with verbs.

If you want to say "because of" in the *middle* of a sentence, take a verb stem and attach 기 때문에 after it.

돈이 있기 때문에 기쁩니다.
"I am happy because I have money."

학교에 가기 때문에 숙제가 있습니다.
"I have homework because I go to school."

저는 미국 사람이기 때문에 영어를 잘합니다.
"Because I am an American I speak English well."

> **Adv** — When the adverb 잘 comes before the verb 하다 (잘하다), it can attach *directly* without any space; this is an exception. When used without a space, its meaning also slightly changes from "to do well" to become "to do something skillfully." This is often used when talking about speaking languages.

The above sentence would literally translate as "Because I am an American I *do* English well." However, it's not necessary to say "speak," because using the verb 하다 ("to do") following a language (Korean, English, etc.) implies that you mean "speak."

If you want to say "it is because of" at the *end* of a sentence, take a verb stem and attach 기 때문, followed by 입니다.

자동차가 있기 때문입니다.
"It's because I have a car."

너무 빨리 먹기 때문입니다.
"It's because you eat too fast."

김철수: 저는 슬픕니다.

"I am sad."

Numbers

김영희: 왜 슬픕니까?

"Why are you sad?"

김철수: 저의 일을 싫어하기 때문입니다.

"Because I dislike my work."

Practice

Write the following numbers phonetically in Korean:

1. 15
2. 29
3. 81
4. 99
5. 101
6. 333
7. 500
8. 1,001
9. 9,000
10. 10,112
11. 50,500
12. 900,000
13. 1,000,000

Translate to Korean:

14. "I have 1,000 Won."

_____.

15. "How much is this cat?"

_____.

16. "I am happy because I have a house."

_____.

Chapter 12 — Numbers

17. "I am happy because of my house."

18. "Is this homework so difficult?"

Translate to English:

19. 그것이 얼마입니까?

20. 저는 19,000 원이 있습니다.

21. 숙제가 있기 때문에 슬픕니다.

22. 오늘 저의 숙제 때문에 슬픕니다.

23. 정말 그렇게 쉽습니까?

New Phrases

얼마입니까?	"How much does it cost?"

Numbers

Chapter 12

New Vocabulary

영	0
일	1
이	2
삼	3
사	4
오	5
육	6
칠	7
팔	8
구	9
십	10
백	100
천	1,000
만	10,000
십만	100,000
백만	1,000,000
천만	10,000,000
억	100,000,000
원	"Won" (Korean currency)
기쁘다	"to be happy"
행복하다	"to be happy"
슬프다	"to be sad"
자연	"nature"
자연스럽다	"to be natural"
훌륭하다	"to be wonderful"
결혼	"marriage"
결혼(을) 하다	"to marry"
무례하다	"to be impolite"
예의(가) 바르다	"to be polite"
가격	"price," "cost"
손님	"guest," "customer"
이웃	"neighbor"

Chapter 12: Numbers

번호	"number (of something)"
전화	"telephone call"
전화기	"telephone"
전화번호	"phone number"
전화(를) 하다	"to telephone," "to call"
전화(를) 받다	"to answer the phone"
직원	"employee"
회사	"company"
사장님	"boss"
대통령	"the President"
정부	"government"
경제	"economics"
정치	"politics"
자유	"freedom"
사회	"society"
문화	"culture"
표	"ticket"
비행기표	"plane ticket"
감자튀김	"French fries"
숫자	"an integer," "a number"
비밀	"a secret"
비밀 번호	"password"
그렇게	"so," "in that way" (adverb)
너무	"too (much)," "overly" (adverb)

More Numbers

Chapter 13

Last chapter we focused on *Sino-Korean numbers* (we'll cover what this means), and this chapter we'll introduce *Pure Korean numbers*, as well as how and when to use them. We'll also learn what the distinction between Sino-Korean numbers and Pure Korean numbers is, and why it's important to know both of them.

Conversation

A:	몇 명이 옵니까?
B:	세 명이 옵니다. 저와 김 씨와 제 친구도 옵니다.
A:	그 친구는 제주도에서 여기까지 옵니까?
B:	네, 맞습니다. 그리고 그분의 고양이도 데리고 옵니다.
A:	고양이라고요? 몇 마리를 데리고 옵니까?
B:	한 마리지만, 그 한 마리가 개보다 더 큽니다.
A:	아이고! 정말 고양이가 맞습니까?

Pure Korean and Sino-Korean Numbers

In the last chapter, we learned how to count in Korean using *Sino-Korean numbers*. "Sino" is a word that means "China," and Sino-Korean numbers are numbers that originated from the *Chinese language*. Some things, such as money (원) are counted using Sino-Korean numbers, as we learned in the last chapter, but other things are counted using Pure Korean numbers.

Chapter 13

More Numbers

Pure Korean numbers are numbers which did not originate from China, but developed within Korea. You will need to become familiar with both Sino and Pure Korean numbers in order to properly speak Korean.

But don't worry! In some ways, Pure Korean numbers are simpler than Sino-Korean numbers. Pure Korean numbers have different uses than Sino-Korean numbers. We'll go over these in a bit.

If you're simply counting numbers *on their own*, such as when teaching someone how to count to ten in Korean, and not counting anything, it's much more common and preferred to use Sino-Korean numbers.

This chapter will focus on Pure Korean numbers and how to use them. We'll also learn how to count things besides only 원.

Let's go over the Pure Korean numbers.

1	하나
2	둘
3	셋
4	넷
5	다섯
6	여섯
7	일곱
8	여덟
9	아홉
10	열
20	스물
30	서른
40	마흔

Remember from the rules of reading 한글 that 여덟 is pronounced as 여덜.

Fortunately, counting Pure Korean numbers is done in the same way as Sino-Korean numbers. However, Pure Korean has special numbers for 20, 30, and 40.

> **Adv** Also notice the unique *spacing* used with Pure Korean numbers and also with counters. It's not required that you know exactly how to space words in Korean, as many Koreans are unaware of the rules as well; improper spacing will not severely impact your Korean, but proper spacing does show a stronger understanding of the written language.

More Numbers

11 = 10 & 1	열 하나
19 = 10 & 9	열 아홉
21 = 20 & 1	스물 하나
39 = 30 & 9	서른 아홉
41 = 40 & 1	마흔 하나

This is in contrast to Sino-Korean numbers, such as the following example:

21 = 2 & 10 & 1	이십일

Once we reach 50, things go back to normal.

50 = 5 & 10	오십
65 = 6 & 10 & 5	육십오
100	백

See what happened? Once we pass 49, we can simply switch to Sino-Korean again. This is because many of the larger Pure Korean numbers are now no longer used anymore (such as 100 and above).

In fact, if you want to, feel free to switch back to Sino-Korean once you've hit 40, and it'll still be acceptable.

> **Advanced**
>
> There are actually Pure Korean numbers that go up extremely high, though these are no longer in use and most people do not know them. However, there are also numbers for **50**, **60**, **70**, **80**, and **90** which are still in use today; Koreans might not use these numbers often, but it would be useful to know them, especially if you have plans to visit Korea in the future. Here are those numbers:
>
> 50 → 쉰
> 60 → 예순
> 70 → 일흔
> 80 → 여든
> 90 → 아흔
>
> And here are some examples of numbers within this range.
>
> 51 → 쉰 하나
> 64 → 예순 넷
> 72 → 일흔 둘
> 85 → 여든 다섯
> 99 → 아흔 아홉
>
> 100 → 백
>
> Regardless of how high you wish to count in Pure Korean numbers, you will still switch back to Sino-Korean once you hit 100, as Pure Korean numbers for 100 and above are no longer used in Korea.

Chapter 13: More Numbers

Counting and Counters

Now that we've learned how to count with both Sino-Korean and Pure Korean numbers, let's see what we can do with them.

In the last chapter we learned how to use Sino-Korean numbers to count South Korean Won.

> 1,000 Won   천원

And of course, we can use Sino-Korean numbers to say numbers on their own.

> 112   백십이

But what if you want to count other things, like people?

You will need to learn what is called *counters* in order to do this. A *counter* is a word that is only used when counting something. In order to say "1 person," you will need to know the *person counter*, and in order to say "1 animal" you will need to know the *animal counter*. English actually also has a similar concept.

"a *swarm* of bees" / "a *pack* of wolves" / "a *herd* of buffalo" / "a *flock* of geese"

But imagine having to learn a different counter, such as "swarm" or "pack," for every different type of animal. In Korean, things are much less complicated.

What you are counting will determine whether you will need to use Sino-Korean or Pure Korean. For 원, use Sino-Korean as we learned in the last chapter.

Let's go over some things that are counted using Pure Korean numbers.

Animals are counted using 마리.

소 아홉 마리 "nine cows"

물고기 일곱 마리 "seven fish"

Notice how we name the animal first, followed by the Korean number, and then the counter. This is how all counting works in Korean – first specify *what* you are counting (here 소 or 물고기), followed by the *number*, and then the *counter*.

개 여섯 마리 "six dogs"

More Numbers

Chapter 13

고양이 한 마리 "one cat"

For this example, 하나 becomes 한. This is because the first four numbers (1, 2, 3, and 4) in Pure Korean are special, and change form when used before a counter.

1	하나	→	한
2	둘	→	두
3	셋	→	세
4	넷	→	네

In addition, the number 20 also changes when used directly before a counter.

| 20 | 스물 | → | 스무 |

개 한 마리 "one dog"

쥐 두 마리 "two mice"

뱀 세 마리 "three snakes"

사자 네 마리 "four lions"

Let's look at a few examples.

저는 고양이 한 마리가 있습니다.
"I have one cat."

여기에 뱀 여섯 마리가 있습니다.
"Here are six snakes."

Remember that although we're using counters, you will still need to attach whatever *marker* you would normally use – above, we're attaching the *Subject Marker*.

닭 백 마리를 먹고 싶습니다.
"I want to eat 100 chickens."

And here we attached the *Object Marker*. Remember that for any number 50 or above (even 40 or above if you'd like), feel free to switch to Sino-Korean numbers (here 백마리).

People are counted using 명.

사람 세 명 "3 people"

Chapter 13: More Numbers

사람 여섯 명 "6 people"

사람 만 명 "10,000 people"

Or, you can simply use a Pure Korean number with the counter 명 all by itself, and it will still have the same meaning.

세 명 "3 people"

오십 명 "50 people"

저는 (사람) 다섯 명을 초대합니다.
"I'm inviting 5 people."

Items (including things for which there is no specific counter) are counted using 개.

의자 일곱 개 "7 chairs"

펜 열 두 개 "12 pens"

상자 세 개 "3 boxes"

저는 컴퓨터 한 개가 있습니다.
"I have one computer."

의자 두 개를 원합니다.
"I want two chairs."

Age is counted using 살.

세 살 "3 years old"

스무 살 "20 years old"

저는 스물 일곱 살입니다.
"I am 27 years old."

김 선생님은 서른 두 살입니다.
"Mr. Kim is 32 years old."

More Numbers

Chapter 13

> **Advanced**
>
> 살 is a bit of an exception; it should only be used with Pure Korean numbers. However, this doesn't mean that you need to learn all numbers to 100 in order to say a person's age; instead, once you are no longer able to use Pure Korean numbers (above 40), it's more common to use the counter 세 instead of 살.
>
> While 살 is used with Pure Korean numbers, 세 is used with Sino-Korean numbers.
>
> 30 years old → 서른 살
> 50 years old → 오십 세
> 73 years old → 칠십삼 세
> 82 years old → 팔십이 세

몇 can be used before a counter to mean "how many," and is used for asking about quantities.

몇 명입니까?
"How many people?"

몇 명이 있습니까?
"How many people are there?"

닭 몇 마리를 먹고 싶습니까?
"How many chickens do you want to eat?"

김 씨는 몇 살입니까?
"As for Mr. Kim, how old is he?"

몇 살입니까?
"How old are you?"

Asking someone his or her age with 몇 살입니까? is only acceptable to people who are *younger* than yourself. In Chapter 15 we will cover a more polite, standard way of asking a person's age.

> **Advanced**
>
> 몇 can also mean "some" or "a few." Whether it is being used to mean "how many," "some," or "a few," will be clear from the context. It is used in the same way, before a *counter*.
>
> 몇 명이 옵니까?
> "How many people are coming?"
>
> 몇 명이 옵니다.
> "A few people are coming."

Measuring things is done using Sino-Korean numbers. Like most countries besides the United States, Korea uses the metric system.

미터 "meter"
→ 이 미터 "2 meters"

Chapter 13

More Numbers

센티미터 "centimeter"
→ 십 센티미터 "10 centimeters"

밀리미터 "millimeter"
→ 육 밀리미터 "6 millimeters"

킬로(그램) "kilo(gram)"
→ 이백 킬로 "200 kilos"

그램 "gram"
→ 백오십 그램 "150 grams"

리터 "liter"
→ 팔 리터 "8 liters"

도 "degrees"
→ 사십 도 "40 degrees"

Note that Korea uses Celsius for measuring degrees.

Although Korea uses the metric system, if you're in the United States, you can use your local measurement system in Korean as well.

갤런 "gallon"
→ 삼 갤런 "3 gallons"

마일 "mile"
→ 백 마일 "100 miles"

톤 "ton"
→ 오천 톤 "5,000 tons"

Want to Have

몇 개를 가지고 싶습니까?
"How many do you want to have?"

The above sentence uses the verb 가지다 instead of 원하다. In fact, using the verb 원하다 to express that you want something (which we've used up until this point) is actually a bit direct – "I *want*." A more natural way to say this is by using the verb 가지다, which means "to have (on your person)" or "to hold." 가지고 싶다 therefore means "to want to have." Also note that 싶다 is the original verb where 싶습니다 comes from.

More Numbers

Chapter 13

저는 새로운 핸드폰을 가지고 싶습니다.
"I want to have a new cell phone."

However, do not use the verb 가지다 by itself to say that you have something on your person yet, as it must be conjugated another way that this book does not cover. Continue to use the verb 있다 to express that you have something.

> **Adv**: You may also come across the verb 갖다. Both 갖다 and 가지다 have the same meaning, and are interchangeable. 갖다 is an abbreviation of 가지다.

Flat items, such as paper items and shirts, are counted using 장.

종이 한 장
"1 sheet of paper"

종이 백 장
"100 sheets of paper"

셔츠 열 두 장
"12 shirts"

Books are counted using 권.

책 한 권
"1 book"

책 서른 권
"30 books"

As I mentioned for the counter 명, if it's already clear what you are referring to, feel free to leave off the first noun (*what* you are counting), and simply say the Pure Korean number with its counter.

거기에 사람 몇 명이 갑니까?
"How many people are going there?"

세 명이 갑니다.
"3 people are going."

It would be fine to say 사람 세 명이 갑니다, though it's unnecessary since it's already clear that you're talking about people simply by using the 명 counter.

More Numbers

Let's go over some more counters. This is not a complete list of every counter, but includes most of the common ones you will find in Korean.

Remember that saying *what* you are counting before the number and counter is *optional*.

벌 clothing counter
→ (양복) 한 벌 "1 suit"

마디 word counter
→ (말) 한 마디 "1 word"

병 bottle counter
→ (맥주) 열 두 병 "12 bottles of beer"
→ (물) 세 병 "3 bottles of water"

자루 long, thin item counter
→ (연필) 세 자루 "3 pencils"
→ (칼) 한 자루 "1 knife"

켤레 pairs (of shoes or socks) counter
→ (양말) 두 켤레 "2 pairs of socks"
→ (신발) 한 켤레 "1 pair of shoes"

판 pizza counter
→ (피자) 스물 다섯 판 "25 pizzas"

접시 plate counter
→ (볶음밥) 일곱 접시 "7 plates of fried rice"

컵 cup counter
→ (물) 한 컵 "1 cup of water"

그루 tree counter
→ (나무) 한 그루 "1 tree"

대 appliance or car counter
→ (자동차) 두 대 "2 cars"
→ (컴퓨터) 세 대 "3 computers"

조각 piece counter
→ (빵) 한 조각 "1 piece of bread"
→ (피자) 세 조각 "3 pieces of pizza"

번 times counter
→ 한 번 "once," "one time"
→ 두 번 "twice," "two times"

저는 이 음식을 **백 번** 더 먹고 싶습니다.
"I want to eat this food 100 more times."

Now that we've got everything about numbers cleared up, let's go over the conversation.

A: 몇 명이 옵니까?

"How many people are coming?"

More Numbers

Chapter 13

Although it would be grammatically fine to say 사람 몇 명이 옵니까? here, it isn't necessary because the counter 명 is only used in reference to *people*. Unless it were vague that you were referring to people (such as in the middle of talking about something completely different), it's fine to leave off 사람.

> B: 세 명이 옵니다. 저와 김 씨와 제 친구도 옵니다.
> "3 people are coming. Me and Mr. Kim and my friend are coming too."

> A: 그 친구는 제주도에서 여기까지 옵니까?
> "Is that friend coming from Jeju Island to here?"

A 에서 B 까지

This is how to say "*from A to B*" when talking about *locations*. 에서 here means "from," and 까지 means "until" or "(up) to."

> 저는 저의 집에서 김 씨의 집까지 걸어갑니다.
> "I'm walking from my house to Mr. Kim's house."

> 김 씨는 거기에서 여기까지 옵니다.
> "Mr. Kim is coming from there to here."

> 학교에서 병원까지 갑니다.
> "I'm going from the school to the hospital."

Adv: In other situations, 에서 can also mean "at" or "in," but we'll go over these situations in Chapter 15. For now, just remember that 에서 means "from a location." Note that this is not how you would say "from person A to person B," but that this is *only* used for locations. We'll go over how to say "from person A to person B" in Chapter 17.

Culture Notes

To many in Korea, 제주도 is known as the Hawaii of South Korea, and rightly so. Located between South Korea and Japan, 제주도 has warmer weather year-round; in winter it rarely drops below freezing. 제주도 is home to many popular nature-related attractions, such as waterfalls, underground lava tubes, and Mt. Halla (한라산).

Chapter 13 — More Numbers

B: 네, 맞습니다. 그리고 그분의 고양이도 데리고 옵니다.
"Yes, that's right. And he is bringing his cat too."

맞다 means "to be correct," but can also translate as "to be right."

> **Adv**: 맞다, when meaning "to be correct," conjugates to an *adjective* as 맞는 ("correct").

그분 – "he," "she," "*that person*"

그분 literally means "that person" (분 is a special, polite word that means "person"). You can use it to refer to anyone with whom you are not acquainted, or for anyone who you do not know the name of. Remember that it means "that person," so you would not use this if the person is standing in the same room as you, just as you would not call someone "that person" in English if he or she is present.

You can use 그분 for both males and females, making it a convenient way to say "he" or "she" in Korean.

Nevertheless, it's best to refer to people by their names when possible.

그분이 좋은 사람입니다.
"He/she is a good person."

그분이 누구입니까?
"Who is he/she?"

그분은 저의 친구 입니다.
"As for him/her, he/she is my friend."

그분을 만나고 싶습니다.
"I want to meet him/her."

데리다 and 가지다

These two verbs both mean "to take," but are used a bit differently. 데리다 is used for *people* or *animals* (never for things), while 가지다 is used exclusively for *things* (never for people).

Combined with the verbs 가다 and 오다 (using 고), these verbs mean "to take" and "to bring."

More Numbers

Chapter 13

파티에 김 씨를 데리고 갑니다.
"I'm taking Mr. Kim to the party."

그분은 파티에 김 씨를 데리고 옵니다.
"He's bringing Mr. Kim to the party."

파티에 김치를 가지고 갑니다.
"I'm taking kimchi to the party."

그분은 파티에 김치를 가지고 옵니다.
"He's bringing kimchi to the party."

> **Adv** Alternate versions of 데리고 가다 and 데리고 오다 are 데려가다 and 데려오다. Alternate versions of 가지고 가다 and 가지고 오다 are 가져가다 and 가져오다. These can be used in the same way as the versions taught above, and have the same meaning.

A: 고양이라고요? 몇 마리를 데리고 옵니까?
"Did you say cat? How many is he bringing?"

(이)라고요?

Use this after a word to confirm whether or not someone said something. An equivalent expression in English would be "Did you say...?"

Use 이라고요 if the word ends in a *consonant*, or use 라고요 if the word ends in a *vowel*.

저라고요?
"Did you say me?"

선생님이라고요?
"Did you say the teacher?"

치즈라고요?
"Did you say cheese?"

This form can also be used in statements to repeat something that someone said.

김 선생님이라고요.
"He said Mr. Kim."

사과 두 개라고요.
"I said 2 apples."

Chapter 13

More Numbers

B: 한 마리지만, 그 한 마리가 개보다 더 큽니다.
"It's one cat, but that one cat is bigger than a dog."

Noun + 보다 (더)

Saying that something is *more* (adjective) than something else is simple.

Take a noun and attach 보다 to the end. You can also *optionally* add 더 after as an *adverb*, which means "more."

이것이 그것보다 어렵습니다.
"This is more difficult than that."

사이다가 우유보다 더 맛있습니다.
"Soda is more delicious than milk."

소고기가 돼지고기보다 비쌉니다.
"Beef is more expensive than pork."

You can also use 더 in other situations.

더 먹고 싶습니다.
"I want to eat more."

더 주세요.
"Please give me more."

그분은 저보다 키가 더 큽니다.
"He is taller than me."

In the example above, 키(가) 크다 means "to be tall (height)," but literally means that a person's 키 ("height," "stature") is 크다 ("big"). Because 더 is an *adverb* it must modify a verb, so in 키(가) 크다 the verb is the *descriptive verb* 크다; therefore 더 should appear before 크다 and not before 키.

더 can also be used to add the meaning of "*er*" to any *descriptive verb*.

더 큰 케이크를 원합니다.
"I want a bigger cake."

더 좋은 생각
"a better idea"

More Numbers

Chapter 13

더 빠른 자동차
"a faster car"

더 예쁜 여자
"a prettier girl"

더 똑똑한 사람
"a smarter person"

A: 아이고! 정말 고양이가 맞습니까?
"Oh my! Is it really a cat?"

Noun + (이/가) 맞다

Here's how to ask if something is correct, or to claim that it is. Use the verb 맞다 after a noun with a Subject Marker.

제가 미국 사람이 맞습니다.
"It's correct that I'm an American."

그것이 카메라가 맞습니까?
"Is that really a camera?"

그분이 정말 선생님이 맞습니까?
"Is he really a teacher?"

Adv

In this chapter we learned how to use *counters*, and how to use *markers* appropriately with them. Take the following sentence for example:

사과 몇 개를 먹고 싶습니까?
"How many apples do you want to eat?"

Notice how we used the *Object Marker* after 개, and not after 사과. In fact, all of our examples in this chapter use markers *after* counters in this way. But it doesn't have to be this way. The above sentence could just as well be this:

사과를 몇 개 먹고 싶습니까?
"How many apples do you want to eat?"

To keep things simple, this chapters' examples only show using markers after counters – but feel free to use markers directly after *what* it is that you're counting. There is no significant difference, and both ways are correct.

Chapter 13

More Numbers

Practice

Write the following numbers in Pure Korean:

a. 1
b. 2
c. 3
d. 4
e. 5
f. 6
g. 7
h. 8
i. 9
j. 10
k. 20
l. 22
m. 27
n. 30

Translate to Korean:

1. "I want to see 10 monkeys."

_____.

2. "Please give me 3 notebooks."

_____.

3. "There are 2 people in my house."

_____.

4. "He is 30 years old."

_____.

More Numbers

Chapter 13

5. "How old is he?"

_____.

6. "I'm walking from home to the store."

_____.

7. "Is that really a cake?"

_____.

8. "I will bring my friend to school."

_____.

9. "Did you say Korean food?"

_____.

10. "This is better than that."

_____.

Translate to English:

11. 소 두 마리를 먹고 싶습니다.

_____.

12. 사람 한 명이 옵니다.

_____.

13. 저는 열 여덟 살입니다.

_____.

Chapter 13   **More Numbers**

14. 서울에서 부산까지 운전합니다.

_____.

15. 고양이는 몇 마리가 있습니까?

_____.

16. 그것이 정말 물고기가 맞습니다.

_____.

17. 제 집이 김 선생님의 집보다 큽니다.

_____.

18. 종이 한 장만 주세요.

_____.

19. 그분은 선물도 가지고 갑니다.

_____.

20. 선물이라고요?

_____.

21. 저는 이 고양이가 저 고양이보다 더 귀엽기 때문에 이 고양이를 더 좋아합니다.

_____.

New Phrases

아이고!	"Oh my!"

More Numbers

Chapter 13

New Vocabulary

하나	1
한	1 (adjective)
둘	2
두	2 (adjective)
셋	3
세	3 (adjective)
넷	4
네	4 (adjective)
다섯	5
여섯	6
일곱	7
여덟	8
아홉	9
열	10
스물	20
스무	20 (adjective)
서른	30
마흔	40
마리	animal counter
명	person counter
개	item counter
살	age counter
장	flat item counter
권	book counter
몇	"how many" (adjective)
소	"cow"
공책	"(study) notebook"
상자	"box"
맥주	"beer"
소주	"(Korean) alcohol"
나무	"tree," "wood"
꽃	"flower"

Chapter 13: More Numbers

장미	"rose"
하늘	"sky"
땅	"earth," "dirt"
바람	"wind"
불	"fire"
세계	"world"
지구	"the Earth"
우주	"universe"
해	"the sun"
잔디	"grass," "lawn"
숲	"forest"
종이	"paper"
물고기	"(alive) fish"
고기	"meat"
쇠고기	"beef"
돼지고기	"pork"
돌	"stone"
가지다	"to hold," "to have (on your person)"
가게	"store"
운전(을) 하다	"to drive"
운동(을) 하다	"to exercise"
똑똑하다	"to be smart"
쥐	"mouse," "rat"
칼	"knife," "blade"
검	"sword"
컵	"cup"
사자	"lion"
닭	"chicken"
게	"crab"
당근	"carrot"
똥	"poop"
초대(를) 하다	"to invite"
양복	"a suit"
신발	"shoes"

More Numbers

Chapter 13

양말	"socks"
맞다	"to be correct"
틀리다	"to be incorrect"
에서	"from," "at," "in" (particle)
만나다	"to meet"
제주도	"Jeju Island"
그분	"him," "her," "that person"
가지고 오다	"to bring (something here)"
가지고 가다	"to take (something somewhere else)"
데리고 오다	"to take (someone here)"
데리고 가다	"to take (someone somewhere else)"
파티	"party"
보다 (더)	"more than"
키(가) 크다	"to be tall (height)"
키(가) 작다	"to be short (height)"
키	"height," "stature"
불편하다	"to be uncomfortable"
편하다	"to be comfortable"
필요하다	"to be necessary"
갤런	"gallon"
마일	"mile"
톤	"ton"
미터	"meter"
센티미터	"centimeter"
밀리미터	"millimeter"
킬로(그램)	"kilo(gram)"
그램	"gram"
리터	"liter"
밀리리터	"milliliter"
도	"degrees"

Chapter 13

More Numbers

Negative Sentences

Chapter 14

In this chapter we'll learn how to make *negative* sentences – "I do not want to eat it," as opposed to "I want to eat it." We'll also learn about negative verbs.

Conversation

양태용:	오늘도 저와 함께 공원에 갑니까?
최소영:	아니요. 안 갑니다.
양태용:	왜 가지 않습니까?
최소영:	시간이 없기 때문에 갈 수 없습니다.

Making Verbs Negative

Up until now we've only worked with verbs that are *positive* – what I mean by positive is they've all been about things you *do*, as opposed to things that you *don't* do. For example:

저는 갑니다.
"I'm going."

저는 미국 사람입니다.
"I'm an American."

This chapter will cover how to make *negative* sentences.

저는 안 갑니다.
"I'm not going."

199

Chapter 14

Negative Sentences

저는 미국 사람이 아닙니다.
"I'm not an American."

Before we can learn how these work, we need to learn a little bit more about how the Korean language works. In English, to make a verb negative in the *present tense*, you can simply add "not."

"I am a student." ←→ "I am *not* a student."

"I'm going." ←→ "I'm *not* going."

Korean has a similar way to make verbs negative too, but some verbs act differently than others.

Verb Stem + 지 않다

You can use this form to turn *any verb* into a negative.

Take the verb stem and attach 지, followed by the verb 않다 conjugated; in *present tense*, this would become 않습니다.

공부하다
→ 공부하지 않다

가다
→ 가지 않다

먹다
→ 먹지 않다

공부합니다.
"I'm studying"

공부하지 않습니다.
"I'm not studying."

학교에 갑니다.
"I'm going to school."

학교에 가지 않습니다.
"I'm not going to school."

Negative Sentences

김치를 먹습니다.
"I'm eating kimchi."

김치를 먹지 않습니다.
"I'm not eating kimchi."

When changing a *descriptive verb* into an *adjective*, using this negative form, 지 않다 will become 지 않은.

덥지 않은 날씨
"weather that isn't hot"

피곤하지 않은 사람
"a person who isn't tired"

높지 않은 산
"a mountain that isn't tall"

안 + Verb

Some verbs are a bit special, and have a second, extra way of making them negative.

For these type of verbs, all you need to do is add 안 before them to make them negative.

가다
→ 안 가다

먹다
→ 안 먹다

갑니다.
"I'm going"

안 갑니다.
"I'm not going."

김치를 먹습니다.
"I'm eating kimchi."

김치를 안 먹습니다.
"I'm not eating kimchi."

Chapter 14

Negative Sentences

Seems simple, right? But how do you know when you should use 안 before the verb, or 지 않다 after it? Here's the answer:

When to Use 안 or 지 않다

First of all, if you've seen or heard a verb used before with 안 to make it negative, you can (probably) do the same. This is a skill that will come with time and practice, but it's not the only tip you can use.

Second, if the verb only has two syllables (one syllable and 다) then it can use both methods. There are many of these verbs. For example, 가다 ("to go") and 먹다 ("to eat") only have two syllables.

안 가다 "to not go"

        저는 안 갑니다.
        "I'm not going."

가지 않다 "to not go"

        저는 가지 않습니다.
        "I'm not going."

안 먹다 "to not eat"

        저는 안 먹습니다.
        "I'm not eating it."

먹지 않다 "to not eat"

        저는 먹지 않습니다.
        "I'm not eating it."

These above two methods are identical. Feel free to use whichever you feel more comfortable with.

Third, if the verb ends with 하다, pay close attention. If the verb can be separated with the Object Marker, then you can use both methods with 하다 (and only 하다). For example, the verb 공부(를) 하다 ends with 하다, and can be separated by the Object Marker to become 공부를 하다; here, this can become 공부(를) 안 하다 (since 하다 is now separated) or 공부(를) 하지 않다. However, this cannot become 안 공부(를) 하다. This is because 하다 itself is a two-syllable verb and can use both methods. Again, this only applies to verbs that can be separated with the Object Marker and 하다.

Negative Sentences

공부하지 않다 "to not study"

저는 공부하지 않습니다.
"I'm not studying."

안 공부하다 would be incorrect, since 공부하다 can be separated with the Object Marker.

수영하지 않다 "to not swim"

저는 수영하지 않습니다.
"I'm not swimming."

안 수영하다 would also be incorrect because it can be separated with the Object Marker.

> **Adv**: The difference between using 안 and using 지 않다 is that 지 않다 is used a *tiny bit* more in formal situations or when trying to be polite. This difference is really small, and will not matter at all, but there is a difference.

Fourth, any descriptive verb can use both methods. For example, 춥다 can become both 안 춥다 or 춥지 않다.

In fact, even if a descriptive verb ends with 하다, it can still use both methods. For example, 피곤하다 ("to be tired," "to be exhausted") can become 안 피곤하다 and 피곤하지 않다. This is because in an action verb, 하다 has the meaning of "to do." Remember that 공부(를) 하다 literally means "to do studying." However, descriptive verbs are not actions and this does not apply.

Keep in mind the only one exception to this rule – the verb 하다. Except when 하다 is all on its own in a sentence (or separated with the Object Marker), you'll have to pay close attention to the verb to know whether it can use 안 or 지 않다 to become negative.

안 하다 is okay (하다 is on its own), as is 하지 않다, but 안 공부하다 is incorrect (공부하다 can be separated with the Object Marker).

안 심심하다 is okay (심심하다 is a descriptive verb), and 심심하지 않다 is also okay.

Chapter 14

Negative Sentences

> All verbs in this book containing 하다 that are listed with an *Object Marker* before them can also be used with *both* 안 and 지 않다. This is because these verbs are a *combination* of a noun and the verb 하다, and can be separated into two pieces as such.
>
> Remember that 안 will still come directly before the verb itself, just as usual. Here are some example conjugations.
>
> 공부(를) 하다 "to study"
>
> 공부하지 않다 "to not study"
>
> *공부를 안 하다 "to not study"
>
> 안 공부하다 would still be *incorrect*, for the same reasons as explained above.
>
> Just to reiterate once more, not all verbs containing 하다 can be separated in this way, such as 심심하다 which is mentioned above. Be certain the verb can be separated in this way before using 안 before 하다.

However, sometimes the only way to tell whether a verb uses 안 or 지 않다 to become negative is through paying close attention to how each verb is used in real conversation. If you notice a certain verb being used with 안 or with 지 않다 more often, then you can know for the future that it can be used that way.

But when all else fails, use 지 않다. Every verb can become negative using the 지 않다 form, so this is a safe bet when you're not sure whether a verb can use 안 or 지 않다 to become negative.

Already Negative Verbs

Korean is a bit unique in another way from English. Saying "I know" and "I don't know" in English uses the same verb – "to know." However there are some cases in Korean where a separate verb exists that can be used instead.

Take the verb 알다 which means "to know."

저는 압니다.
"I know."

Since this verb (알다) only has two syllables, we can know for sure that it can become negative with either 안 or 지 않다.

But there's actually already a negative verb for 알다 that exists in Korean – 모르다, which means "to not know."

Instead of using 안 알다 or 알지 않다, you would use 모르다.

Negative Sentences

저는 모릅니다.
"I don't know."

김 선생님을 모릅니까?
"You don't know Mr. Kim?"

Another common verb which has a negative version already in Korean is 있다 ("to exist"). Its opposite is 없다 ("to not exist").

저는 돈이 있습니다.
"I have money."

저는 돈이 없습니다.
"I don't have money."

철수 씨가 지금 집에 없습니다.
"Chul-soo is not at home now."

이 음식은 맛이 없습니다.
"This food is not delicious."

재미없습니다.
"It's not entertaining."

When used as an adjective, 없다 becomes 없는.

맛없는 음식
"food that doesn't taste good"

재미없는 이야기
"a story that's not entertaining"

> **Adv**: For verbs that contain 없다 and 있다, the Subject Marker is optional, as indicated by being surrounded in parentheses. However, these types of verbs are most often used without the Subject Marker. Instead of 재미(가) 있다, it's more common to see 재미있다, and instead of 맛(이) 없다, it's more common to see 맛없다.

Chapter 14: Negative Sentences

이다 and 아니다

Let's go over another useful negative verb.

아니다 ("to not be") is the opposite of 이다 ("to be").

아니다 is used slightly differently than 이다, in that when you use 아니다 you must mark what it is that you *aren't* (or what *isn't*) by using the *Subject Marker*.

저는 미국 사람입니다.
"I'm an American."

저는 미국 사람이 아닙니다.
"I'm not an American."

그것은 고양이입니다.
"As for that, it is a cat."

그것은 고양이가 아닙니다.
"As for that, it is not a cat."

> **Adv** Even for verbs that already have negatives such as 알다, 있다, and 이다 feel free to use 지 않다 instead if you are unable to remember their negative forms. This is why I recommend falling back on 지 않다 if you're not sure. Of course, if you know the negative form of the verb, it's much preferred to use it instead.

> **Adv** There are also a small number of verbs ending with 하다 that cannot be separated with the Object Marker, but can still use 안 before them; these are exceptions and not the norm, and these are typically verbs with one syllable followed by 하다. One common example is 통하다 ("to go through").

Now that we can make verbs negative, let's go over the conversation.

Negative Sentences

Chapter 14

양태용: 오늘도 저와 함께 공원에 갑니까?

"Are you going to the park with me today too?"

Noun + 와/과 함께

Saying "together with" is simple.

Take a noun and attach 와/과 followed by 함께.

저와 함께 집에 걸어가고 싶습니까?
"Do you want to walk home together with me?"

김 씨와 함께 있습니까?
"Are you together with Mr. Kim?"

Although 오늘도 means "also today" or "today too," in this context it translates much better as "today again."

> **Advanced**
>
> In the above form, 함께 is actually *optional*, but using it gives a stronger meaning of "together." Using 와/과 on its own after a noun will mean simply "with."
>
> 저와 가고 싶습니까?
> "Do you want to go with me?"
>
> 저는 김 선생님과 있습니다.
> "I am with Mr. Kim."

최소영: 아니요. 안 갑니다.

"No. I'm not going."

양태용: 왜 가지 않습니까?

"Why aren't you going?"

Remember that since 가다 has only two syllables, it can become negative by either adding 안 before it, or by adding 지 않다 after it.

최소영: 시간이 없기 때문에 갈 수 없습니다.

"I'm not going because I don't have time."

Chapter 14

Negative Sentences

Can and Can't
Verb Stem + (을/ㄹ) 수 있다/없다

To say *can* or *can't*, take the verb stem and attach 을 if it ends in a *consonant*, or ㄹ if it ends in a *vowel*. Then add 수. Finally, use 있다 if you want to say "can," or use 없다 if you want to say "can't."

저는 그것을 먹을 수 있습니다.
"I can eat that."

저는 그것을 먹을 수 없습니다.
"I can't eat that."

그분은 노래를 부를 수 있습니다.
"He/she can sing."

그분은 노래를 부를 수 없습니다.
"He/she can't sing."

주제를 이해할 수 있습니다.
"I can understand the topic."

주제를 이해할 수 없습니다.
"I can't understand the topic."

저도 갈 수 있습니다.
"I can go too."

저도 갈 수 없습니다.
"I can't go either."

> **Adv** It's also common for 수 to be followed by a marker, such as the Subject Marker (가) or Topic Marker (는). Although the meaning will stay the same, doing so will slightly alter the nuance of the sentence. We'll learn more about how these markers can affect the nuance of a sentence in the next chapter.

In negative sentences, 도 can also translate to "either."

저도 이해할 수 없습니다.
"I can't understand it either."

저도 쇠고기를 먹을 수 없습니다.
"I can't eat beef either."

Negative Sentences

> Chapter 14

Advanced

Here's an extra trick. If you know that a verb can use both 안 and 지 않다 to become negative, there is a much easier way to say "can't" than the above method. Instead, attach 못 before the verb, then conjugate it normally. As with 안, this does not work for some verbs.

저는 갈 수 없습니다.
"I can't go."

저는 못 갑니다.
"I can't go."

먹을 수 없습니다.
"I can't eat it."

못 먹습니다.
"I can't eat it."

그분도 할 수 없습니다.
"He can't do it either."

그분도 못 합니다.
"He can't do it either."

However, you will still need to use the above form like normal if you want to say "can."

저는 갈 수 있습니다.
"I can go."

Using the 수 없다 form is a *tiny bit* more formal than using 못, but feel free to use either one. Remember that using 못 and using 안 have different meanings – while 못 is used to mean "can't" (unable to), 안 means "doesn't" (maybe can, but does not).

Let's look at an example with the verb 이해(를) 하다 ("to understand"). Using 이해(를) 안 하다 would be *incorrect*, as using 안 means that you are not doing something on your own free will – instead, this verb would need to be either 이해(를) 못 하다, or 이해(를) 할 수 없다.

Culture Notes

노래방 and PC 방

노래방 ("song room") and PC 방 (피시방 – "personal computer room") are popular places for Koreans, both young and old, to meet with each other.

A 노래방 is a private room for karaoke with friends and family. You are not expected to sing well, so relax and enjoy the time. If you are able to learn and sing a song in Korean at a 노래방, your experience will be even more memorable.

A typical PC 방 will contain several dozens of high-end computers, as well as pre-installed popular games. Instead of owning a powerful gaming computer at home, most Koreans will simply spend money in a PC 방 when they want to play games, which charge by the hour and are quite inexpensive.

Chapter 14: Negative Sentences

Practice

Translate to Korean:

1. "I'm not going to school today." (Using 안)

   _____.

2. "He is not going to the hospital." (Using 지 않다)

   _____.

3. "You're not coming to my house?" (Using 안)

   _____.

4. "He is not at school." (Using 없다)

   _____.

5. "I do not know him."

   _____.

6. "I can swim quickly."

   _____.

7. "Do you want to go together with me to the party?"

   _____.

8. "I am not a Korean."

   _____.

Negative Sentences

Translate to English:

9. 왜 병원에 안 갑니까?

_____.

10. 정말 숙제를 하지 않습니까?

_____.

11. 저는 학교에 가고 싶지 않습니다.

_____.

12. 저는 소고기를 싫어하기 때문에 먹고 싶지 않습니다.

_____.

13. 영희 씨를 압니까?

_____.

14. 아니요. 저는 영희 씨를 모릅니다.

_____.

15. 저는 영국 사람이 아닙니다.

_____.

16. 저는 돈이 없기 때문에 영희 씨와 함께 놀이 공원에 갈 수 없습니다.

_____.

Chapter 14

Negative Sentences

New Vocabulary

노래	"song"
부르다	"to sing"
노래(를) 부르다	"to sing a song"
이야기	"story"
이야기(를) 하다	"to chat," "to gossip"
외우다	"to memorize"
기억(을) 하다	"to remember"
공원	"a park"
놀이 공원	"amusement park"
심심하다	"to be bored"
지루하다	"to be boring"
유명하다	"to be famous"
아니다	"to not be"
없다	"to not exist"
재미(가) 없다	"to not be fun," "to not be entertaining"
맛(이) 없다	"to not be delicious," "to not taste good"
멋(이) 없다	"to not be cool," "to be unstylish"
인기(가) 있다	"to be popular"
인기(가) 없다	"to be unpopular"
인기	"popularity"
주제	"topic," "theme"
알다	"to know"
모르다	"to not know"
이해(를) 하다	"to understand"
빨리	"quickly," "fast" (adverb)
꼭	"surely," "certainly" (adverb)
일찍	"early" (adverb)
늦게	"late" (adverb)
늦다	"to be late"
와/과 함께	"together with"

Korean Markers

Chapter 15

We've talked about markers in previous chapters, but here we'll review all of them in more detail, along with examples, to help you know the difference between each of them. Before passing this chapter, make sure you have a good understanding of each of them, as you'll be using these markers daily in your Korean practice.

Conversation

김철수:	안녕하세요. 저는 철수라고 합니다.
김영희:	안녕하세요. 저는 영희라고 합니다.
김철수:	취미가 어떻게 됩니까?
김영희:	제 취미는 컴퓨터 게임과 독서입니다.
김철수:	저는 낚시와 운동입니다. 그리고 미국에서 삽니다.
김영희:	저는 한국에서 삽니다. 나이가 어떻게 됩니까?
김철수:	저는 스물 한 살입니다.
김영희:	저는 스물 일곱 살입니다. 만나서 반갑습니다.
김철수:	네, 반갑습니다.

This chapter will go back and review some of the concepts we've learned in earlier lessons – specifically markers such as the Topic Marker, the Subject Marker, and the Object Marker. Then we'll go back and re-learn how to introduce ourselves in Korean, but with a much larger vocabulary.

Korean Markers

Topic Marker – 은/는

How to use it: Use 은 after a *consonant* and 는 after a *vowel*.

집은
학교는

What it does: The Topic Marker marks what the topic of a sentence is. You can think of it translating as "as for," or "when it comes to." Let's look at some examples.

저는 김치를 싫어합니다.
"As for me, I dislike kimchi."
"When it comes to me, I dislike kimchi."

김치는 맛이 있습니다.
"As for kimchi, it is delicious."
"When it comes to kimchi, it is delicious."

Think of the Topic Marker as meaning "as for" – by "as for," I mean "as for (as opposed to someone or something else)."

강 씨는 김치를 좋아하지만, 저는 싫어합니다.
"As for Mrs. Kang, she likes kimchi, but as for me, I dislike it."

Although the above sentence uses two Topic Markers appropriately, be extra careful when using more than one in the same sentence as it can be awkward. For example, take the following sentence:

김치는 저는 좋아합니다.
"As for kimchi, as for me I like it."

The above type of repetition is awkward even in English, and should be avoided in Korean as well. Most of the time, a sentence will not have more than one Topic Marker, if it even has one at all.

저는 김치를 좋아합니다.
"As for me, I like kimchi."

왜 좋아합니까?
"Why do you like it?"

맛이 있기 때문에 좋아합니다.
"I like it because it is delicious."

Korean Markers

Chapter 15

Subject Marker – 이/가

How to use it: Use 이 after a *consonant* and 가 after a *vowel*.

집**이**
학교**가**

What it does: The Subject Marker marks a subject – whatever is doing an action in a sentence, or whatever is being described. Let's look at some examples.

강 씨가 친절한 사람입니다.
"Mrs. Kang is a nice person."

빨간색이 예쁜 색입니다.
"Red is a pretty color."

제가 미국 사람입니다.
"I'm an American."

But the Subject Marker works differently from the Topic Marker; this difference is easier to see in Korean than in English, as often translations in English will be similar. Take the following two sentences for example:

저는 한국 사람입니다.
"I'm a Korean."

제가 한국 사람입니다.
"I'm a Korean."

In order to better understand the difference between using the Topic Marker and the Subject Marker, try translating the Topic Marker as "as for" in your head when using it.

저는 한국 사람입니다.
"As for me, I'm a Korean."

Using the Topic Marker expresses distinction – you're specifying "as for me," as opposed to someone else.

저는 한국 사람입니다.
"As for me, I'm a Korean."

그렇습니까? 저는 미국 사람입니다.
"Is that so? As for me, I'm an American."

Chapter 15

Korean Markers

제가 한국 사람입니다.
"I'm a Korean."

Using the Subject Marker expresses emphasis – you're simply marking something or someone as the subject of a verb (here the verb is 이다, "to be").

김치는 맛이 있습니다.
"As for kimchi, it's delicious."

김치가 맛이 있습니다.
"Kimchi is delicious."

Which sentence sounds better in English? In most situations, the second one will be preferred. Grammatically, both sentences are correct.

As for our two sentences, let's take one more look:

저는 한국 사람입니다.
"As for me, I'm a Korean."

제가 한국 사람입니다.
"I'm a Korean."

Can't tell which one is better? Don't worry – both of them are fine. Their meanings are slightly different, as we've learned, but being used in context will help you pick which one you'd want to use.

Topic Markers and Subject Markers are often confused by beginning speakers because of their seemingly similar meanings when translated into English. Frequent practice will help you to distinguish when to use one or the other.

The Topic Marker and Subject Marker Together

Let's take a look at a few examples which use both the Topic Marker and the Subject Marker in the same sentence.

저는 김치가 맛이 있습니다.
"As for me, kimchi is delicious."

강 씨는 취미가 독서입니다.
"As for Mrs. Kang, her hobby is reading."

Korean Markers

Chapter 15

생선은 고등어가 최고입니다.
"As for fish, mackerel is the best."

> Adv: 생선 means "fish," and is what you would call the fish on your plate at a restaurant – specifically, *dead* fish. This is different from 물고기, which refers to *live* fish.

Most of the time the Topic Marker will come first after the topic of the sentence, followed by the Subject Marker marking the subject of the verb.

Object Marker – 을/를

How to use it: Use 을 after a *consonant* and 를 after a *vowel*.

집을
학교를

What it does: The Object Marker marks the object of a verb – whatever is receiving an action.

저는 김치를 먹습니다.
"I eat kimchi."

강 씨는 저를 사랑합니다.
"Mrs. Kang loves me."

새로운 수학 선생님을 좋아합니까?
"Do you like the new math teacher?"

If you're still feeling a little confused about any of these markers even after several reviews, don't stress. Instead, try to absorb as much Korean as you can. As these concepts do not translate well into English, they may feel foreign at first, but with practice will become second nature.

Now let's look over the conversation.

김철수: 안녕하세요. 저는 철수라고 합니다.

"Hello. My name is Chul-soo."

Chapter 15

Korean Markers

저는 ____(이)라고 합니다.

In addition to 제 이름은 ____입니다 which we learned in Chapter 11, here is one more useful way that you can say your name. Literally it means "I am called ____."

Use 이라고 합니다 after a *consonant*, or 라고 합니다 after a *vowel*.

저는 빌리라고 합니다.
"My name is Billy."

저는 메릴이라고 합니다.
"My name is Merrill."

Remember to not use 씨 after your own name; this is only used when referring to other people. Simply use your name as it is.

> **Adv**: This form originally comes from the verbs 이다 ("to be") and 하다 ("to do"); here 하다 is being used to mean "to say" or "to call" – just like 말(을) 하다.

김영희: 안녕하세요. 저는 김영희라고 합니다.

"Hello. My name is Yung-hee."

김철수: 취미가 어떻게 됩니까?

"Tell me about your hobbies."

"Tell me about..."

Noun + (이/가) 어떻게 됩니까?

Take a noun and attach the Subject Marker, followed by 어떻게 ("how") and then 됩니까?

You can use this form to say "tell me about," such as in this chapter's conversation.

Korean Markers

Chapter 15

취미가 어떻게 됩니까?
"Tell me about your hobbies?"

A more natural translation of the above sentence could be "What are your hobbies?"

This form has limited usage, and can't be used to ask about *people*.

Asking **김철수 씨**가 어떻게 됩니까 would therefore be *incorrect*.

> **Adv** 됩니까? comes from the verb 되다 which means "to become," which we'll learn about in Chapter 17. 어떻게 됩니까? literally means "how does it become?" It might sound strange now, but it will make more sense later when we go over it.

김영희: 제 취미는 컴퓨터 게임과 독서입니다.
"My hobbies are computer games and reading."

김철수: 저는 낚시와 운동입니다. 그리고 미국에서 삽니다.
"My hobbies are fishing and exercise. And I live in America."

"at," "in" – 에서

When using *action verbs*, such as "to do" or "to meet" (action verbs are all verbs that involve doing something), mark the location of where that action is taking place *at* or *in* by using 에서.

어디에서 공부합니까?
"Where do you study at?"

> **Adv** 어디에서 can be shortened to 어디서 with no change in meaning. In addition, 어디서 is easier to say than 어디에서, so feel free to use it yourself instead.

저는 학교에서 공부합니다.
"I study at school."

저는 미국에서 삽니다.
"I live in America."

식당에서 밥을 먹습니다.
"I eat (a meal) at the restaurant."

병원에서 의사를 만납니다.
"I meet a doctor at the hospital."

Chapter 15

Korean Markers

Note that this particle (에서) is different from 에, which simply marks the location of where something is going or coming (verbs that show *movement*), or where something *exists*.

> 저는 한국에서 여행하고 싶습니다.
> "I want to travel in Korea."

> 저는 한국에 여행하고 싶습니다.
> "I want to travel to Korea."

> 저는 한국에 갑니다.
> "I go to Korea."

> 저는 한국에 있습니다.
> "I am in Korea."

> 저의 자동차가 미국에 있습니다.
> "My car is in America."

Note that the verb 있다 ("to exist"), although an action verb, does not use 에서. This is an exception.

> 김영희: 저는 한국에서 삽니다. 나이가 어떻게 됩니까?
> "I live in Korea. How old are you?"

Adv
The verb 살다 is special, in that although it is an action verb it can use either 에 or 에서. Therefore, the two following sentences are both correct:

> 한국에서 삽니다.
> 한국에 삽니다.
> "I live in Korea."

The standard way of asking a person's age is by using 나이가 어떻게 됩니까? Although above we said that 어떻게 됩니까? can translate as "tell me about," a much better translation in this situation would simply be "how old are you?"

Using 몇 살입니까?, as covered in Chapter 13, is acceptable only when speaking to people *younger* than yourself (using it to anyone older can be impolite, as it is a direct way of asking a person's age). Therefore, in most situations you should use 나이가 어떻게 됩니까? to ask someone's age.

Korean Markers

김철수: 저는 스물 한 살입니다.

"I'm 21 years old."

김영희: 저는 스물 일곱 살입니다. 만나서 반갑습니다.

"I'm 27 years old. Nice to meet you."

김철수: 네, 반갑습니다.

"Yes, nice to meet you."

Don't expect to master these concepts in an afternoon, but know that it's possible to master them with practice. The more you become familiar with seeing them, hearing them, and using them yourself, the better you will understand when to use each one. As usual, practice using them all wherever you can.

Practice

Translate to English:

1. 제가 중국 사람이 아닙니다.

   _____.

2. 김 씨는 친절한 한국 남자입니다.

   _____.

3. 도시는 서울이 최고입니다.

   _____.

4. 저는 김철수라고 합니다.

   _____.

5. 오늘 학교에서 공부하고 싶습니까?

   _____.

Chapter 15 — Korean Markers

6. 저는 정말 영화관에 가고 싶습니다.

_____.

Translate to Korean:

7. "How old is Mr. Kim?"

_____.

8. "As for me, I like school."

_____.

9. "I do not want to eat cold steak."

_____.

10. "My name is [your name]."

_____.

11. "What are your hobbies?"

_____.

12. "I want to do homework at home."

_____.

New Phrases

저는 ____(이)라고 합니다.	"My name is ____."
어떻게 됩니까?	"Tell me about..."
나이가 어떻게 됩니까?	"How old are you?"

Korean Markers

New Vocabulary

나이	"age"
취미	"hobby"
운동	"exercise"
독서	"reading"
낚시	"fishing"
컴퓨터 게임	"computer game"
언어	"language"
언어학	"linguistics"
여행	"travel," "a trip"
여행(을) 하다	"to travel," "to take a trip"
생선	"(dead) fish"
고등어	"mackerel"
최고	"(the) best"
최악	"(the) worst"
치과 의사	"dentist"
경찰	"police"
경찰관	"policeman"
약	"medicine," "drugs"
약국	"pharmacy"
지갑	"wallet"

Chapter 15

Korean Markers

Telling Time

Chapter 16

Taking what we've learned from Chapter 12 and Chapter 13 on Korean numbers (Sino-Korean numbers and Pure Korean numbers), let's learn how to tell the time.

Conversation

A:	지금 몇 시입니까?
B:	저녁 열 시 사십 분입니다.
A:	오늘 며칠입니까?
B:	이십육 일입니다.
A:	감사합니다.
B:	천만에요.

Time Counters

This chapter introduces a few new counters we can use to count lengths of time.

시 "o'clock"
시간 hour counter
분 minute counter
초 second counter

While 시 and 시간 both use *Pure Korean numbers*, 분 and 초 use *Sino-Korean numbers*.

Let's first take a look at 시.

225

Chapter 16

Telling Time

1 o'clock	한 시
2 o'clock	두 시
3 o'clock	세 시
4 o'clock	네 시
5 o'clock	다섯 시
6 o'clock	여섯 시
7 o'clock	일곱 시
8 o'clock	여덟 시
9 o'clock	아홉 시
10 o'clock	열 시
11 o'clock	열 한 시
12 o'clock	열 두 시

To specify whether you're referring to A.M. or P.M., add either 오전 ("before noon") or 오후 ("after noon") before saying the time. Or alternatively, you could also add 저녁 ("evening") or 아침 ("morning") before it instead. Pick whichever way you'd like.

오전 열 시
"10 o'clock A.M."

아침 열 시
"10 o'clock A.M."

오후 열 시
"10 o'clock P.M."

저녁 열 시
"10 o'clock P.M."

Remember that A.M. or P.M. in Korean always comes *before* the time, and not after like in English.

Another useful word is 새벽 ("after midnight"), for marking times that are before people would normally wake up in the morning. Although it would also be grammatically correct in these situations to use 오전 or 아침, using 새벽 emphasizes that the time is before the morning, and therefore sounds more natural.

새벽 두 시
"2 o'clock past midnight"

Telling Time

새벽 일곱 시
"7 o'clock past midnight"

It's acceptable to use 새벽 for times between 1 o'clock and 7 o'clock, but not afterward.

Counting hours uses Pure Korean numbers and the hour counter 시간.

1 hour	한 시간
2 hours	두 시간
3 hours	세 시간
4 hours	네 시간
5 hours	다섯 시간
10 hours	열 시간
24 hours	스물 네 시간

For minutes (분) and seconds (초), attach Sino-Korean numbers to the beginning.

1 minute	일 분
10 minutes	십 분
59 minutes	오십구 분

1 second	일 초
20 seconds	이십 초
50 seconds	오십 초

And just like in English, *counting* time goes in order from *hours* to *minutes* to *seconds*.

세 시간 오십 분 이십이 초
"3 hours, 50 minutes, 22 seconds"

열 시간 이 분 삼십 초
"10 hours, 2 minutes, 30 seconds"

네 시간 삼십 분
"4 hours, 30 minutes"

Chapter 16: Telling Time

The same goes for *telling* the time.

세 시 오십 분 이십이 초
"3 o'clock, 50 minutes, and 22 seconds"

Most often when telling time, saying just the hour and minutes is sufficient.

세 시 오십 분
"3:50"

열 시 삼 분
"10:03"

열 두 시 삼십 분
"12:30"

In the above sentence, instead of saying "30 minutes" (삼십 분) you can also use 반, which means "half."

열 두 시 반
"12:30"

네 시간 반
"4 and a half hours," or "4 hours, 30 minutes"

네 시 반
"4:30"

Adding 오전 or 오후, among others that we've learned, will specify the time of day.

오후 네 시 반
"4:30 P.M."

오전 열 시 반
"10:30 A.M."

새벽 두 시 반
"2:30 past midnight"

Now that we can count and tell time, let's learn how to work with days, weeks, months, and years.

Telling Time

Chapter 16

First let's look at days. We'll start with the names of the days of the week.

Monday	월요일
Tuesday	화요일
Wednesday	수요일
Thursday	목요일
Friday	금요일
Saturday	토요일
Sunday	일요일

Notice how all of them end in 요일. This makes memorizing them quicker. Simply memorize 월, 화, 수, 목, 금, 토, and 일.

Now let's learn how to count days, weeks, months, and years. All of these use Sino-Korean numbers.

일 day counter
→ 일 일 "1 day"
→ 이 일 "2 days"
→ 삼 일 "3 days"
→ 삼백육십오 일 "365 days"

주일 week counter
→ 일 주일 "1 week"
→ 이 주일 "2 weeks"
→ 사 주일 "4 weeks"
→ 오십이 주일 "52 weeks"

개월 month counter
→ 일 개월 "1 month"
→ 사 개월 "4 months"
→ 육 개월 "6 months"
→ 십이 개월 "12 months"

년 year counter
→ 일 년 "1 year"
→ 십 년 "10 years"
→ 백 년 "100 years"
→ 이천십사 년 "the year 2014"

Chapter 16

Telling Time

You'll use 년 not only when counting numbers of years, but when saying what year it currently is too, as in the previous example.

> **Advanced**
>
> There is also an additional counter for *month* that uses Pure Korean numbers instead. Let's go over it so you're familiar with how it works, but feel free to stick with using 개월 until you're more comfortable. Although 개월 is more widely used, either is acceptable.
>
> 달 month counter
> → 한 달 "1 month"
> → 두 달 "2 months"
> → 세 달 "3 months"
> → 다섯 달 "5 months"
>
> I should also note that 달 means "moon."
>
> In addition to *month*, when counting *days* you have two additional options. There are also Pure Korean versions of "1 day" and "2 days" which you can use instead of their Sino-Korean versions. In fact, the Pure Korean versions of "1 day" and "2 days" will be more preferred, although both versions are acceptable.
>
> 일 일 "1 day"
> **하루** "1 day"
>
> 이 일 "2 days"
> **이틀** "2 days"
>
> Beyond two days, switch back to using Sino-Korean numbers and 일.
>
> 삼 일 "3 days"
> 오 일 "5 days"
> 십 일 "10 days"

You can also add 동안 ("a period of time") after an amount of time (hours, months, years, etc.) to express that something happens "for" that amount of time.

한 시간 동안
"for 1 hour"

삼십 분 동안
"for 30 minutes"

몇 시간 동안
"for *how many* hours"

삼 일 동안
"for 3 days"

삼 개월 동안
"for 3 months"

Telling Time

팔 년 동안
"for 8 years"

한국어를 십 년 동안 공부하고 싶습니다.
"I want to study Korean for 10 years."

> **Adv**: Both 한국말 and 한국어 mean "Korean (language)," but 한국어 is much more commonly used than 한국말. Feel free to use either one, but be aware of both words. The same thing applies to 일본어 and 중국어, among others.

There's just one more thing to go over before we start the conversation, and that is the names of the months. Fortunately, you're in luck. Although English has a separate name for each month of the year, Korean simply numbers the months from 1 to 12, with 1 being January, 2 being February, and so on. When saying the name of the month, use the counter 월.

January	일월
February	이월
March	삼월
April	사월
May	오월
June*	유월*
July	칠월
August	팔월
September	구월
October*	시월*
November	십일월
December	십이월

There are only two exceptions here, "June" and "October," which I've marked above with an asterisk. These names changed over time to make them easier to pronounce.

Remember that using 월 to *name* the months is different from 개월, which is for *counting* how many months.

일 개월
"1 month"

일월
"January"

Chapter 16

Telling Time

이 개월
"2 months"

이월
"February"

Let's go over the conversation for this chapter.

A: 지금 몇 시입니까?

"What time is it now?"

You can ask someone the time by using 몇 시입니까?

B: 저녁 열 시 사십 분입니다.

"It's 10:40 P.M."

A: 오늘 며칠입니까?

"What day (of the month) is it today?"

> **Advanced**
>
> Although 며칠 is used for asking the day of the month, you can also find out the day of the week by asking 무슨 요일입니까?
>
> 요일 is a noun that means "a day of the week"
>
> **Q.** 오늘이 무슨 요일입니까?
> "What day (of the week) is today?"
>
> **A.** 수요일입니다.
> "It is Wednesday."
>
> Notice how in the above question 오늘 is followed by the Subject Marker (here, 이). This is because the Subject Marker, as we learned in Chapter 8, often appears in questions to mark what it is that you're asking about.

B: 이십육 일입니다.

"It's the 26th."

A: 감사합니다.

"Thank you."

Telling Time

Chapter 16

B: 천만에요.

"You're welcome."

| Adv | Although 천만에요 is the proper way to say "you're welcome," it's not used as often as you might think. It's actually more common to hear people replying with **아니에요** ("no," "it isn't"), which comes from the verb 아니다, in real world situations. Feel free to use whichever you'd like. We'll learn how to conjugate 아니에요 later in Chapter 19. |

Now let's go over the journal for this chapter.

Journal

일요일 – 이천십사 년 유월 십오 일

오늘 오후 세 시에 비행기를 타고 제 친구의 집에 갑니다.

제 친구는 한국에서 삽니다.

저는 제 친구를 정말 보고 싶습니다.

한국에서 한국말을 삼 개월 동안 공부합니다.

많이 기대합니다.

구월 십오 일까지 한국에 있습니다.

이미 한 시이기 때문에 지금부터 준비합니다.

안녕히 계세요.

Telling Time

일요일 – 이천십사 년 유월 십오 일

"Sunday – June 15th, 2014"

Complete dates in Korean are written with the *year* first, followed by the *month*, and then the *day*.

오늘 오후 세 시에 비행기를 타고 제 친구의 집에 갑니다.

"Today at 3 o'clock P.M. I am taking an airplane and going to my friend's house."

The Verb 타다

You can use the verb 타다 ("to ride") with any method of transportation, including airplanes, cars, bicycles, and buses, among others.

차를 타고 학교에 갑니다.
"I'm riding a car and going to school."

A more natural sounding translation would be "I'm going to school by car."

배를 타고 싶습니까?
"Do you want to ride a boat?"

저는 자전거를 탈 수 없습니다.
"I can't ride a bicycle."

제 친구는 한국에서 삽니다.
"My friend lives in Korea."

Telling Time

Chapter 16

> 저는 제 친구를 정말 보고 싶습니다.
> "I really miss my friend."

보고 싶다 literally means "to want to see," but is the most common way of saying "to miss (someone)."

> 한국에서 한국말을 삼 개월 동안 공부합니다.
> "In Korea I'll study Korean for 3 months."

Since the previous sentence already mentioned that "I" am the topic of this sentence (using 저는), it's not necessary to repeat it here.

> 많이 기대합니다.
> "I'm really looking forward to it."

기대하다 can be used with the Object Marker after something you are *looking forward to*, or *expecting*.

> 선물을 기대합니다.
> "I'm expecting a present."

> 내일을 기대합니다.
> "I'm looking forward to tomorrow."

Although 많이 is an *adverb* that means "a lot," here it would translate better as "really."

> 구월 십오 일까지 한국에 있습니다.
> "I'll be in Korea until September 15th."

까지 can be used for not just locations, but for conveying "until" or "up to" in regards to *time*.

> 일요일까지
> "until Sunday"

> 세시까지
> "until 3 o'clock"

> 유월까지 기다릴 수 없습니다.
> "I can't wait until June."

Chapter 16

Telling Time

> 이미 한 시이기 때문에 지금부터 준비합니다.
> "Because it's already 1 o'clock I'll prepare from now."

We learned 에서 in Chapter 13 as a way of saying "from (a location)." There's one additional way to say "from" – 부터.

Specifically, 부터 is used to say "from (a *time* or *location*)." You can use 까지 together with it to mean "until."

지금부터
"from now"

지금부터 두 시까지
"from now until 2 o'clock"

삼 일부터
"from the 3rd"

삼 일부터 이십구 일까지
"from the 3rd to the 29th"

시월부터
"from October"

시월부터 십이월까지
"from October to December"

> 안녕히 계세요.
> "Goodbye."

It should be noted again that although this chapter and the previous chapter use numbers written *phonetically* in 한글, this is only to help explain how numbers work. In real Korean, numbers are written using Arabic numerals (and *without* a space between the number and the counter). Here are just a few real world examples:

1 시
"1 o'clock"

10 시간
"10 hours"

Chapter 16

Telling Time

50 분
"50 minutes"

20 초
"20 seconds"

5 개월
"5 months"

3 월
"March"

2014 년 9 월 12 일
"September 12th, 2014"

Once you are comfortable with how to pronounce Pure Korean and Sino-Korean numbers, as well as when to use each one, it is preferred to write them in this way.

Practice

Translate to Korean:

1. 1 o'clock P.M.
2. 11 o'clock in the morning
3. 6 o'clock in the evening
4. 3 o'clock past midnight
5. 8 o'clock A.M.
6. 3 hours
7. 2 hours and 12 minutes
8. 17 seconds
9. 3 days
10. 2 weeks
11. 8 months
12. 10 years

Write the names of the months in Korean:

13. January
14. June

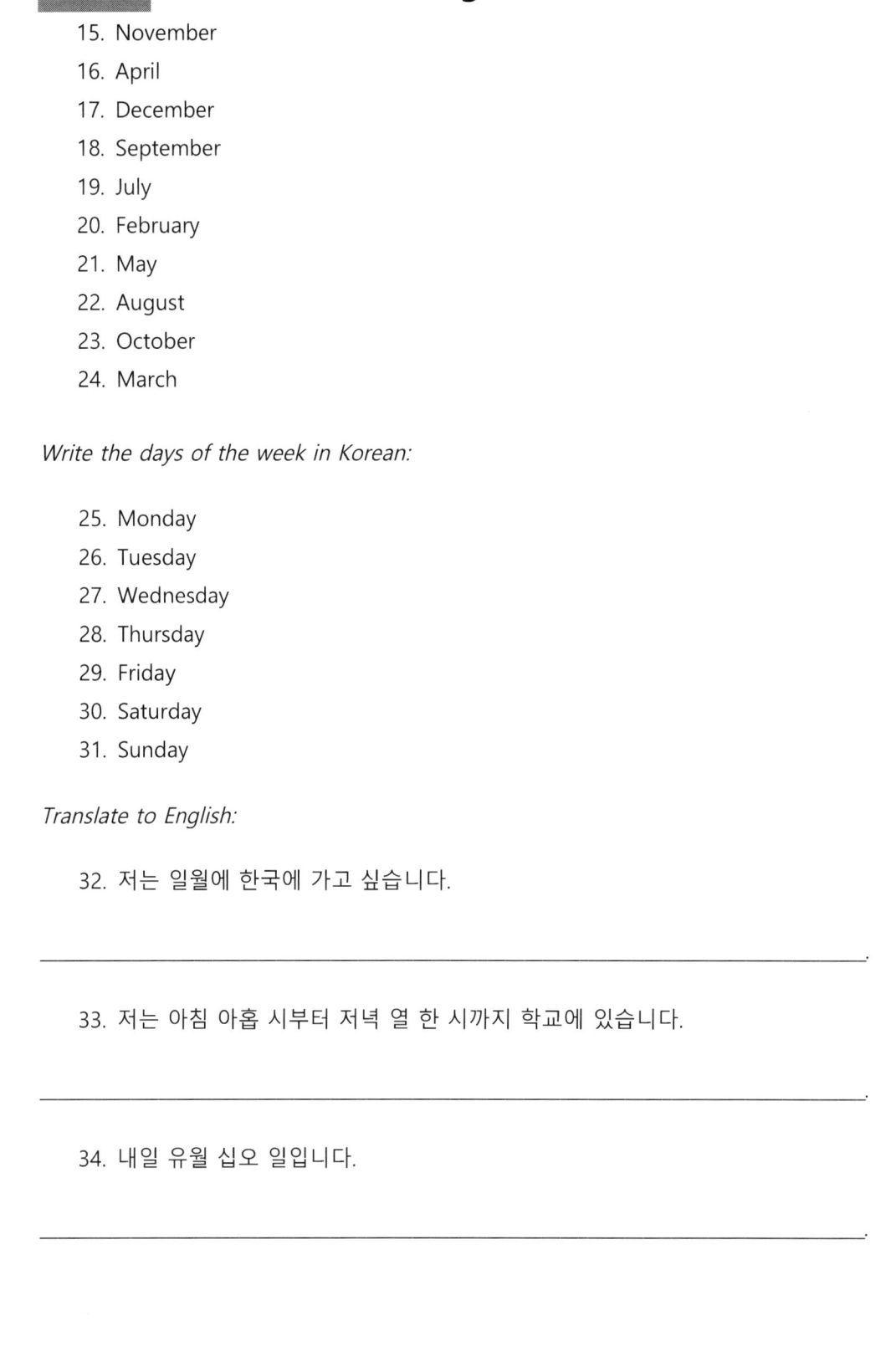

Chapter 16   **Telling Time**

15. November
16. April
17. December
18. September
19. July
20. February
21. May
22. August
23. October
24. March

Write the days of the week in Korean:

25. Monday
26. Tuesday
27. Wednesday
28. Thursday
29. Friday
30. Saturday
31. Sunday

Translate to English:

32. 저는 일월에 한국에 가고 싶습니다.

_____.

33. 저는 아침 아홉 시부터 저녁 열 한 시까지 학교에 있습니다.

_____.

34. 내일 유월 십오 일입니다.

_____.

Telling Time

Chapter 16

35. 저는 오후 한 시에 김 씨를 만납니다.

36. 화요일에 파티에 갈 수 있습니까?

37. 이번 주에 시간이 있습니까?

Translate to Korean:

38. "What time is it?"

39. "What day of the month is it?"

40. "I love December. December is the best."

41. "I also miss Mr. Kim."

42. "Today is (month) (day), (year)."

43. "Tomorrow is Friday."

Chapter 16

Telling Time

New Phrases

몇 시입니까?	"What time is it?"
며칠입니까?	"What day (of the month) is it?"
괜찮습니다.	"No, thank you."
천만에요.	"You're welcome."
좋은 아침입니다.	"Good morning."
좋은 하루 되세요.	"Have a nice day."

New Vocabulary

기대(를) 하다	"to look forward to," "to expect"
보고 싶다	"to miss," "to want to see"
지금부터	"from now"
부터	"from (a time or location)"
한국어	"Korean (language)"
일본어	"Japanese (language)"
중국어	"Chinese (language)"
이미	"already" (adverb)
다시	"again" (adverb)
한 번 더	"once more" (adverb)
비행기	"airplane"
타다	"to ride"
저녁	"evening"
아침	"morning"
오후	"after noon," "P.M."
오전	"before noon," "A.M."
정오	"noon"
새벽	"past midnight"
몇 시	"what time"
며칠	"what day"
몇 월	"what month"
몇 년	"what year," "how many years"
시	"o'clock"

Telling Time

> Chapter 16

시간	hour counter
분	minute counter
초	second counter
반	"half"
달	"month," "moon"
날	"day"
해	"year"
하루	"one day"
이틀	"two days"
일	day counter
주일	week counter
개월	month counter
년	year counter
월	month name counter
일월	"January"
이월	"February"
삼월	"March"
사월	"April"
오월	"May"
유월	"June"
칠월	"July"
팔월	"August"
구월	"September"
시월	"October"
십일월	"November"
십이월	"December"
일요일	"Sunday"
월요일	"Monday"
화요일	"Tuesday"
수요일	"Wednesday"
목요일	"Thursday"
금요일	"Friday"
토요일	"Saturday"
자전거	"bicycle"

Chapter 16: Telling Time

버스	"bus"
지하철	"subway"
기차	"(electric) train"
열차	"(ordinary) train"
택시	"taxi"
이번 주	"this week"
지난 주	"last week"
다음 주	"next week"
이번 달	"this month"
지난 달	"last month"
다음 달	"next month"
봄	"spring"
여름	"summer"
가을	"autumn"
겨울	"winter"
동안	"a period of time"
오랫동안	"for a long time" (adverb)
준비(를) 하다	"to prepare"

Shopping

Chapter 17

In this chapter we'll learn how to count money, purchase things, and ask for things. We'll also cover grammar forms for expressing "to" and "from" a person.

Conversation

김철수:	저기요. 이 시계가 얼마입니까?
직원:	삼만구천원입니다.
김철수:	조금 깎아주세요.
직원:	알겠습니다. 그럼 삼만원입니다.
김철수:	조금 더 깎아주세요. 이만오천원은 어떻습니까?
직원:	안 됩니다. 그럼 저에게 이만구천원을 주세요.
김철수:	여기 이만구천원입니다. 감사합니다!
직원:	안녕히 가세요.
김철수:	네, 많이 파세요!

Counting Dollars

In Chapter 12 we learned how to count 원 using Sino-Korean numbers. Now let's take a quick moment to learn how to count *dollars* and *cents*.

Chapter 17

Shopping

불 dollar counter
→ 일불 "1 dollar"
→ 십불 "10 dollars"
→ 만불 "10,000 dollars"

전 penny counter
→ 일전 "1 cent"
→ 십이전 "12 cents"
→ 오십구전 "59 cents"

Dollars and cents are both counted using Sino-Korean numbers. Say the dollar amount, followed directly by the amount of cents.

일불 삼십전
"$1.30"

삼불 이십전
"$3.20"

십불 이전
"$10.02"

백불
"$100"

Note that foreign currencies (such as the dollar) will be *written* the same way they would be normally – $1.30, for example. In order to *say* them, you will need to know how to use their counters, 불 and 전.

"Please"
Verb Stem + (으)세요

Let's learn how to tell someone to do something for you – "please go to the store," or "please do it." We've already learned how to use 주세요 to say "please give me." This actually comes from the verb 주다, which means "to give." The ending part, 세요, is used to make the verb a *polite command*. By polite command, I mean it is similar to asking someone "please."

Take the verb stem and add 으세요 if it ends in a *consonant*, or add 세요 if it ends in a *vowel*.

Shopping

Chapter 17

주다 → 주 + 세요

주세요
"Please give me."

하다 → 하 + 세요

하세요
"Please do it."

가다 → 가 + 세요

가세요
"Please go."

들어오다 → 들어오 + 세요

들어오세요.
"Please come in."

찾다 → 찾 + 으세요

찾으세요
"Please look for it."

놓다 → 놓 → 놓 + 으세요

놓으세요
"Please put it down."

For verbs ending in a single ㄹ, remove the ㄹ before doing the above step.

팔다 → 팔 → 파 + 세요

파세요
"Please sell."

> **Adv** This is the same form used in the phrases 안녕히 가세요 and 안녕히 계세요. However, 안녕히 가세요 and 안녕히 계세요 are instead used more like regular phrases. This is because this form, (으)세요, has an additional use in speaking *politely* (specifically, when using what's called *honorific speech*). This book doesn't have room to cover how to use this form in this way, but just know that they are formed the same way.

Chapter 17

Shopping

김철수: 저기요. 이 시계가 얼마입니까?

"Excuse me. How much is this watch?"

"Excuse me!"

As we learned in Chapter 11, 저기 means "there (farther)" and 여기 means "here." However, when using them to call people they have a different usage. You can call out to someone else by saying either 저기요 ("You over there!") or 여기요 ("Hey, I'm over here!"). Only use these words when you need to get an employee's attention, whether at a restaurant or in a store.

여기요!
저기요!
"Excuse me!"

However, this does not mean "excuse me" when you are apologizing to someone, or recognizing that you may be interrupting someone – perhaps after bumping into a stranger on the street, or when trying to ask directions. For these situations, use the verb 실례하다 ("to do a discourtesy").

실례합니다.
"Excuse me."

실례하지만...
"Excuse me but..."

The above sentence could then be followed by your request.

> **Adv** You might see and hear 실례지만 used as well. This has the same meaning as 실례하지만, but is a more common, quicker way of expressing the same thing.

Shopping

Chapter 17

직원: 삼만구천원입니다.

"It's 39,000 Won."

김철수: 조금 깎아주세요.

"Please give me a discount."

Adv 깎아주다 translates as "to give a discount," but literally it means "to trim down." Figuratively, by saying 깎아주세요 you're asking the employee to trim down the price.

직원: 알겠습니다. 그럼 삼만원입니다.

"Understood. Well then it is 30,000 Won."

김철수: 조금 더 깎아주세요. 이만오천원은 어떻습니까?

"Please give me a little more of a discount. How is 25,000 Won?"

조금 더 can be used anywhere as an *adverb* to mean "a little more."

조금 더 주세요.
"Please give me a little more."

조금 더 연습하세요.
"Please practice a little more."

조금 더 노력하세요.
"Please try a little more."

We first saw the verb 어떻다 ("to be how") in Chapter 8 when we learned the *adverb* 어떻게 ("how"). Then we saw it make another appearance in Chapter 10 when we learned the *adjective* 어떤 ("what kind of"). Now we're going to be using it as a regular descriptive verb.

어떻습니까?
"How is it?"

You can use the verb 어떻다 anywhere to ask someone "how" *something* is.

학교가 어떻습니까?
"How is school?"

그 영화가 어떻습니까?
"How is that movie?"

Chapter 17

Shopping

음식이 어떻습니까?
"How is the food?"

When asking "how" *someone* is, instead ask 어떻게 지내세요 – "how are you doing?" You can ask this in the same situations as 잘 지내세요, which we learned in Chapter 7.

Q. 어떻게 지내세요?
"How are you doing?"

A. 아주 좋습니다.
"I'm very good."

> **Adv**
> Using the verb 어떻다 to ask how *someone* is has a different meaning – it asks about them as a person, or their personality.
>
> 친구들이 어떻습니까?
> "How are your friends?"
>
> The above could be asked if you were wondering what type of people their friends are. If you are wondering how the friends are doing, instead use 어떻게 지내세요.
>
> 친구들이 어떻게 지내세요?
> "How are your friends doing?"

Let's take one more look at the second part of this sentence.

이만오천원은 어떻습니까?
"How is 25,000 Won?"

Remembering what we learned about the Topic Marker in Chapter 15, this sentence would literally translate to "*As for* 25,000 Won, how is it?"

직원: 안 됩니다. 그럼 저에게 이만구천원을 주세요.
"That won't work. Well then, give me 29,000 Won."

되다 and 안 되다

되다 and 안 되다 are opposites. In the above sentence, 되다 means "to be okay" and 안 되다 means "to not be okay."

Q. 오늘 학교가 있지만 공원에 가고 싶습니다.
"I have school today, but I want to go to the park."

248

Shopping

A. 안 됩니다.
"No."
"That's not okay."

되다 can also mean "to work," and 안 되다 can mean "to not work."

제 컴퓨터가 안 됩니다.
"My computer doesn't work."

지금 됩니까?
"Does it work now?"

저의 핸드폰이 안 됩니다.
"My cell phone doesn't work."

> **Adv** Although 핸드폰 is certainly the most common word for "cell phone," you may also choose to use either 휴대폰 ("mobile phone") or 휴대 전화 ("mobile telephone") instead.

And finally, 되다 can also mean "to become," and 안 되다 can mean "to not become."

왜 선생님이 되고 싶습니까?
"Why do you want to become a teacher."

저는 더 좋은 사람이 되고 싶습니다.
"I want to become a better person."

저는 프로 선수가 되고 싶지 않습니다.
"I don't want to become a professional athlete."

Most often, as in the examples above, you will see 되다 and 안 되다 used together with the *Subject Marker*.

To and From a Person
에게 and 에게(서)

We've learned how to say "to" and "from" a *location* (에서...까지), and "to" and "from" a *time* (부터...까지). Here we'll learn how to say "to" and "from" a *person*.

To say "to" someone, attach 에게 after the person.

저**에게** 주세요.
"Please give it to me."

Chapter 17

Shopping

김 씨**에게** 편지를 보내고 싶습니다.
"I want to send a letter to Mr. Kim."

김 씨**에게** 말하세요.
"Speak to Mr. Kim."

> **Adv**
> Both the verbs 말(을) 하다 and 물어보다 will use 에게, and *not* the Object Marker, when stating to whom it is you are talking or asking. The same applies to any verb that shows *communication*, such as 전화(를) 하다.
>
> 박 씨**에게** 물어보세요.
> "Ask Mr. Park."
>
> 내일 정 씨**에게** 전화하세요.
> "Call Mr. Jeong tomorrow."

김 씨**에게** 주세요.
"Please give it to Mr. Kim."

To say "from" someone, attach 에게서 after the person.

저**에게서** 배우고 싶습니까?
"Do you want to learn from me?"

김 씨**에게서** 받습니다.
"I receive it from Mr. Kim."

However, the 서 in 에게서 is *optional*. Feel free to simply use 에게 for both "to" and "from" as long as the meaning isn't completely vague by doing so.

김 씨**에게** 줍니다.
"I give it to Mr. Kim."

김 씨**에게** 받습니다.
"I receive it from Mr. Kim."

> **Adv**
> You can use the same 에게(서) to say "to" and "from" an *animal* as well.

김철수: 여기 이만구천원입니다. 감사합니다!
"Here is 29,000 Won. Thank you!"

직원: 안녕히 가세요.
"Goodbye."

Shopping

Chapter 17

김철수: 네, 많이 파세요!

"Okay, sell a lot!"

많이 파세요 comes from 많이 팔다 ("to sell a lot"), and is a common phrase you can say to a store employee after purchasing something. This phrase is similar to saying "I hope your business does well."

Practice

Write the following amounts in Korean:

1. $0.10
2. $1.00
3. $1.50
4. $5.25
5. $80.11
6. $1,020.33

Translate to Korean:

7. "Please give me $10."

_____.

8. "Please take a shower."

_____.

9. "My car does not work. Please help me."

_____.

10. "I want to be a doctor."

_____.

11. "Please buy medicine at the pharmacy."

_____.

Chapter 17

Shopping

Translate to English:

12. 돈을 조금 더 주세요.

13. 왜 선생님이 되고 싶지 않습니까?

14. 저는 김 씨에게서 한국말을 배웁니다.

15. 한국 음식이 어떻습니까? 맛있습니까?

16. 빨리 숙제하세요.

New Phrases

(조금) 깎아주세요.	"Please give me a discount."
(을/를) 더 주세요.	"Please give me more…"
많이 파세요.	"Sell a lot."
여기요.	"Over here." ("Excuse me.")
저기요.	"Over here." ("Excuse me.")
어떻게 지내세요?	"How are you doing?"
실례합니다.	"Excuse me."
실례하지만…	"Excuse me but…"

Shopping

Chapter 17

New Vocabulary

되다	"to become," "to be okay," "to work"
안 되다	"to not become," "to not be okay," "to not work"
들어오다	"to come in"
들어가다	"to go in"
실례하다	"to do a discourtesy"
물어보다	"to ask"
(대)답	"answer"
(대)답(을) 하다	"to answer"
계획	"plan"
계획(을) 하다	"to plan"
결정	"decision"
결정(을) 하다	"to decide," "to make a decision"
사다	"to buy"
팔다	"to sell"
주문(을) 하다	"to order (something)"
빌리다	"to borrow," "to lend"
놓다	"to put down," "to let go"
넣다	"to put in"
보내다	"to send"
도와주다	"to help"
주다	"to give"
쓰다	"to use," "to write"
사용(을) 하다	"to utilize," "to use"
나누다	"to share," "to divide"
샤워(를) 하다	"to take a shower"
씻다	"to wash," "to bathe"
세수(를) 하다	"to wash one's face and hands," "to wash up"
빨래	"laundry"
빨래(를) 하다	"to do the laundry"
설거지	"(dirty) dishes"

Chapter 17: Shopping

설거지(를) 하다	"to do the dishes"
쓰레기	"garbage," "trash"
버리다	"to throw away"
목표	"a goal"
부럽다	"to be jealous"
연습(을) 하다	"to practice"
노력	"effort"
노력(을) 하다	"to try," "to put forth effort"
샴푸	"shampoo"
칫솔	"toothbrush"
치약	"toothpaste"
시계	"clock," "watch"
편지	"(written) letter"
메시지	"message"
쪽지	"note"
프로 선수	"professional athlete"
팀	"team"
껌	"gum"
씹다	"to chew"
불	dollar counter
전	penny counter
에게	"to (a person)"
에게(서)	"from (a person)"
조금 더	"a little more" (adverb)

Relationships

Chapter 18

In this chapter we'll learn essential vocabulary related to the family, and relationships.

Read through the chapter first, then come back here as necessary to review using the following illustration. It might look a bit overwhelming at first, but once you've learned the basic vocabulary for relationships, it's simple.

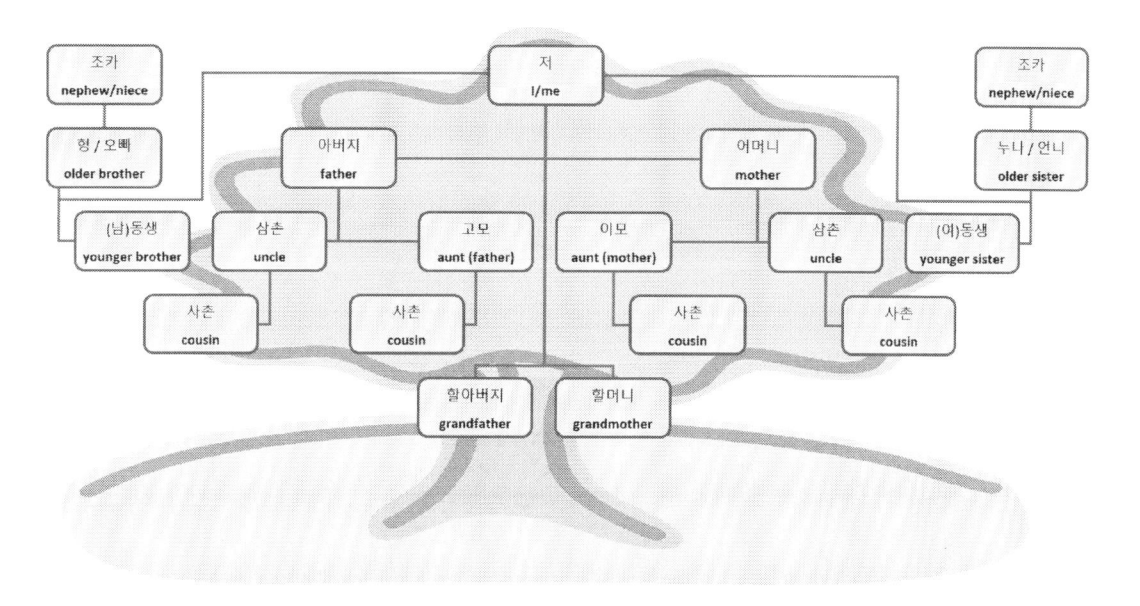

조카	nephew/niece
저	I/me
조카	nephew/niece
형 / 오빠	older brother
아버지	father
어머니	mother
누나 / 언니	older sister
(남)동생	younger brother
삼촌	uncle
고모	aunt (father)
이모	aunt (mother)
삼촌	uncle
(여)동생	younger sister
사촌	cousin
할아버지	grandfather
할머니	grandmother

Conversation

Chapter 18

Relationships

김철수:	가족이 어떻게 됩니까?
김영희:	부모님과 오빠가 한 명 있습니다. 당신은요?
김철수:	저는 부모님과 누나가 한 명 있고, 형도 한 명 있고, 동생도 한 명 있습니다.
김영희:	정말 대가족입니다.
김철수:	네, 사람이 많고 재미있습니다.

Family Vocabulary

Historically as well as today, family is everything to Koreans, so it's no surprise that Korean vocabulary can be a bit extensive when it comes to words related to family members. I created this chapter as a guide to teach you the most common, most useful words for referring to family members.

부모님	"parents"
아이	"child"
아들	"son"
딸	"daughter"

Adv: You'll see words with 님 attached to the end frequently in Korean. 님 attaches to titles, such as "teacher," "parent" or "boss," when used to refer to that person *politely*.

First let's take a look at the words for "older brother" and "older sister."

형	"older brother" (said by *males*)
오빠	"older brother" (said by *females*)

누나	"older sister" (said by *males*)
언니	"older sister" (said by *females*)

Depending on whether you are a boy or a girl, there will be a different word you will use for "older brother" and "older sister." Be careful to learn these correctly, because using the wrong word will sound strange to a Korean.

If you are male, focus on learning 형 and 누나 first, before learning how a female would say them.

Relationships

Chapter 18

If you are female, focus on learning 오빠 and 언니 first, before learning how a male would say them.

The words for "younger brother" and "younger sister" are much simpler. It is the same word, whether you are male or female.

동생	"younger sibling"
남동생	"male younger sibling"
여동생	"female younger sibling"

You could therefore say 남동생 to refer to a *male* younger sibling, or 여동생 to refer to a *female* younger sibling. Or, simply say 동생 to refer to a younger sibling without having to specify the gender.

The words for "mother" and "father" are also simple.

어머니	"mother"
엄마	"mom"

아버지	"father"
아빠	"dad"

Use 엄마 or 아빠 as a more *friendly* version of 어머니 and 아버지, such as to your own parents. However, note that these words are not appropriate for people with whom you are not close and well acquainted. It would not be appropriate to refer to a stranger's parents using 엄마 and 아빠.

할아버지	"grandfather"
할머니	"grandmother"
증조할아버지	"great grandfather"
증조할머니	"great grandmother"
손자	"grandson"
손녀	"granddaughter"

Once you've learned 할아버지 and 할머니, learning 증조할아버지 and 증조할머니 should be easy.

English only has one word for "aunt," but Korean has two, depending on whether you're referring to an aunt on your *mother's* side of the family, or your *father's* side.

257

Chapter 18

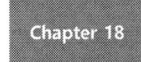

Relationships

이모	"aunt" (*mother's* side)
고모	"aunt" (*father's* side)

However, there is just one word to learn for "uncle."

삼촌	"uncle"

> **Adv**
> There is actually a second word for "uncle," but it's not always necessary to use it. This is because 삼촌 actually means an uncle on your *father's* side of the family. To refer to an uncle on your *mother's* side, use 외삼촌. However, unless you need to specify which side of the family the uncle is from, it's not necessary to use 외삼촌 – you can use 삼촌 to refer to an uncle on either side.

Here's how to refer to your uncles' and aunts' children.

사촌	"cousin"

And finally, you only need to know one word to refer to your siblings' children (a niece or nephew).

조카	"niece," "nephew"

Review these terms one more time, then let's take a look at the conversation.

김철수: 가족이 어떻게 됩니까?

"How many people are in your family?"

Previously we learned that 어떻게 됩니까? was used to mean "tell me about." In this situation, what the speaker actually wants to know is how her family is composed – specifically, how many family members 영희 has. This is why 가족이 어떻게 됩니까? translates better as "How many people are in your family?"

김영희: 부모님과 오빠가 한 명 있습니다. 당신은요?

"There are my parents and one older brother. And you?"

Notice how there is no need to refer to "my" parents, as 부모님 is enough. The same goes here for 오빠, or for any family terms.

Relationships

Chapter 18

Advanced

You may hear 우리 used directly before family member vocabulary in Korean speech. This literally means "our," but is used to mean that the family member the speaker is talking about does not only belong to him or herself. English uses "my" to refer to family members, but Korean does not assume that a family member belongs to only you.

우리 부모님
"our parents" → "my parents"

우리 어머니
"our mother" → "my mother"

Using 저의 (or 제) is also acceptable, and is not incorrect, but using 우리 or nothing at all is more preferred.

Also note how when counting siblings in the previous sentence, the family member comes before the *Subject Marker*, followed by the number.

저는 오빠가 한 명 있습니다.
"I have one older brother."

당신

Although I said that Koreans will use a person's name instead of saying "you," there actually is a word for "you" in Korean – 당신. *However!* You should avoid 당신 except in the following situations only:

1. You do not know the other person's name, status, or anything about them at all.

2. You're talking to your spouse (당신 can also mean "dear" in this way).

3. You're angry at another person, and refuse to even call them by their name.

An example of 1 would be if you were talking to someone who you couldn't see, or to someone who suddenly came to you and began talking without any sort of introduction. Not knowing whether you need to be polite to them or not, it would be acceptable to ask them who they are using 당신 for "you."

An example of 2 would be if you are speaking politely to your spouse. However, this is more of a traditional usage, as younger couples will call each other by their first names, or nicknames. You might also see this usage in books.

An example of 3 would be similar to 1 – you're calling them 당신 because you do not know anything about them, or no longer wish to. Using 당신 can cause the listener to feel distanced from you, so it should be avoided outside of these three cases.

Chapter 18 — Relationships

Besides these few cases, you shouldn't use 당신. However, in the previous conversation I included it only to show you that a word for "you" does exist, and to demonstrate how it works. It can be rude when used in other situations.

> **Advanced**
>
> There are many other words for "you," but they are not acceptable in polite situations (but are acceptable around close friends who are younger than you). Be careful when using any translation you may find for "you," as *all of them* can be rude, even when used with close friends, unless you know their usage.
>
> One more word for "you" I'll introduce is an alternative to 당신; the word is 그쪽. You can use 그쪽 only in one situation.
>
> 1. You do not know the other person's name, status, or anything about them at all.
>
> As such, 그쪽 is more limited than 당신, but there is one more difference. Using 그쪽 to a stranger is not impolite.
>
> 그쪽 literally means "that way." It loosely translates as "you, the person that way."
>
> 그쪽은요?
> "How about you?"
>
> 그쪽은 가족이 어떻게 됩니까?
> "How many people are in your family?"
>
> However, with this said, it's still important to quickly assess the other person's name or status, and then to cease using 그쪽 or 당신 as soon as you can.

그 and 그녀

These are not good words to use either, but I want to let you know that they exist.

그	"he," "him"
그녀	"she," "her"

These two words are solely to be used within *textbooks* as direct translations for the English words "he/him" and "she/her." They shouldn't be used in real Korean speech, as they sound rude when spoken. Hopefully due to the way that I've arranged the lessons in this book, you should be able to see by now that these words aren't really necessary for speaking Korean. Still, you should be able to recognize them and know what they mean.

Remember that if you need to say "he" or "she" and can't remember a person's name or title (김철수 씨, or 선생님, for example), you can still sound polite using 그분.

김철수: 저는 부모님과 누나가 한 명 있고, 형도 한 명 있고, 동생도 한 명 있습니다.
"As for me, there are my parents and one older sister, and one older brother, and also one younger sibling."

Relationships

Chapter 18

김영희: 정말 대가족입니다.

"It's really a big family."

In Korean, "big family" has its own vocabulary word – 대가족. Although you might be tempted to conjugate the descriptive verb 크다, "to be big," this would sound awkward in Korean as 크다 refers to something's actual *size*. Instead, in English a "big family" refers to having many family members, so 대가족 should be used.

김철수: 네, 사람이 많고 재미있습니다.

"Yes, there are many people and it's entertaining."

Culture Notes

Before reading further, make sure that you have a good understanding of how to use each of the four words 형, 오빠, 누나, and 언니.

These four words are a bit special, in that they can also be used to refer to *friends*, and not only family members.

형

"older male friend" (said by *males*)

오빠

"older male friend" (said by *females*)

누나

"older female friend" (said by *males*)

언니

"older female friend" (said by *females*)

Just like before, remember that each word is to be used by either *males* or *females*, and to be careful to use the right ones.

Adv In addition, 삼촌 and 이모 have one more use – when calling out to strangers who are *older* than yourself. If you want to get the attention of a man or a woman who you are not close to, such as a waiter or waitress in a restaurant, you may use 삼촌 ("uncle") to *males*, or 이모 ("aunt") to *females*.

Practice

How would **you** say the following words:

1. Older brother
2. Older sister
3. Younger brother
4. Younger sister

Chapter 18

Relationships

Translate to Korean:

5. "I also have a big family."

6. "How many people are in your family, Mr. Kim?"

7. "I really love my mother."

8. "I want to study with my older sister."

Translate to English:

9. 저의 형도 김치를 싫어합니다.

10. 저의 언니는 유명한 가수입니다.

11. 오늘 학교에서 저의 누나를 만납니다.

12. 저의 형을 왜 미워합니까?

New Phrases

Relationships

Chapter 18

가족이 어떻게 됩니까?	"How many people are in your family?"
축하합니다.	"Congratulations."

New Vocabulary

걱정(을) 하다	"to worry"
약속(을) 하다	"to promise"
관계	"relationship"
부모님	"parents"
아이	"child"
아기	"baby"
당신	"you" (not polite)
그	"he/him" (not polite)
그녀	"she/her" (not polite)
가족	"family"
대가족	"big family"
축하(를) 하다	"to congratulate"
형	"older brother" (used by males)
오빠	"older brother" (used by females)
누나	"older sister" (used by males)
언니	"older sister" (used by females)
동생	"younger sibling"
남동생	"male younger sibling"
여동생	"female younger sibling"
어머니	"mother"
엄마	"mom"
아버지	"father"
아빠	"dad"
할아버지	"grandfather"
할머니	"grandmother"
이모	"aunt" (mother's side)
고모	"aunt" (father's side)
조카	"niece," "nephew"

Chapter 18: Relationships

삼촌	"uncle"
사촌	"cousin"
아들	"son"
딸	"daughter"
손자	"grandson"
손녀	"granddaughter"
증조할아버지	"great grandfather"
증조할머니	"great grandmother"
남편	"husband"
아내	"wife"
노인	"old person"
어른	"adult"
삶	"life"
죽음	"death"

Informal Korean

> Chapter 19

The time has come for us to switch from formal to informal Korean. We'll learn how to conjugate the 요 form – the most common, popular form in use in Korean. We'll also learn about when it's necessary to use formal, as well as informal Korean.

I recommend that you spend extra time reading over this chapter to make sure you know each and every rule. These conjugation rules will also be essential as you learn additional grammar rules in the future.

Conversation

조지:	안녕하세요!
임이랑:	안녕하세요! 아, 혹시 한국 사람이에요?
조지:	아니에요. 저는 미국 사람이에요.
임이랑:	정말이요? 한국어도 할 수 있어요?
조지:	네, 미국 사람이지만 한국어를 조금 해요. 하지만 완벽하지 않아요.

Formal vs. Informal Korean

Up until now, everything we have learned in this book has been *formal* Korean. By *formal*, I mean *extra polite*. This is because all of the concepts we've learned so far can be taught more clearly using formal Korean, instead of using informal Korean. Specifically, using the 니다 and 니까 endings is considered formal.

Chapter 19

Informal Korean

But knowing a foreign language means being able to speak and understand it in all situations, including both formal and informal situations. By *informal*, I mean *polite* – but less polite than formal. We've now learned a good portion of the basics of the Korean language already, and this is why it is time for us to begin covering informal Korean.

So what is *informal* Korean, and when do we use it? An easier way to answer this question is by first showing you when you should use *formal* Korean (such as the 니다 and 니까 endings).

Formal Korean is used in these situations:

1. Meeting people for the first time who are older than you

2. Job interviews

3. Business relations

4. When you want to sound extra polite

Informal Korean can be used in all other situations.

Using the wrong kind of Korean (*formal* or *informal*) in any situation can come across as either rude, or overly polite. As a non-Korean, you won't be held to the same high standards as a native Korean speaker at first, but as your Korean improves you will be expected to know which kind of language to use with each person you communicate with. It's much easier to learn proper, formal Korean at first, and then to learn informal Korean, than it is to go the other way; it's better to be overly polite than rude.

The 요 Form

In this chapter we will be learning how to conjugate verbs into a new *informal* form – the 요 form. Previously, we've only been working with the 니다 and 니까 forms. But informal does not mean rude; on the contrary, *informal* Korean is still polite, but less polite than *formal*. As such, it should not be used in situations where you want to sound more formal, such as the four situations listed previously.

The 요 form isn't as straightforward to conjugate as the 니다 or 니까 forms, but it does have a set of rules which it follows nicely. With a bit of practice, it will become second nature.

The meaning of the 요 form is the same as the 니다 or 니까 form – yes, it can be used for making both *statements* and *questions* – simply add a question mark to turn the sentence into a question. The only difference is that the 요 form is not formal.

Informal Korean

Chapter 19

The basic steps to conjugating the 요 form are as so:

1. Get the verb stem.

2. Add 아 after ㅏ or ㅗ, or add 어 after anything else.

3. Attach 요.

Remove the 다 at the end of a verb to get the verb stem. Then look at the vowel in the last syllable. If that vowel is ㅏ or ㅗ, then attach 아 to the end of it. If that vowel is anything else, then attach 어 to the end of it. Then attach 요.

Before we get into any more rules, let's take a look at some examples of this in action.

먹다 → 먹
먹 (ㅓ) → 먹어
→ 먹어요

After getting the verb stem of 먹다, which is 먹, we look at the vowel in the last syllable. The last vowel in 먹 is ㅓ, which isn't ㅏ or ㅗ, so we attach 어 to the end. Then we attach 요, and we're finished.

Let's look at another example.

좋다 → 좋
좋 (ㅗ) → 좋아
→ 좋아요

First we take the verb stem of 좋다, which is 좋. Then we look at the vowel in the last syllable. Here, the last vowel of 좋 is ㅗ, so we attach 아 to the end. Finally we attach 요 to the end.

Although this is the basic rule for conjugating the 요 form, there are also some other rules to consider depending on the type of verb. Let's go over each of them one at a time.

Rule 1: Ends in a vowel with no consonants

If the verb stem ends in a vowel without any consonants on the *bottom*, then instead of adding 아 or 어 to the end of it like we did in the above examples, the 아 or 어 ending will *combine* into the last syllable. This is much simpler than it sounds.

267

Chapter 19

Informal Korean

가다 → 가
가 (ㅏ) → 가아 → 가
→ 가요

After taking the verb stem of 가다, which is 가, we look at the vowel in the last syllable. The last vowel is ㅏ, so we would normally attach 아 to the end.

But see how the 아 combined into 가? This is because it has the same vowel sound as it. It would be unnecessary to drag out the sound and say 가아요, so this is why this rule exists in the first place. This rule makes it easier for us to say these types of verbs more quickly.

오다 → 오
오 (ㅗ) → 오아 → 와
→ 와요

Saying 오아 quickly will sound like 와 anyway.

주다 → 주
주 (ㅜ) → 주어 → 줘
→ 줘요

Let's take a look at one more.

보다 → 보
보 (ㅗ) → 보아 → 봐
→ 봐요

Rule 2: Ends in ㅣ

If the verb stem ends with ㅣ, then instead of adding 아 or 어 to the end of it, the 아 or 어 ending will *combine* into the last syllable. This is similar to Rule 1, and works in the same way. However, since ㅣ is not ㅗ or ㅏ, you will always add ㅓ to the end.

마시다 → 마시
마시 (ㅣ) → 마시어 → 마셔
→ 마셔요

It should feel natural to apply this rule as well.

가르치다 → 가르치
가르치 (ㅣ) → 가르치어 → 가르쳐
→ 가르쳐요

Informal Korean

Chapter 19

Here's one more example.

피다 → 피
피 (ㅣ) → 피어 → 펴
펴요

Rule 3: Ends in ㅡ

If the verb stem ends with ㅡ, first remove the ㅡ. Then you will need to look at the *2nd to last syllable*. If the 2nd to last syllable ends in ㅗ or ㅏ, add ㅏ to the end. If it's any other vowel, add ㅓ to the end.

바쁘다 → 바쁘
바쁘 (ㅡ) → 바ㅃ
바ㅃ + ㅏ → 바빠
→ 바빠요

In the above example, after we removed the ㅡ we were left with 바ㅃ, so we had to then look at the 2nd to last syllable – 바. Since 바 ends in ㅏ, we added ㅏ to the end. Then we finished by attaching 요.

예쁘다 → 예쁘
예쁘 (ㅡ) → 예ㅃ
예ㅃ + ㅓ → 예뻐
→ 예뻐요

In this example, after we removed the ㅡ, the 2nd to last syllable is 예 so we added ㅓ to the end.

쓰다 → 쓰
쓰 (ㅡ) → ㅆ
ㅆ + ㅓ → 써
→ 써요

Here, there is no 2nd to last syllable, because the entire verb is only two syllables. In this case, you'll always add ㅓ to the end.

> **Adv** The reason you'd always add ㅓ to the end in this situation is because the only syllable to look at is the last one remaining. In the above example, 쓰 is all that's left, and if you remember from our basic rules of conjugation, ㅡ is neither ㅏ or ㅗ so it would require adding ㅓ to the end.

269

Informal Korean

Rule 4: Ends in 르

Although 르 technically also ends in ㅡ like in Rule 3, this is a special case. When the verb stem ends in 르, first remove the ㅡ. Then add an extra ㄹ to the bottom of the *2nd to last syllable*. Finally, look again at the *2nd to last syllable*; if it's ㅏ or ㅗ, add ㅏ to the end, else add ㅓ to the end.

모르다 → 모르
모르 (르) → 모ㄹ
몰ㄹ (ㅗ) → 몰ㄹ + ㅏ → 몰라
→ 몰라요

This might seem a bit confusing since there are multiple steps, but don't worry about it. There are only a few of these verbs in Korean, and the ones you will use are so common that you will be able to memorize them easily just from using them often.

부르다 → 부르
부르 (르) → 부ㄹ
불ㄹ (ㅜ) → 불ㄹ + ㅓ → 불러
→ 불러요

Let's take a look at one more example.

마르다 → 마르
마르 (르) → 마ㄹ
말ㄹ (ㅏ) → 말ㄹ + ㅏ → 말라
→ 말라요

Rule 5: Ends in ㅂ (Descriptive Verb)

This rule only applies to *descriptive verbs*. When the verb stem ends in ㅂ (and no other *consonants*), first remove the ㅂ. Then add 우. Next (since 우 does not end in ㅗ or ㅏ), add ㅓ. Then, remember Rule 1; 우 and ㅓ combine to become 워.

부럽다 → 부럽
부럽 (ㅂ) → 부러
부러 + 우 → 부러우
부러우 + ㅓ → 부러워
→ 부러워요

Let's look at another example.

Informal Korean

Chapter 19

맵다 → 맵
맵 (ㅂ) → 매
매 + 우 → 매우
매우 + ㅓ → 매워
→ 매워요

Here's one more example.

덥다 → 덥
덥 (ㅂ) → 더
더 + 우 → 더우
더우 + ㅓ → 더워
→ 더워요

Remember that this rule only applies to *descriptive verbs*. Action verbs that end in ㅂ will not conjugate using any of these special rules, but will conjugate completely normally.

> **Advanced**
>
> An exception to this rule is the *action verb* 굽다 ("to bake") which conjugates to become 구워요.
>
> In addition, some *descriptive verbs* that end with the sound 옵다 (곱다, 롭다, 좁다, etc.) will also conjugate uniquely.
>
> 곱다 → 고와요
>
> 좁다 → 좁아요
>
> But many will still follow the general rules.
>
> 새롭다 → 새로워요
>
> 외롭다 → 외로워요
>
> 까다롭다 → 까다로워요
>
> Take heed of exceptions as you see them, but remember that most verbs will follow the rules.

Rule 6: Ends in ㅐ

If the verb stem ends in ㅐ, then you don't need to add anything other than 요 to the end.

보내다 → 보내
→ 보내요

Here's one more example.

새다 → 새
→ 새요

271

Chapter 19

Informal Korean

Rule 7: Ends in ㄷ

If the verb ends in ㄷ, the ㄷ will change into ㄹ.

걷다 → 걷
걷 (ㄷ) → 거 + ㄹ → 걸
걸어요

Here's another example.

듣다 → 듣
듣 (ㄷ) → 드 + ㄹ → 들
들어요

And here's one last example.

묻다 → 묻
묻 (ㄷ) → 무 + ㄹ → 물
물어요

However, there are also a few common verbs that do not follow this rule that you should keep in mind.

믿다 → 믿어요
받다 → 받아요
얻다 → 얻어요

Rule 8: 어떻다, 그렇다, 이렇다

These three verbs conjugate differently.

어떻다 becomes **어때요**.

수업이 어때요?
"How are your classes?"

그렇다 becomes **그래요**.

아, 그래요?
"Ah, really?"

Informal Korean

Chapter 19

이렇다 becomes **이래요**.

항상 이래요.
"It's always this way."

Rule 9: 하다 and 되다

If the verb ends in 하다, or if the verb is just 하다, it simply becomes 해요. This rule applies to any verb that ends in 하다, whether it's a *descriptive verb* or an *action verb*.

하다 → 해
→ 해요

Here's one more example.

공부하다 → 공부해
→ 공부해요

> **Adv:** You might also see 하여 instead of 해 in some situations, such as books. This is an older form of 해. Don't use it yourself in spoken Korean, but know what it means when you see it.

If the verb ends in 되다, or if the verb is just 되다, you have two options. First, you could conjugate it normally using the basic rule.

되다 → 되
되 + 어 → 되어
→ 되어요

Or, 되다 can simply become 돼요.

되다 → 돼
→ 돼요

Although either one is correct, 돼요 is definitely the more popular choice.

> **Adv:** 돼 comes from a combination of the diphthong ㅚ and the vowel ㅓ. Imagine ㅓ attaching itself on the right side of 되, and you'd get 돼.

Rule 10: 이다 and 아니다

It's best to simply memorize how these verbs conjugate in the 요 form.

Chapter 19: Informal Korean

이다 → 이에요 or 예요

아니다 → 아니에요

이다 becomes 이에요 when following a *consonant*, or 예요 when following a *vowel*.

저는 미국 사람**이에요**.
"I am an American."

저는 남자**예요**.
"I am a man."

아니다 simply becomes 아니에요.

저는 한국 사람이 **아니에요**.
"I am not a Korean."

Remember that 아니다 is used together with the *Subject Marker* (이/가).

> **Adv** A common mistake that native Korean speakers will make is writing 예요 as 에요. This is because 예요 when spoken in conversation is actually pronounced 에요 – this is much easier to say.

Rule 11: Irregular Verbs

There is no Rule 11, but Korean does have many *irregular verbs* which have their own way of conjugating. A few examples I gave specifically are 하다, 되다, 이다, and 아니다, but there are others too.

Instead of teaching every single additional irregular verb in this book, it's best to go out and learn them on your own. I've covered some of them already, and I will be covering more in the future.

Don't be afraid of a few verbs not conforming to the rules. The vast majority of verbs do follow the rules, but there are some here and there that do not.

Learn these rules as well as you possibly can before continuing on. Knowing how to conjugate the 요 form correctly is one of the most commonly needed skills to have in speaking Korean.

Now that we've got all of that out of the way, let's go over the conversation.

Informal Korean

Chapter 19

A d v

Although we won't learn it in this book, you will come across spoken and written Korean verbs that are conjugated in this same way, but simply lack the 요 at the end. This is known as *casual* Korean, and is not *polite* or *formal*. However, it's a bit tricky to work with; in order to avoid offending people and being rude, you need to know exactly when it is okay and not okay to use casual Korean. Be aware of its existence, and don't be offended if you hear it, but avoid using it for the time being.

조지: 안녕하세요!
"Hello!"

Common Greetings

Even in informal Korean, some greetings will stay the same because they are so common, such as 안녕하세요.

Other greetings may change, such as 안녕히 가세요 and 안녕히 계세요.

The informal version of 안녕히 가세요 is 잘 가요 ("Go well.").

There are a few informal versions of 안녕히 계세요, one of which is 먼저 갈게요 ("I'll go first."). The grammar used in this form has not been covered yet, but simply memorizing this phrase is sufficient for now.

Another important greeting to know is 여보세요, which means "hello" when answering the phone.

여보세요 is used to get the other person's attention, just like "hello?" is asked when answering the phone in English. As such, it can also be used to get someone's attention in a public place – perhaps if someone dropped their wallet.

여보세요?
"Hello?" (on the phone)

여보세요?
"Excuse me?" ("Hello?" to someone in public)

임이랑: 안녕하세요! 아, 혹시 한국 사람이에요?
"Hello! Ah, by chance are you a Korean?"

Chapter 19

Informal Korean

The Adverb 혹시

혹시 is an *adverb* that means "by chance," and can be used to soften the tone of a question.

혹시 차가 있어요?
"Do you have a car by chance?"

그분이 **혹시** 유명한 사람이에요?
"Is he by chance a famous person?"

혹시... 저에게 돈을 조금 줄 수 있어요?
"By chance... can you give a little money to me?"

> 조지: 아니에요. 저는 미국 사람이에요.
> "I'm not. I am an American."

Remember that 아니에요 is different from 아니요 – which simply means "no." Using 아니에요 here is in response to the previous question. In this case, saying just 아니에요 is a shorter way of saying 한국 사람이 아니에요.

> 임이랑: 정말이요? 한국어도 할 수 있어요?
> "Really? Can you speak Korean too?"

Ending Sentences Using 요

In the above sentence we have 정말이요, which is 정말 ("really") combined with 이요. Simply ending the question with 정말 on its own would be impolite when speaking to older people. Even for informal Korean like we're learning, it's important to not be rude. If there is no verb at the end of the sentence, or you're not using 은요 or 는요 (which we covered in Chapter 7), add 요 to the end to make the sentence sound more polite.

Informal Korean

Chapter 19

Add 요 to the end of a word ending with a *vowel*, or 이요 if it ends with a *consonant*. Words ending with ㄹ can use either.

저**요**?
"Me?"

저**요**.
"Me."

한글**이요**.
"Hangul."

김 씨**요**?
"Mr. Kim?"

가방**이요**.
"(A/The) bag."

Remember that using 요 is different from using 은요 or 는요.

저는요?
"How about me?"

김 씨는요?
"What about Mr. Kim?"

조지: 네, 미국 사람이지만 한국어를 조금 해요. 하지만 완벽하지 않아요.
"Yes, I am an American but I can speak a little Korean. But I'm not perfect."

As mentioned in Chapter 12, adding 하다 ("to do") after a *language* is a common way to express that you can *speak* it.

저도 한국어를 해요.
"I speak Korean too."

Using 하다 in this way is actually an abbreviation of 말(을) 하다 ("to speak").

277

Chapter 19 — Informal Korean

Practice

Complete the following exercises using informal Korean.

Conjugate the following verbs:

1. 사다
2. 팔다
3. 내다
4. 뜨겁다
5. 끄다
6. 수영하다
7. 선생님이 되다
8. 바르다
9. 말리다
10. 아니다
11. 켜다

Translate to Korean:

12. "By chance can you speak English?"

13. "I dry my clothes at home."

14. "Where does Mr. Kim eat lunch?"

15. "I don't know. I'm not meeting him today."

Informal Korean

Chapter 19

Translate to English:

16. 화장실이 어디 있어요?

_____.

17. 저는 피부에 로션을 발라요.

_____.

18. 과학 선생님을 좋아해요?

_____.

19. 안 좋아해요. 똑똑하지만 조금 이상한 사람이에요.

_____.

New Phrases

잘 가요.	"Go well."
먼저 갈게요.	"I'll go first."
여보세요?	"Hello?" (on the phone)

New Vocabulary

완벽하다	"to be perfect"
이상하다	"to be strange"
묻다	"to inquire"
끄다	"to turn off"
켜다	"to turn on"
바르다	"to spread (on)," "to apply"
말리다	"to (make) dry," "to dry (something)"
피부	"skin"
로션	"lotion"
항상	"always" (adverb)

Chapter 19: Informal Korean

먼저	"first (before anything/anyone else)" (adverb)
처음	"first" (noun), "for the first time" (adverb)
첫	"first" (adjective)
첫인상	"first impression"
인상	"impression"
마지막	"last" (noun)
가끔	"sometimes" (adverb)
자주	"often" (adverb)
때때로	"from time to time" (adverb)
혹시	"by chance" (adverb)
특히	"especially" (adverb)

Past Tense

Chapter 20

Using the 요 form we learned in the last chapter, this lesson will cover how to speak using the *past tense*.

Conversation

A:	철수 씨가 어디에 있어요?
B:	아마 학교에서 공부해요.
A:	왜 학교에 갔어요? 수업이 이미 끝나지 않았어요?
B:	아니요. 밤에도 수업이 있어요.
A:	철수 씨가 그 수업을 왜 선택했어요?
B:	그 수업에 예쁜 여자가 많기 때문에 선택했어요.

Make sure you've got a good grasp of conjugating the 요 form, which we covered in Chapter 19, before beginning this chapter. Fortunately, things get a bit easier now that you're able to conjugate the 요 form. This chapter will cover how to make the *past tense*.

Past Tense

Up until now, everything we've learned has been only in the *present tense*. The present tense is used to describe things that are currently happening in the present.

저는 학교에 갑니다.
저는 학교에 가요.
"I go to school."

Chapter 20: Past Tense

In this chapter we'll learn how to make the *past tense*. The past tense is used to describe things that have happened in the past.

The steps to conjugating the past tense are as so:

1. Conjugate the verb to the 요 form.

2. Remove the 요.

3. Attach ㅆ to the bottom.

4. Attach 습니다/습니까 or 어요, depending on politeness.

For step 4, you can attach 습니다 (or 습니까?) to speak *formally*, or attach 어요 to speak *informally*.

공부하다 → 공부해요
공부해요 – 요 → 공부해
공부해 + ㅆ → 공부했
→ 공부했습니다 or 공부했어요

Let's look at another example.

놀다 → 놀아요
놀아요 – 요 → 놀아
놀아 + ㅆ → 놀았
→ 놀았습니다 or 놀았어요

Here's an example using the verb 어떻다 – "to be how."

어떻다 → 어때요
어때요 – 요 → 어때
어때 + ㅆ → 어땠
→ 어땠습니까? or 어땠어요?

And here's an example with a *descriptive verb*. The steps for turning it into the past tense form are the same.

덥다 → 더워요
더워 – 요 → 더워
더워 + ㅆ → 더웠
→ 더웠습니다 or 더웠어요

Past Tense

If you know how to conjugate the 요 form, turning present tense into past tense is simple.

저는 학교에 갔습니다.
저는 학교에 갔어요.
"I went to school."

이다 and 아니다

There is one additional rule to consider when conjugating the past tense, and it applies to the verbs 이다 and 아니다. It's best to simply memorize these.

이다 becomes 이었습니다 or 이었어요 when following a *consonant*, and 였습니다 or 였어요 when following a *vowel*.

After a *consonant*:
이다 → 이었습니다 or 이었어요

저는 학생**이었습니다**.
저는 학생**이었어요**.
"I was a student."

After a *vowel*:
이다 → 였습니다 or 였어요

저는 박사**였습니다**.
저는 박사**였어요**.
"I was a doctor."

아니다 becomes 아니었습니다 or 아니었어요, *regardless* of whether it comes after a consonant or vowel.

아니다 → 아니었습니다 or 아니었어요

저는 학생이 **아니었습니다**.
저는 학생이 **아니었어요**.
"I was not a student."

Now that we can correctly conjugate the past tense, let's go over the conversation.

Chapter 20

Past Tense

A: 철수 씨가 어디에 있어요?

"Where is Chul-soo?"

Remember that when asking questions, it's most common to mark the *subject* of that sentence (whoever or whatever it is that you are specifically asking about) with the *Subject Marker* – in this case, the subject of this question is 철수 씨.

More on 에 있다

So far we've been able to express that something is "at," or "in" somewhere, or is going "to" somewhere by using the particle 에 with the verb 있다. But English has *prepositions* – "The book is *under* the desk," "I am *in front of* the house," or "We're *outside* the school." Korean also has these kinds of words, but they're actually called *postpositions* – "post" because they are used *after*, instead of before what you are referring to. They're simple to use. Let's look at the most standard, and common postpositions.

위 "above," "on (top of)"

> 책은 책상 **위**에 있어요.
> "The book is *on top of* the desk."

밑 "underneath"

> 고양이는 제 자동차 **밑**에 있어요.
> "The cat is *underneath* my car."

앞 "in front of"

> 저 **앞**에 있어요.
> "It's *in front of* me."

뒤 "behind," "after"

> 원숭이는 개 **뒤**에 있어요.
> "The monkey is *behind* the dog."

옆 "beside," "(right) next to"

> 제 친구는 저 **옆**에 있어요.
> "My friend is *next to* me."

Past Tense

Chapter 20

안 "inside"

아이는 집 안에 있어요.
"The child is <i>inside</i> the house."</p>

밖 "outside"

우리는 학교 밖에 있어요.
"We are <i>outside</i> the school."</p>

> B: 아마 학교에서 공부해요.
> "Maybe he's studying at school."

You can express "maybe" or "probably" in Korean with the adverb 아마(도) – the 도 is optional, and if used makes the meaning *stronger*. You can think of 아마 as meaning "maybe" or "probably," and think of 아마도 as meaning "*maybe*" or "*probably.*"

Although in English, "maybe" and "probably" express two different possibilities, in Korean they are the same; 아마(도) can be used to mean both.

The above sentence could therefore also translate as, "He's probably studying at school."

> A: 왜 학교에 갔어요? 수업이 이미 끝나지 않았어요?
> "Why did he go to school? Didn't classes already finish?"

Notes on Sentence Order

Let's take a look at the following two sentences:

A. 왜 학교에 갔어요?
B. 학교에 왜 갔어요?
"Why did he go to school?"

Both of the above two sentences are correct, and have the same meaning. However, there is a difference between them.

Sentence A uses a question word (왜, 언제, 어디, 무엇, 누구/누가, 어떻게, etc.) at the *beginning* of the sentence.

Sentence B uses a *question word* as an *adverb*, right *before* the verb.

285

Chapter 20 — Past Tense

The easiest way to know how these two sentences are different is by looking at sentence B. Using a question word directly before a verb adds more *emphasis* to the question word.

학교에 왜 갔어요?
"*Why* did he go to school?"

Using a question word at the beginning of a sentence adds no additional emphasis.

왜 학교에 갔어요?
"Why did he go to school?"

Let's take a look at a couple of different examples.

어디에서 숙제를 해요?
"Where are you doing homework at?"

숙제를 어디에서 해요?
"*Where* are you doing homework at?"

누가 병원에 갔어요?
"Who went to the hospital?"

병원에 누가 갔어요?
"*Who* went to the hospital?"

언제 밥을 먹었어요?
"When did you eat?"

밥을 언제 먹었어요?
"*When* did you eat?"

Remember that both usages are correct, and both can be used. Don't worry about making mistakes with this. When in doubt, use question words at the beginning of a sentence or phrase.

잘생기다

Previously in Chapter 10 we learned to only use 잘생기다 as an *adjective* – 잘생긴. Now we can use it at the end of a sentence too.

This verb is an exception, and *must* be conjugated in the *past tense* to be used at the end of a sentence.

Past Tense

저 남자가 잘생겼어요.
"That man over there is handsome."

제가 잘생겼어요?
"Am I handsome?"

끝나다 and 끝내다

Before finishing the conversation, we need to cover how to use the verbs 끝나다 and 끝내다. The same concepts that apply to these two verbs will apply to numerous other verbs that you will come across in the future. Let's go over each of them first.

끝나다 means "to be finish," "to end," or "to be over." It can be used with a variety of markers.

수업**이** 끝났어요.
"Class is over."

수업**은** 끝났어요.
"As for the class, it's over."

수업**도** 끝났어요.
"Even the class is over."

끝내다 means "to finish (something)," or "to end (something)." It can also be used with a variety of markers.

숙제를 끝냈어요.
"I finished the homework."

철수 씨**가** 시험을 끝냈어요.
"Chul-soo finished the test."

Can you tell how 끝나다 and 끝내다 are different? 끝나다 refers to *something finishing*, and 끝내다 refers to *someone finishing something*. They are certainly different. For example, the following sentence is *incorrect*:

숙제를 끝났어요.

Past Tense

Since 끝나다 means "to be finished," this would not translate. 끝나다 does not indicate an action, but something finishing, and does not need an object. The following sentence is also *incorrect*:

숙제가 끝냈어요.

Since the Subject Marker shows the subject of a sentence (here, *who* or *what* that is doing the verb), using it after 숙제 would imply that "homework" is finishing something. If "homework" starts to finish things, it's time to start running for your life (or stop drinking).

However, the following sentence would be *correct*:

숙제는 끝났어요.
"As for homework, it's finished."

In addition, this sentence would also be *correct*:

숙제는 끝냈어요.
"As for homework, I finished it."

And these two sentences as well would be *correct*:

숙제도 끝냈어요.
"I also finished the homework."

숙제도 끝났어요.
"The homework is finished too."

It's important to distinguish whether a verb indicates that something is being done (끝나다), or indicating that someone or something is doing something (끝내다). Knowing this difference will help you learn new verbs in the future, such as 움직이다 and 옮기다 – verbs that indicate physical *movement*.

박스가 움직였어요.
"The box moved."

제가 박스를 옮겼어요.
"I moved the box."

Now let's continue the conversation.

Past Tense

> B: 아니요. 밤에도 수업이 있어요.
> "No. He has class at night also."

More than one particle can appear after a noun, such as 에 and 도 in the above sentence. However, particles that indicate *direction*, such as 에 or 에게, must come first. Particles such as 도 or 만, if used, must come after.

Here are some more basic examples.

> 저에게**도** 주세요.
> "Please give it to me too."

> 한국에**만** 가고 싶어요.
> "I only want to go to Korea."

> 김 씨에게**는** 주고 싶지 않아요.
> "As for Mr. Kim, I don't want to give it to him."

However, the *Subject Marker* cannot be used after a particle that indicates *direction* (such as 에 and 에게). The following sentence would be *incorrect*:

> 저에게가 주세요.

To be safe, if you are not certain how to combine particles, experiment only using combinations which you have seen used before. Some will be more common than others, such as the above examples.

> A: 철수 씨가 그 수업을 왜 선택했어요?
> "Why did Chul-soo choose that class?"

In the above sentence, remember that 왜 is being *emphasized* since it appears directly before the verb.

> B: 그 수업에 예쁜 여자가 많기 때문에 선택했어요.
> "He chose it because there are many pretty girls in that class."

Chapter 20

Past Tense

"To Wear"

Expressing "to wear" can be a bit complicated in Korean at first glance, as there are multiple verbs that can all translate as "to wear" depending on where it is being worn. Let's go over a few of the most common ones.

For general items such as shirts and pants, use the verb 입다.

셔츠를 입다
"to wear a shirt"

바지를 입다
"to wear pants"

For items you can wear on your feet, such as shoes and socks, use the verb 신다.

양말을 신다
"to wear socks"

신발을 신다
"to wear shoes"

> **Adv**: The verb 신다 is pronounced 신따, and is an exception to the sound change rules.

For items you can wear on your head, use the verb 쓰다.

모자를 쓰다
"to wear a hat"

Past Tense

Chapter 20

You can also use the verb 벗다, "to take off (clothing)" as the opposite of 입다, for any type of clothing worn on the body.

셔츠를 벗다
"to take off one's shirt"

양말을 벗다
"to take off one's socks"

모자를 벗다
"to take off a hat"

Although there are other, less common verbs for expressing "to wear," these are the most important ones to remember for the time being.

> **Advanced**
>
> Two more verbs that you might want to learn are 끼다 and 차다.
>
> For items you wear on your hands, use the verb 끼다.
>
>
>
> 장갑을 **끼다**
> "to wear gloves"
>
> 반지를 **끼다**
> "to wear a ring"
>
>
>
> For items you wear on your wrists, use the verb 차다.
>
>
>
> 손목 시계를 **차다**
> "to wear a wristwatch"
>
>

Culture Notes

The traditional Korean dress is known as 한복. There are both male and female styles of 한복. 한복 can be very expensive, and like a tuxedo, are custom tailored to fit each individual. Nowadays, such clothing is only seen on special occasions, such as in traditional Korean wedding ceremonies.

Past Tense

Practice

Complete the following exercises using informal Korean in the past tense.

Conjugate the following verbs:

1. 하다
2. 가다
3. 춥다
4. 차갑다
5. 좋아하다
6. 아니다
7. 버리다
8. 쓰다
9. 가르치다
10. 배우다

Translate to Korean:

11. "I do not want to go to school today."

_____.

12. "I did not want to go to school yesterday."

_____.

13. "Yesterday I went to the store, and I bought milk and cheese."

_____.

14. "From what time did you study?"

_____.

15. "From what time, until what time, did you work yesterday?"

_____.

Past Tense

16. "Who went to the hospital?"

_____.

Translate to English:

17. 제 샌드위치를 왜 먹었어요?

_____.

18. 누가 제 피자를 훔쳤어요?

_____.

19. 저는 안 갔지만 정말 가고 싶었어요.

_____.

20. 언제 김 씨를 만났어요? 왜 만났어요?

_____.

21. 지난 주 너무 더웠기 때문에 반바지를 입었어요.

_____.

22. 오늘 집에서 한국어를 두 시간 동안 열심히 공부했어요.

_____.

New Phrases

행운(을) 빌어요!	"Good luck!"

New Vocabulary

행운(을) 빌다	"to wish (someone) good luck"
한복	"Hanbok"

Chapter 20 — Past Tense

농담	"joke"
농담(을) 하다	"to tell a joke," "to joke"
웃기다	"to be humorous," "to be funny"
훔치다	"to steal"
샌드위치	"sandwich"
반바지	"shorts" (literally, "half pants")
바지	"pants"
코트	"coat"
입다	"to wear (on body)"
쓰다	"to wear (on head)"
신다	"to wear (on feet)"
끼다	"to wear (on hands)"
차다	"to wear (on wrists)"
손목시계	"wristwatch"
반지	"ring"
벗다	"to take off (clothing)"
구두	"dress shoes"
아마(도)	"maybe," "possibly"
수업	"lesson," "course," "class"
끝나다	"to be finished," "to end," "to be over"
끝내다	"to finish (something)," "to end (something)"
끝	"the end"
시작	"beginning," "start"
시작(을) 하다	"to begin," "to start"
선택(을) 하다	"to choose," "to select"
움직이다	"to move"
옮기다	"to move (something)"
책상	"desk," "(writing) table"
가구	"furniture"
유리	"glass"
램프	"lamp"
과거	"the past"
현재	"the present"

Past Tense

미래	"the future"
위	"above," "on top of"
밑	"underneath"
앞	"in front of"
뒤	"behind," "after"
옆	"beside," "(right) next to"
안	"inside"
밖	"outside"
중	"center"
광고	"advertisement"
사랑에 빠지다	"to fall in love"
열심히	"diligently," "hard" (adverb)
역시	"(just) as expected" (adverb)
갑자기	"all of the sudden," "suddenly" (adverb)
매일	"every day"
매주	"every week"
매월	"every month"
매년	"every year"
작년	"last year"
올해	"this year"
내년	"next year"

Chapter 20

Past Tense

Answer Keys

Chapter 1

a) 안녕하세요.
b) 안녕하세요. 저는 철수입니다.
c) 저는 영희입니다. 만나서 반갑습니다.
d) 네, (만나서) 반갑습니다.
e) 안녕히 가세요.
f) 안녕히 계세요.
g) "Hello. I am Chul-soo. Nice to meet you. Goodbye."
h) 안녕하세요. (만나서) 반갑습니다. 저는 [your name]입니다. 안녕히 계세요.

Chapter 2

4) Hello. I am Chul-soo. I like music. I dislike dance."
5) 저는 스포츠를 사랑합니다. 미식축구를 좋아합니다. 수영을 싫어합니다.

Chapter 3

1) "I like cats more."
2) "I like dogs more."
3) 저는 영화를 좋아합니다.
4) 저는 책을 더 좋아합니다.
5) 저는 벌레를 싫어합니다.
6) 저는 거미를 더 싫어합니다.

Chapter 4

1) "I want to eat tomatoes too."
2) "I want to eat only tomatoes."
3) "I also want to earn money."
4) "Only I want to earn money."
5) 저만 김치를 좋아합니다.
6) 저는 김치만 좋아합니다.
7) 저도 채소를 먹고 싶습니다.
8) 저는 채소도 먹고 싶습니다.

Answer Keys

Chapter 5

1) 저는 병원에 갑니다.
2) 저는 병원에 옵니다.
3) 저는 학교에 가고 싶습니다.
4) 저는 놀고 싶습니다.
5) "I play games."
6) "I go to the museum."
7) "I go to the beach."
8) "I want to eat cheese too."

Chapter 6

1) "I'm going to Europe now."
2) "I have a cell phone."
3) "I have a car in America."
4) "I want to go to Korea, but I also want to go to America."
5) 저는 한국에 갑니다.
6) 저는 지금 미국에 갑니다.
7) 저는 자동차가 있습니다.
8) 한국에 김치가 있습니다.
9) 미국에 미국 사람이 있습니다.
10) 저는 영국에 가고 싶지만 한국에도 가고 싶습니다.

Chapter 7

1) "Mr. Kim Chul-soo and Mrs. Kim Yung-hee are Koreans."
2) "I like kimchi and pork belly."
3) "I really like math."
4) "How about Mr. Kim Chul-soo?"
5) "What do you want to eat?"
6) "What do you do these days?"
7) 안녕하세요. 잘 지내세요?
8) 저도 미국 사람입니다.
9) 김철수 씨는 정말 한국 사람입니다.

Answer Keys

10) 저는 숙제를 싫어하지만 수학과 과학을 좋아합니다.
11) 무엇을 하고 싶습니까?
12) 피자는요?
13) 원숭이를 사랑합니까?

Chapter 8

1) "I'm going to eat."
2) "Where is Mr. Kim going today?"
3) "We are walking to school."
4) "I'm going to work."
5) "Where is the bathroom?"
6) 박 씨가 누구입니까?
7) 누구를 사랑합니까?
8) 우리는 가고 싶습니다.
9) 언제 밥을 먹고 싶습니까?
10) 집이 어디에 있습니까?

Chapter 9

1) descriptive verb
2) action verb
3) descriptive verb
4) action verb
5) action verb
6) descriptive verb
7) "Mr. Kim really drinks a lot of alcohol."
8) "Today I am a little cold."
9) "Is the water cold?"
10) 수프가 조금 차갑습니다.
11) 오늘 아주 춥습니다.
12) 저는 한국을 정말 좋아합니다.

Answer Keys

Chapter 10

1) "What kind of person is Mr. Kim Chul-soo?"
2) "What kind of movies do you like?"
3) "I like entertaining movies."
4) "Do you want to eat spicy food?"
5) "Do you like short movies?"
6) "I dislike that kind of movie."
7) "Today I'll go to school and do homework."
8) 제가 어떤 사람입니까?
9) 저는 그런 음식을 싫어합니다.
10) 제가 좋은 사람입니다.
11) 예쁜 여자가 어디에 있습니까?
12) 김영희 씨가 아주 예쁩니다.
13) 긴 영화를 좋아합니까?
14) 아니요. 저는 짧고 재미있는 영화를 좋아합니다.

Chapter 11

1) "I want a black bag."
2) "That house is big."
3) "My face is red."
4) "That far mountain is green."
5) "My house is here."
6) "This is the same as that."
7) "Is Mr. Kim Chul-soo the same person as that man?"
8) 저는 초록색 사과를 먹고 싶습니다.
9) 저의 옷이 빨간색입니다.
10) 고양이는 귀엽습니다.
11) 저는 거기에 가고 싶습니다.
12) 이 영화가 재미있습니다.
13) 이 모자가 그 모자와 같습니다.
14) 그 셔츠가 저의 셔츠와 똑같습니다.

Answer Keys

Chapter 12

1. 십오
2. 이십구
3. 팔십일
4. 구십구
5. 백일
6. 삼백삼십삼
7. 오백
8. 천일
9. 구천
10. 만백십이
11. 오만오백
12. 구십만
13. 백만
14. 저는 천원이 있습니다.
15. 이 고양이가 얼마입니까?
16. 저는 집이 있기 때문에 기쁩니다.
17. 저의 집 덕분에 기쁩니다.
18. 이 숙제가 그렇게 어렵습니까?
19. "How much is that?"
20. "I have 19,000 Won."
21. "I am sad because I have homework."
22. "Today I am sad because of my homework."
23. "Is it really so easy?"

Chapter 13

a) 하나
b) 둘
c) 셋
d) 넷
e) 다섯
f) 여섯
g) 일곱

Answer Keys

h) 여덟

i) 아홉

j) 열

k) 스물

l) 스물 둘

m) 스물 일곱

n) 서른

1) 저는 원숭이 열 마리를 보고 싶습니다.
2) 공책 세 개를 주세요
3) 저의 집에 두 명이 있습니다.
4) 그분은 서른 살입니다.
5) 그분은 몇 살입니까?
6) 저는 집에서 가게까지 걸어갑니다.
7) 그것이 정말 케이크입니까?
8) 학교에 저의 친구를 데리고 갑니다.
9) 한국 음식이라고요?
10) 이것이 그것보다 더 좋습니다.
11) "I want to eat two cows."
12) "One person is coming."
13) "I am 18 years old."
14) "I'm driving from Seoul to Busan."
15) "How many cats are there?"
16) "That is really a fish."
17) "My house is bigger than Mr. Kim's house."
18) "Give me only one sheet of paper."
19) "He is bringing presents too."
20) "Did you say presents?"
21) "Because this cat is cuter than that cat, I like this cat more."

Chapter 14

1) 오늘 저는 학교에 안 갑니다.
2) 그분은 병원에 가지 않습니다.
3) 저의 집에 안 옵니까?

Answer Keys

4) 그분은 학교에 없습니다.
5) 저는 그분을 모릅니다.
6) 저는 빨리 수영할 수 있습니다.
7) 저와 함께 파티에 가고 싶습니까?
8) 저는 한국 사람이 아닙니다.
9) "Why aren't you going to the hospital?"
10) "Are you really not doing your homework?"
11) "I don't want to go to school."
12) "I don't want to eat beef because I dislike it."
13) "Do you know Mrs. Yung-hee?"
14) "No. I don't know Mrs. Yung-hee."
15) "I'm not an English person."
16) "I can't go to the park with Mrs. Yung-hee because I don't have money."

Chapter 15

1) "I am not a Chinese person."
2) "Mr. Kim is a friendly Korean man."
3) "When it comes to cities, Seoul is the best."
4) "My name is Kim Chul-soo."
5) "Do you want to study at school today?"
6) "I really want to go to the movie theater."
7) 김 씨는 나이가 어떻게 됩니까?
8) 저는 학교를 좋아합니다.
9) 저는 차가운 스테이크를 먹고 싶지 않습니다.
10) 저는 [your name](이)라고 합니다.
11) 취미가 어떻게 됩니까?
12) 저는 집에서 숙제를 하고 싶습니다.

Chapter 16

1) 오후 한 시
2) 아침 열 한 시
3) 저녁 여섯 시
4) 새벽 세 시

Answer Keys

5) 아침 여덟 시
6) 세 시간
7) 두 시간 십이 분
8) 십칠 초
9) 삼일
10) 이 주일
11) 팔 개월
12) 십 년
13) 일월
14) 유월
15) 십일월
16) 사월
17) 십이월
18) 구월
19) 칠월
20) 이월
21) 오월
22) 팔월
23) 시월
24) 삼월
25) 월요일
26) 화요일
27) 수요일
28) 목요일
29) 금요일
30) 토요일
31) 일요일
32) "I want to go to Korea in January."
33) "I'm at school from 9 o'clock in the morning until 11 o'clock in the evening."
34) "Tomorrow is June 15th."
35) "I'm meeting Mr. Kim at 1 o'clock P.M.."
36) "Can you go to the party on Tuesday?"
37) "Do you have time this week?"
38) 몇 시입니까?
39) 며칠입니까?

Answer Keys

40) 저는 십이월을 사랑합니다. 십이월이 최고입니다.
41) 저도 김 씨를 보고 싶습니다.
42) 오늘 (month) (day), (year)입니다.
43) 내일 금요일입니다.

Chapter 17

1) 십전
2) 일불
3) 일불 오십전
4) 오불 이십오전
5) 팔십불 십일전
6) 천이십불 삼십삼전
7) 십불을 주세요.
8) 샤워하세요.
9) 저의 차가 안 됩니다. 도와주세요.
10) 저는 의사가 되고 싶습니다.
11) 약국에서 약을 사세요.
12) "Please give me a little more money."
13) "Why do you not want to become a teacher?"
14) "I learn Korean from Mr. Kim."
15) "How is Korean food? Is it delicious?"
16) "Do your homework quickly."

Chapter 18

1) 형 or 오빠
2) 누나 or 언니
3) 남동생
4) 여동생
5) 저도 대가족이 있습니다.
6) 김 씨는 가족이 어떻게 됩니까?
7) 저는 어머니를 정말 사랑합니다.
8) 저의 (누나/언니)와 함께 공부하고 싶습니다.
9) "My brother also dislikes kimchi."

305

Answer Keys

10) "My older sister is a famous singer."

11) "Today I'm meeting my older sister at school."

12) "Why do you hate my older brother?"

Chapter 19

1) 사요
2) 팔아요
3) 내요
4) 뜨거워요
5) 꺼요
6) 수영해요
7) 선생님이 돼요
8) 발라요
9) 말려요
10) 아니에요
11) 켜요
12) 혹시 영어를 할 수 있어요?
13) 저는 집에서 옷을 말려요.
14) 김 씨가 어디에서 점심을 먹어요?
15) 몰라요. 오늘 안 만나요.
16) "Where is the bathroom?"
17) "I apply lotion on my skin."
18) "Do you like the science teacher?"
19) "I don't like him/her. He/she's smart, but kind of a strange person."

Chapter 20

1) 했어요
2) 갔어요
3) 추웠어요
4) 차가웠어요
5) 좋아했어요
6) 아니었어요
7) 버렸어요

Answer Keys

8) 썼어요

9) 가르쳤어요

10) 배웠어요

11) 오늘 학교에 가고 싶지 않아요.

12) 어제 학교에 가고 싶지 않았어요.

13) 어제 제가 가게에 갔고, 우유와 치즈를 샀어요.

14) 몇 시부터 공부했어요?

15) 어제 몇 시부터 몇 시까지 일했어요?

16) 누가 병원에 갔어요?

17) "Why did you eat my sandwich?"

18) "Who stole my pizza?"

19) "I didn't go, but I really wanted to go."

20) "When did you meet Mr. Kim? Why did you meet him?"

21) "Because it was too hot last week I wore shorts."

22) "Today I studied Korean hard at home for 2 hours."

Answer Keys

Appendix A. Typing in Korean

In addition to being able to write in Korean, you may want to be able to type in Korean. While this book is not a complete guide on doing this, take a look at the image below which shows the layout of a typical Korean keyboard as a quick reference.

Switching your computer's keyboard to Korean is something you can easily look up how to do online. I also recommend purchasing some 한글 stickers to put on your keyboard, as they're inexpensive and can be helpful for becoming adjusted to the layout.

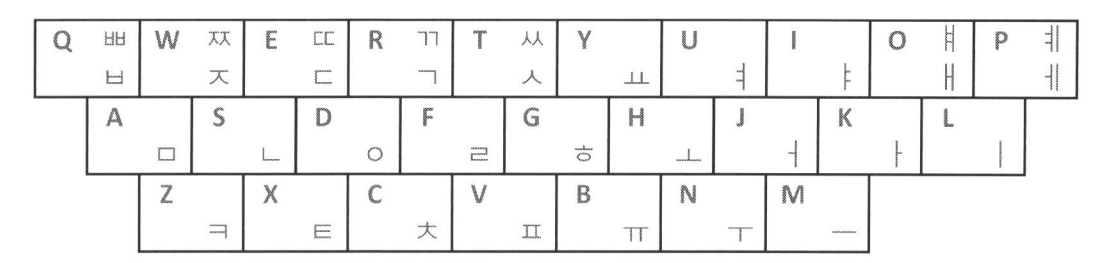

Q ㅃ/ㅂ	W ㅉ/ㅈ	E ㄸ/ㄷ	R ㄲ/ㄱ	T ㅆ/ㅅ	Y ㅛ	U ㅕ	I ㅑ	O ㅐ/ㅒ	P ㅔ/ㅖ
A ㅁ	S ㄴ	D ㅇ	F ㄹ	G ㅎ	H ㅗ	J ㅓ	K ㅏ	L ㅣ	
Z ㅋ	X ㅌ	C ㅊ	V ㅍ	B ㅠ	N ㅜ	M ㅡ			

One thing you might notice right away is how the *consonants* are on the *left* of the keyboard, and *vowels* are on the *right*. In addition, the bottom row contains *strong consonants*.

Typing a syllable is done by typing the individual letters in order from *left to right*, and *top to bottom*, just as they would be pronounced. For example, 간 is made by first typing ㄱ, then ㅏ, and finally ㄴ (this corresponds to "r," "k," and "s" on the keyboard, so typing "rks" will become 간).

In order to type the letter on the top of the key, such as typing ㅃ instead of ㅂ (top left), hold down the *Shift* key. Switching between English and Korean input can be done using the right *Alt* key (or 한/영 key, if you have a Korean keyboard).

Diphthongs are created by typing two vowels – the first being the horizontal vowel, and the second being the vertical vowel. For example, ㅢ would be made by first typing ㅡ, followed by ㅣ.

Other than that, the rest should be self explanatory. While I don't recommend learning to type until you're able to write, once you've got the basics down, feel free to practice using a computer.

Appendix A. Typing in Korean

Appendix B. Hangul Chart and Names of Letters

Use the following chart for reference purposes only. Although it correctly shows every possible single consonant and single vowel combination in Korean (note that it does not include syllables with 3 letters or more), many of the combinations below will not be found in modern Korean. Nevertheless, it will benefit you to be able to know how to write and read any of the following combinations below; pronouncing some of them (ones that aren't used) might be difficult, even for native Korean speakers.

ㅇ	ㄱ	ㄴ	ㄷ	ㄹ	ㅁ	ㅂ	ㅅ	ㅇ	ㅈ	ㅊ	ㅋ	ㅌ	ㅍ	ㅎ	ㄲ	ㄸ	ㅃ	ㅆ	ㅉ
ㅏ	가	나	다	라	마	바	사	아	자	차	카	타	파	하	까	따	빠	싸	짜
ㅑ	야	냐	댜	랴	먀	뱌	샤	야	쟈	챠	캬	탸	퍄	햐	꺄	땨	뺘	쌰	쨔
ㅓ	거	너	더	러	머	버	서	어	저	처	커	터	퍼	허	꺼	떠	뻐	써	쩌
ㅕ	겨	녀	뎌	려	며	벼	셔	여	져	쳐	켜	텨	펴	혀	껴	뗘	뼈	쎠	쪄
ㅗ	고	노	도	로	모	보	소	오	조	초	코	토	포	호	꼬	또	뽀	쏘	쪼
ㅛ	교	뇨	됴	료	묘	뵤	쇼	요	죠	쵸	쿄	툐	표	효	꾜	뚀	뾰	쑈	쬬
ㅜ	구	누	두	루	무	부	수	우	주	추	쿠	투	푸	후	꾸	뚜	뿌	쑤	쭈
ㅠ	규	뉴	듀	류	뮤	뷰	슈	유	쥬	츄	큐	튜	퓨	휴	뀨	뜌	쀼	쓔	쮸
ㅡ	그	느	드	르	므	브	스	으	즈	츠	크	트	프	흐	끄	뜨	쁘	쓰	쯔
ㅣ	기	니	디	리	미	비	시	이	지	치	키	티	피	히	끼	띠	삐	씨	찌
ㅐ	개	내	대	래	매	배	새	애	재	채	캐	태	패	해	깨	때	빼	쌔	째
ㅒ	걔	냬	댸	럐	먜	뱨	섀	얘	쟤	챼	컈	턔	퍠	햬	꺠	떄	뺴	썌	쨰
ㅔ	게	네	데	레	메	베	세	에	제	체	케	테	페	헤	께	떼	뻬	쎄	쩨
ㅖ	계	녜	뎨	례	몌	볘	셰	예	졔	쳬	켸	톄	폐	혜	꼐	뗴	뻬	쎼	쪠
ㅘ	과	놔	돠	롸	뫄	봐	솨	와	좌	촤	콰	톼	퐈	화	꽈	똬	뽜	쏴	쫘
ㅙ	괘	놰	돼	뢔	뫠	봬	쇄	왜	좨	쵀	쾌	퇘	퐤	홰	꽤	뙈	뽸	쐐	쫴
ㅚ	괴	뇌	되	뢰	뫼	뵈	쇠	외	죄	최	쾨	퇴	푀	회	꾀	뙤	뾔	쐬	쬐
ㅝ	궈	눠	둬	뤄	뭐	붜	숴	워	줘	춰	쿼	퉈	풔	훠	꿔	뚸	뿨	쒀	쭤
ㅞ	궤	눼	뒈	뤠	뭬	붸	쉐	웨	줴	췌	퀘	퉤	풰	훼	꿰	뛔	뿨	쒜	쮀
ㅟ	귀	뉘	뒤	뤼	뮈	뷔	쉬	위	쥐	취	퀴	튀	퓌	휘	뀌	뛰	쀠	쒸	쮜
ㅢ	긔	늬	듸	릐	믜	븨	싀	의	즤	츼	킈	틔	픠	희	끠	띄	쁴	씌	쯰

Appendix B. Hangul Chart and Names of Letters

It's also important to know the names of the consonants in Korean. These will be useful when spelling Korean words. Fortunately, most of them work in the same format (*consonant* + ㅣ + ㅇ + *consonant*), as you will find below. I've marked the *three* consonants that have their own unique names with asterisks.

Letter	Name
*ㄱ	기역
ㄴ	니은
*ㄷ	디귿
ㄹ	리을
ㅁ	미음
ㅂ	비읍
*ㅅ	시옷 (pronounced 시온)
ㅇ	이응
ㅈ	지읒 (pronounced 지읃)
ㅊ	치읓 (pronounced 치읃)
ㅋ	키읔 (pronounced 키윽)
ㅌ	티읕 (pronounced 티읃)
ㅍ	피읖 (pronounced 피읍)
ㅎ	히읗 (pronounced 히읃)

Appendix C. Sound Change Rules

Once you've got the hang of the basic rules regarding 받침 sounds, let's go over some more rules regarding sound changes that take place *between* syllables.

Although the sound change rules contained in this appendix are not required in order to pronounce individual syllables one at a time, they are necessary when speaking Korean at a normal speed.

Do not stress to memorize every rule contained in this appendix on your first time reading it. There are several rules that you will need to learn, and mastering them will require practicing more than it will require studying. Instead, try to speak *slowly* at first, and increase your speed as you become more familiar with these rules.

Base Consonants

In order to start, first we need to learn about *base consonants*.

"We need to learn more consonants?" No, we don't need to learn any more consonants; we've already learned every letter used in 한글. We just need to learn what a *base consonant* is.

The following *five* consonants are the base consonants that we need to know for the purpose of figuring out how to pronounce words in sentences:

ㄱ, ㄷ, ㅂ, ㅅ, ㅈ

You only need to memorize that these 5 consonants make up what we call *base consonants*. Take a moment to put them in your memory.

Now let's learn our first sound change rule for sounds that take place *between* syllables.

1. Consonant + Base Consonant

This rule applies any time you have a consonant – specifically a base consonant, a double consonant, or a strong consonant – that comes *before* a base consonant.

Whenever this happens, the *second* base consonant becomes pronounced like a *double consonant*.

Appendix C. Sound Change Rules

Spelling	Pronunciation
학교	학꾜
받다	받따
돕다	돕따
핫도그	핟또그
옷방	옫빵
찾다	찯따
맡다	맏따
갚다	갑따
샀죠	삳쪼
낯설다	낟썰다
먹자	먹짜
식당	식땅
백보	백뽀
갑부	갑뿌
국수	국쑤
맛술	맏쑬

*double ㄱ → ㄱ+ㄲ

*double ㅂ/ㄷ → ㅂ/ㄸ

This is one of the most commonly used sound change rules, and as such, is at the top of this list.

---

2. Base Consonant + ㅎ
ㅎ + Base Consonant

This rule applies any time you have a base consonant *before* ㅎ, or any time you have ㅎ *followed by* a base consonant.

Whenever this happens, the base consonant becomes pronounced like a strong consonant.

Here are some examples when the base consonant comes *after* ㅎ:

Spelling	Pronunciation
옳게	올케
않다	안타
좋다	조타

Appendix C. Sound Change Rules

괜찮다	괜찬타
많고	만코
많기	만키
쌓자	싸차

When ㅅ comes *after* ㅎ, because ㅅ does not have a *strong consonant* version of itself, it instead becomes pronounced like ㅆ.

Spelling	Pronunciation
않소	안쏘
놓소	노쏘
옳소	올쏘

Here are some examples when the base consonant comes *before* ㅎ:

Spelling	Pronunciation
밟히다	발피다
막히다	마키다
익숙하다	익쑤카다
박하	바카
북한	부칸
착하다	차카다
악하다	아카다
백호	배코
갇히다*	가치다*

To understand how 갇히다 becomes pronounced 가치다, see the next rule.

Since ㅅ is normally pronounced like ㄷ at the end of a syllable, when it comes *before* ㅎ it also behaves like ㄷ. Therefore, when ㅅ comes *before* ㅎ, it becomes pronounced like ㅌ.

Spelling	Pronunciation
못 해	모태
못 하다	모타다

315

Appendix C. Sound Change Rules

3. ㅌ + 이 = 치
ㄷ + 히 = 치
ㄷ + 이 = 지

Whenever you have ㅌ *before* 이, the 이 changes to become 치.

Whenever you have ㄷ *before* 히, the 히 changes to become 치.

Whenever you have ㄷ *before* 이, the 이 changes to become 지.

It might seem strange that this sound change rule exists (changing ㅌ to ㅊ, and changing ㄷ to ㅈ), but there is a similar change in English, although it works a bit differently; notice in English how "train" (ㅌ) is pronounced "*ch*-rain" (ㅊ), and "drain" (ㄷ) is pronounced "*jr*-ain" (ㅈ).

Spelling	Pronunciation
갇히다	가치다
같이	가치
붙이다	부치다
맏이	마지
굳이	구지
맞받이	맏빠지
맡아*	마타*

Note that 맡아 is pronounced like normal (마타), as this rule only applies to syllables that use the vowel ㅣ, such as 이 and 히.

However, this rule also applies to 여/혀 as well; both 여 and 혀 become pronounced like 쳐. This is because 여 is a combination of the sounds 이 and 어, and 혀 is a combination of 히 and 어.

Spelling	Pronunciation
붙여	부쳐
갇혀	가쳐

4. ㄹ + Base Consonant

This rule is an extension of the first rule.

Appendix C. Sound Change Rules

Whenever you have a base consonant *after* ㄹ, the base consonant will become a *double consonant*.

Spelling	Pronunciation
할당	할땅
밀당	밀땅
얼자	얼짜
일자리	일짜리
일세	일쎄

However, this rule does not apply to the base consonant ㅂ.

Spelling	Pronunciation
알바	알바
올바른	올바른
웰빙	웰빙
밀보	밀보

This rule only *sometimes* applies to the base consonant ㄱ.

Spelling	Pronunciation
밀가루	밀까루
물가	물까
할게	할께
얼굴	얼굴
얼간이	얼간이

As with any rule there will be exceptions, but we'll learn those as they come up along the way. For example, here are two common exceptions.

Spelling	Pronunciation
술병	술뼝
물고기	물꼬기

Appendix C. Sound Change Rules

5. ㅂ/ㅍ + ㄴ/ㅁ

Whenever you have ㅂ or ㅍ *before* ㄴ or ㅁ, the ㅂ or ㅍ will become pronounced like ㅁ.

Spelling	Pronunciation
합니다	함니다
같습니다	가씀니다
겁나	검나
잡는	잠는
갑년	감년
굽는	굼는
줍는	줌는
밥먹자	밤먹짜
입무	임무
업무	엄무
업마	엄마
삽목	삼목
합명	함명
갑문	감문
없는	엄는
덮는	덤는
잎나무	임나무
갚나	감나
입 냄새	임냄새

Adv ㅃ is absent from this list because there are no syllables in Korean that end with it at the bottom.

6. ㅂ + ㄹ

Whenever you have ㅂ *before* ㄹ, the ㅂ will become pronounced like ㅁ, and the ㄹ becomes pronounced like ㄴ.

Spelling	Pronunciation
합리	함니

Appendix C. Sound Change Rules

십리	심니
합량	함냥
갑리	감니
겹리	겸니
합류	함뉴
압력	암녁

7. ㄱ + ㄹ

Whenever you have ㄱ *before* ㄹ, the ㄱ becomes pronounced like ㅇ, and the ㄹ becomes pronounced like ㄴ.

Spelling	Pronunciation
백리	뱅니
복리	봉니
막료	망뇨
식량	싱냥
탁류	탕뉴
맥락	맹낙

8. Consonant + ㄴ/ㅁ

Whenever you have a consonant *before* ㄴ or ㅁ, the consonant will become pronounced like ㄴ.

This rule does not apply to the consonants ㄱ, ㄲ, ㅋ, ㅂ, ㅍ, ㅁ, ㄴ, ㅇ or ㄹ – these each have their own rules for interacting with ㄴ/ㅁ which this appendix covers.

Besides the consonants that this rule does not apply to, here are the consonants that it does apply to: ㄷ, ㄸ, ㅌ, ㅈ, ㅉ, ㅊ, ㅅ, ㅆ, and ㅎ.

Spelling	Pronunciation
빛나	빈나
옻나무	온나무
몇 년	면년
맞나	만나
젖니	전니

Appendix C. Sound Change Rules

믿나	민나
닫는	단는
맏나	만나
있는	인는
못 믿어	몬미더
못 먹는다	몬멍는다
못난	몬난
맛나	만나
덧니	던니
여섯마리	여선마리
놓는	논는
잇몸	인몸
맏며느리	만며느리

9. ㄱ/ㄲ/ㅋ + ㄴ/ㅁ

Whenever you have ㄱ (or ㄲ/ㅋ) *before* ㄴ or ㅁ, the ㄱ (or ㄲ/ㅋ) will become pronounced like ㅇ ("ng" at the end of a syllable).

Spelling	Pronunciation
한국말	한궁말
백만	뱅만
부엌문	부엉문
목마르다	몽마르다
국물	궁물
식노	싱노
깎나	깡나
학년	항년
격노	경노
볶나	봉나

320

Appendix C. Sound Change Rules

10. ㅅ + ㅣ/ㅑ/ㅕ/ㅖ/ㅒ/ㅛ/ㅠ

This is an extension of a rule we learned in the "Introduction to Hangul" section of this book, that 시 is pronounced like the English word "she," and not like the English word "see." In addition, when ㅅ comes before the vowels ㅑ, ㅕ, ㅖ, ㅒ, ㅛ, or ㅠ, the ㅅ becomes pronounced like "sh" instead of "s."

Practice reading the following sounds:

시 / 샤 / 셔 / 섀 / 셰 / 쇼 / 슈

This rule exists because the above vowels are combinations of the sounds 시 and 야, 여, 예, 얘, 요, and 유.

This rule does not apply to any other single vowels besides the ones listed above.

> **Adv**: In addition, the diphthongs ㅟ and ㅢ will also produce a sound similar to 시, due to them containing the vowel ㅣ.

11. ㅇ/ㅁ + ㄹ

Whenever you have ㅇ or ㅁ *before* ㄹ, the ㄹ becomes pronounced like ㄴ.

Spelling	Pronunciation
강릉	강능
장로	장노
황률	황뉼
담력	담녁
음료	음뇨
탐라국	탐나국
생략하다	생냐카다

An exception to this rule is the word 장르 ("genre"), which does *not* change its pronunciation.

Appendix C. Sound Change Rules

12. ㄴ + ㄹ
ㄹ + ㄴ

Whenever you have ㄴ *before* or *after* ㄹ, the ㄴ becomes pronounced like ㄹ.

Spelling	Pronunciation
혼란	홀란
만리	말리
신라	실라
간리	갈리
발노	발로
일년	일련
스물넷	스물렛
칼날	칼랄
월남	월람

13. Irregulars

Not all words in Korean follow these rules. But take comfort in the fact that *most* do. Unlike English, where a word's spelling can be completely unrelated to the sound it produces, reading 한글 is mostly straightforward. Although there are words which do not follow the above rules, the majority will. Learn the irregulars as they come up, and don't worry about learning all of them at once.

Here are just a few examples of some common irregulars:

Spelling	Pronunciation
감다	감따
한자	한짜
깻잎	깬닙
십육	심늌
많아*	마나*

For syllables ending in ㅀ or ㄶ, and followed by the vowel ㅇ, the ㅎ will become *silent*.

You will hear the more common irregulars frequently enough to not have to worry about studying them, and the less common ones you can learn as they come up.

Informal Korean Conversations

This section contains every conversation (excluding Chapter 19 and Chapter 20) from the book re-written using the 요 form. As the 요 form and 니다/니까 forms should be used in their own situations (such as *informal* or *formal* situations), these re-written conversations should only be used as practice for familiarizing yourself with the 요 form's conjugation rules. After reading through this book at least once, I recommend coming back here and re-reading each conversation out loud. The more exposure you have to the 요 form, the faster and more accurately you will be able to conjugate it yourself.

Also, all numbers have been re-written using regular numerals; use this for additional practice reading numbers on your own.

Chapter 1

Conversation 1

A:	안녕하세요.
B:	안녕하세요.
A:	안녕히 가세요.
B:	안녕히 계세요.

Conversation 2

철수:	안녕하세요.
영희:	안녕하세요.
철수:	저는 철수예요.
영희:	저는 영희예요.
철수:	만나서 반가워요.
영희:	네, 반가워요.

Chapter 2

Conversation

A:	저는 스포츠를 좋아해요.
B:	저는 음악을 좋아해요. 스포츠를 싫어해요.

Informal Korean Conversations

Chapter 3

Conversation

철수:	저는 고양이를 좋아해요.
영희:	저는 고양이를 싫어해요. 개를 좋아해요.
철수:	저는 김치를 좋아해요.
영희:	저는 삼겹살을 더 좋아해요.

Chapter 4

Conversation

김철수:	저는 아르바이트를 원해요.
김영희:	저도 아르바이트를 원해요.
김철수:	하지만 일을 원하지 않아요. 돈만 원해요.
김영희:	저도 일하고 싶지 않아요. 게임 하고 싶어요.
김철수:	저도 게임을 하고 싶어요. 하지만 돈도 벌고 싶어요.

Chapter 5

Conversation

김철수:	영희 씨, 안녕하세요.
김영희:	안녕하세요. 저는 학교에 가요.
김철수:	저는 집에 가요.
김영희:	저는 공부해요.
김철수:	저는 놀아요.

Chapter 6

Conversation

A:	저는 한국 사람이에요. 한국에 아파트가 있어요.
B:	저는 미국 사람이에요. 미국에 집이 있어요.
A:	저는 미국에 가고 싶어요.

Informal Korean Conversations

| B: | 저는 한국에 가고 싶지만 지금 미국에 있어요. |

Chapter 7

Conversation

김철수:	선생님, 안녕하세요. 잘 지내세요?
김영희:	아, 네. 김철수 씨도 잘 지내세요?
김철수:	네. 요즘 무엇을 해요?
김영희:	저는 학생들을 가르쳐요.
김철수:	무엇을 가르쳐요?
김영희:	저는 수학과 과학을 가르쳐요.
김철수:	저도 수학과 과학을 배우고 싶어요.
김영희:	정말 배우고 싶어요?
김철수:	네. 하지만 숙제와 시험을 싫어해요. 선생님은요?
김영희:	하하. 저도 숙제와 시험을 싫어해요.

Chapter 8

Conversation

A:	언제 밥을 먹으러 나가요?
B:	오늘 밤에 나가요. 어디에 가고 싶어요?
A:	서울에 가고 싶어요. 누가 가요?
B:	저와 김영희 씨와 김철수 선생님이 가요.
A:	김철수 선생님이 누구예요?
B:	서울 대학교 교수예요.
A:	아, 알겠어요. 그러면 어떻게 가요?
B:	우리는 걸어가요.

Chapter 9

Conversation

| 웨이터: | 맛이 괜찮아요? |

325

Informal Korean Conversations

김철수:	김치가 아주 맛이 있어요. 감사해요.
웨이터:	아, 좋아요.
김철수:	하지만 볶음밥이 조금 차가워요.
웨이터:	죄송해요.
김철수:	그리고 식당도 조금 추워요.
웨이터:	많이 추워요?
김철수:	네. 그리고 음식이 많이 비싸요.

Chapter 10

Conversation 1

한승규:	김 선생님이 어떤 사람이에요?
이선주:	아주 좋은 사람이에요.
한승규:	재미있는 사람이에요?
이선주:	네, 재미있고 밝은 사람이에요.

Conversation 2

김영희:	저는 잘생긴 남자를 좋아해요. 철수 씨는요? 어떤 여자를 좋아해요?
김철수:	저는 예쁜 여자를 좋아해요.
김영희:	제가 예쁜 여자예요?
김철수:	글쎄요. 제가 잘생긴 남자예요?

Chapter 11

Conversation

A:	그것이 무엇이에요?
B:	무슨 말이에요?
A:	거기에 그 하얀 것이에요.
B:	아, 이것은 일본 국기예요.
A:	아, 네. 그럼, 저기에 저것은 무엇이에요?
B:	저것은 태극기예요.

Informal Korean Conversations

A:	동그란 것은 무슨 색이에요?
B:	빨간색과 파란색이에요.
A:	저의 옷과 같은 색이에요.

Chapter 12

Conversation 1

김영희:	이것이 얼마예요?
직원:	그것은 35,100 원이에요.
김영희:	여기 40,000 원이에요.
직원:	네, 여기 4,900 원이에요.
김영희:	감사해요. 안녕히 계세요.

Conversation 2

김영희:	아, 저는 오늘 기뻐요.
김철수:	왜 기뻐요? 무엇 때문에 그렇게 기뻐요?
김영희:	저는 일이 있기 때문에 기뻐요. 그것 때문에 돈도 있어요.
김철수:	저는 슬퍼요.
김영희:	왜 슬퍼요?
김철수:	저의 일을 싫어하기 때문이에요.

Chapter 13

Conversation

A:	몇 명이 와요?
B:	3 명이 와요. 저와 김 씨와 제 친구도 와요.
A:	그 친구는 제주도에서 여기까지 와요?
B:	네, 맞아요. 그리고 그분의 고양이도 데리고 와요.
A:	고양이라고요? 몇 마리를 데리고 와요?
B:	1 마리지만, 그 1 마리가 개보다 더 커요.
A:	아이고! 정말 고양이가 맞아요?

Informal Korean Conversations

Chapter 14

Conversation

양태용:	오늘도 저와 함께 공원에 가요?
최소영:	아니요. 안 가요.
양태용:	왜 가지 않아요?
최소영:	시간이 없기 때문에 갈 수 없어요.

Chapter 15

Conversation

김철수:	안녕하세요. 저는 김철수라고 해요.
김영희:	안녕하세요. 저는 김영희라고 해요.
김철수:	취미가 어떻게 돼요?
김영희:	제 취미는 컴퓨터 게임과 독서예요.
김철수:	저는 낚시와 운동이에요. 그리고 미국에서 살아요.
김영희:	저는 한국에서 살아요. 나이가 어떻게 돼요?
김철수:	저는 21 살이에요.
김영희:	저는 27 살입니다. 만나서 반가워요.
김철수:	네, 반가워요.

Chapter 16

Conversation

A:	지금 몇 시예요?
B:	저녁 10 시 40 분이에요.
A:	오늘 며칠이에요?
B:	26 일이에요.
A:	감사해요.
B:	천만에요.

Informal Korean Conversations

Journal

일요일 – 2014 년 6 월 15 일

오늘 오후 3 시에 비행기를 타고 제 친구의 집에 가요.

제 친구는 한국에서 살아요.

저는 제 친구를 정말 보고 싶어요.

한국에서 한국말을 3 개월 동안 공부해요.

많이 기대해요.

9 월 15 일까지 한국에 있어요.

이미 1 시이기 때문에 지금부터 준비해요.

안녕히 계세요.

Chapter 17

Conversation

김철수:	저기요. 이 시계가 얼마예요?
직원:	39,000 원이에요.
김철수:	조금 깎아주세요.
직원:	알겠어요. 그럼 30,000 원이에요.
김철수:	조금 더 깎아주세요. 25,000 원은 어때요?
직원:	안 돼요. 그럼 저에게 29,000 원을 주세요.
김철수:	여기 29,000 원입니다. 감사해요!
직원:	안녕히 가세요.
김철수:	네, 많이 파세요!

Chapter 18

Conversation

김철수:	가족이 어떻게 돼요?
김영희:	부모님과 오빠가 1 명 있어요. 당신은요?
김철수:	저는 부모님과 누나가 1 명 있고, 형도 1 명 있고, 동생도 1 명 있어요.

Informal Korean Conversations

김영희: 정말 대가족이에요.

김철수: 네, 사람이 많고 재미있어요.

Special Thanks

I could not have made this book without the support of the following individuals. You helped to evolve this book into something special. I'd like to give a special thank you to each person here who contributed to this book's creation.

trevarr
Joel Tersigni
Kyle
Jordy Ruiter
Henry Colomb
Richard Hamilton
Mark Harder
Charles Vought
James Straker aka 박민규
George Trombley
Anna Li
Carl Pray
Cindy K
Stephen Johnson
Rachel "토끼" Bibb
Jacob G. Cohen
Eric C.
Edward Voss
Mike Dryer
Catarina Kwan
Hemal Gala (INDIA)
Compcube
Jasmin S
Rebecca
Stephen Santoro
Blake Richardson
Matthieu Hélie
Nelson Morris
Christopher Langdon
Martin Fletcher
Anthony Royce Prudencio
John S. Hudock
Merrill Grady
손소현

Glossary

ㄱ

가게 "store"		Ch. 13
가격 "price," "cost"		Ch. 12
가구 "furniture"		Ch. 20
가끔 "sometimes" (adverb)		Ch. 19
가다 "to go"		Ch. 5
가르치다 "to teach"		Ch. 7
가방 "bag"		Ch. 8
가볍다 "to be light"		Ch. 10
가수 "singer"		Ch. 8
가슴 "chest"		Ch. 10
가위 "scissors"		Ch. 7
가을 "autumn"		Ch. 16
가족이 어떻게 됩니까? "How many people are in your family?"		Ch. 18
가지고 가다 "to take (something somewhere else)"		Ch. 13
가지고 오다 "to bring (something here)"		Ch. 13
가지다 "to hold," "to have (on your person)"		Ch. 13
감사하다 "to be grateful"		Ch. 9
감사합니다. "Thank you."		Ch. 9
감자 "potato"		Ch. 7
감자튀김 "French fries"		Ch. 12
갑자기 "all of the sudden," "suddenly" (adverb)		Ch. 20
강 "river"		Ch. 6
강하다 "to be strong"		Ch. 9
같다 "to be the same," "to be like"		Ch. 11
개 "dog"		Ch. 3
개 item counter		Ch. 13
개구리 "frog"		Ch. 11
개월 month counter		Ch. 16
갤런 "gallon"		Ch. 13
거기 "there"		Ch. 11
거미 "spider"		Ch. 3
거실 "living room"		Ch. 8
거울 "mirror"		Ch. 11
거짓말 "lie"		Ch. 6
거짓말(을) 하다 "to lie"		Ch. 6
걱정(을) 하다 "to worry"		Ch. 18
건강 "health"		Ch. 10
건강하다 "to be healthy"		Ch. 10
건물 "building"		Ch. 11
걷다 "to walk"		Ch. 8
걸어가다 "to walk (somewhere)"		Ch. 8
검 "sword"		Ch. 13
검정 "black" (adjective)		Ch. 11
검정색 "black" (noun)		Ch. 11
것 "a thing"		Ch. 10
게 "crab"		Ch. 13
게임 "game"		Ch. 4
게임(을) 하다 "to play games"		Ch. 4
겨울 "winter"		Ch. 16
결과 "result"		Ch. 7
결정 "decision"		Ch. 17
결정(을) 하다 "to decide," "to make a decision"		Ch. 17
결혼 "marriage"		Ch. 12
결혼(을) 하다 "to marry"		Ch. 12
경제 "economics"		Ch. 12
경찰 "police"		Ch. 15
경찰관 "policeman"		Ch. 15
계단 "stairs"		Ch. 11
계획 "plan"		Ch. 17
계획(을) 하다 "to plan"		Ch. 17
고기 "meat"		Ch. 13
고등어 "mackerel"		Ch. 15
고등학교 "high school"		Ch. 8
고모 "aunt" (father's side)		Ch. 18
고백(을) 하다 "to confess"		Ch. 6
고양이 "cat"		Ch. 3
고향 "hometown"		Ch. 5
골프 "golf"		Ch. 2
곳 "place" (noun)		Ch. 11
공 "ball"		Ch. 11
공부 "study"		Ch. 5
공부(를) 하다 "to study"		Ch. 5
공원 "a park"		Ch. 14
공책 "(study) notebook"		Ch. 13
과거 "the past"		Ch. 20

Glossary

과일 "fruit"		Ch. 4
과자 "snacks"		Ch. 8
과학 "science"		Ch. 7
관계 "relationship"		Ch. 18
광고 "advertisement"		Ch. 20
괜찮다 "to be okay," "to be alright"		Ch. 9
괜찮습니다. "No, thank you."		Ch. 16
괴물 "monster"		Ch. 6
교수 "professor"		Ch. 8
교실 "classroom"		Ch. 8
교육 "education"		Ch. 8
구 9		Ch. 12
구두 "dress shoes"		Ch. 20
구월 "September"		Ch. 16
국기 "flag"		Ch. 11
권 book counter		Ch. 13
귀 "ear"		Ch. 10
귀신 "ghost"		Ch. 6
귀엽다 "to be cute"		Ch. 10
그 "he/him" (not polite)		Ch. 18
그 "that" (adjective)		Ch. 11
그 "Uh..."		Ch. 7
그것 "that thing"		Ch. 11
그녀 "she/her" (not polite)		Ch. 18
그래서 "so," "therefore"		Ch. 9
그램 "gram"		Ch. 13
그러면 "well then"		Ch. 8
그런 "that kind of" (adjective)		Ch. 10
그럼 "well then"		Ch. 11
그렇게 "so," "in that way" (adverb)		Ch. 12
그렇다 "to be so"		Ch. 10
그릇 "bowl"		Ch. 7
그리고 "and," "also"		Ch. 9
그리다 "to draw"		Ch. 6
그림 "drawing"		Ch. 6
그림(을) 그리다 "to draw (a drawing)"		Ch. 6
그분 "him," "her," "that person"		Ch. 13
글쎄요. "Well..."		Ch. 10
금요일 "Friday"		Ch. 16
기다리다 "to wait"		Ch. 7
기대(를) 하다 "to look forward to," "to expect"		Ch. 16
기쁘다 "to be happy"		Ch. 12
기억(을) 하다 "to remember"		Ch. 14
기차 "(electric) train"		Ch. 16
길 "a street," "a road," "a way"		Ch. 5
길다 "to be long"		Ch. 10
김치 "kimchi"		Ch. 3
까만 "black" (adjective)		Ch. 11
까만색 "black" (noun)		Ch. 11
까맣다 "to be black"		Ch. 11
깨끗하다 "to be clean"		Ch. 10
껌 "gum"		Ch. 17
꼭 "surely," "certainly" (adverb)		Ch. 14
꽃 "flower"		Ch. 13
꿀 "honey"		Ch. 8
꿈 "a dream"		Ch. 7
꿈(을) 꾸다 "to dream"		Ch. 7
끄다 "to turn off"		Ch. 19
끝 "the end"		Ch. 20
끝나다 "to be finished," "to end," "to be over"		Ch. 20
끝내다 "to finish (something)," "to end (something)"		Ch. 20
끼다 "to wear (on hands)"		Ch. 20

ㄴ

나가다 "to leave," "to go out"		Ch. 8
나누다 "to share," "to divide"		Ch. 17
나라 "country"		Ch. 8
나무 "tree," "wood"		Ch. 13
나쁘다 "to be bad"		Ch. 9
나오다 "to come out"		Ch. 8
나이 "age"		Ch. 15
나이가 어떻게 됩니까? "How old are you?"		Ch. 15
낚시 "fishing"		Ch. 15
날 "day"		Ch. 16
날씨 "weather"		Ch. 9
남동생 "male younger sibling"		Ch. 18
남자 "boy," "man"		Ch. 6

333

Glossary

남자 친구	"boyfriend"	Ch. 6
남편	"husband"	Ch. 18
낮다	"to be low"	Ch. 10
내년	"next year"	Ch. 20
내다	"to pay (money)"	Ch. 9
내일	"tomorrow"	Ch. 8
냉동실	"freezer"	Ch. 8
냉장고	"refrigerator"	Ch. 8
너무	"too (much)," "overly" (adverb)	Ch. 12
넣다	"to put in"	Ch. 17
네	"yes"	Ch. 1
네	4 (adjective)	Ch. 13
넷	4	Ch. 13
년	year counter	Ch. 16
노란	"yellow" (adjective)	Ch. 11
노란색	"yellow" (noun)	Ch. 11
노랗다	"to be yellow"	Ch. 11
노래	"song"	Ch. 14
노래(를) 부르다	"to sing a song"	Ch. 14
노력	"effort"	Ch. 17
노력(을) 하다	"to try," "to put forth effort"	Ch. 17
노인	"old person"	Ch. 18
노트북	"laptop" (literally, "notebook")	Ch. 11
놀다	"to play," "to hang out"	Ch. 5
놀이 공원	"amusement park"	Ch. 14
농구	"basketball"	Ch. 2
농담	"joke"	Ch. 20
농담(을) 하다	"to tell a joke," "to joke"	Ch. 20
높다	"to be high"	Ch. 10
놓다	"to put down," "to let go"	Ch. 17
누구/누가	"who"	Ch. 8
누나	"older sister" (used by males)	Ch. 18
눈	"eye"	Ch. 10
눈(이) 오다	"to snow"	Ch. 9
눕다	"to lie down"	Ch. 7
뉴스	"news"	Ch. 6
느리다	"to be slow"	Ch. 10
늦게	"late" (adverb)	Ch. 14
늦다	"to be late"	Ch. 14

ㄷ

다니다	"to attend (school)," "to commute (to work)"	Ch. 8
다르다	"to be different"	Ch. 11
다리	"bridge"	Ch. 11
다리	"leg"	Ch. 10
다섯	5	Ch. 13
다시	"again" (adverb)	Ch. 16
다음 달	"next month"	Ch. 16
다음 주	"next week"	Ch. 16
단계	"a step"	Ch. 11
단순하다	"to be simple"	Ch. 10
닫다	"to close (something)"	Ch. 6
달	"month," "moon"	Ch. 16
달다	"to be (sugary) sweet"	Ch. 10
달리다	"to run"	Ch. 8
달콤하다	"to be (deliciously) sweet"	Ch. 10
닭	"chicken"	Ch. 13
담배	"tobacco," "cigarettes"	Ch. 9
당근	"carrot"	Ch. 13
당신	"you" (not polite)	Ch. 18
가족	"family"	Ch. 18
대가족	"big family"	Ch. 18
(대)답	"answer"	Ch. 17
(대)답(을) 하다	"to answer"	Ch. 17
대통령	"the President"	Ch. 12
대학교	"university"	Ch. 8
댄스	"dance"	Ch. 2
더	"more" (adverb)	Ch. 3
더럽다	"to be dirty"	Ch. 10
덜	"less" (adverb)	Ch. 3
덥다	"to be hot" (weather)	Ch. 9
데리고 가다	"to take (someone somewhere else)"	Ch. 13
데리고 오다	"to take (someone here)"	Ch. 13
도	"also," "even," "too" (particle)	Ch. 4
도	"degrees"	Ch. 13

Glossary

도서관	"library"	Ch. 5
도시	"city"	Ch. 5
도와주다	"to help"	Ch. 17
도착(을) 하다	"to arrive"	Ch. 6
독서	"reading"	Ch. 15
독일	"Germany"	Ch. 6
독일 사람	"a German (person)"	Ch. 6
독일어	"German (language)"	Ch. 6
돈	"money"	Ch. 4
돌	"stone"	Ch. 13
동그랗다	"to be round"	Ch. 11
동물	"animal"	Ch. 7
동생	"younger sibling"	Ch. 18
동안	"a period of time"	Ch. 16
돼지	"pig"	Ch. 7
돼지고기	"pork"	Ch. 13
돼지꿈 꾸세요.	"Dream of pigs."	Ch. 7
되다	"to become," "to be okay," "to work"	Ch. 17
두	2 (adjective)	Ch. 13
둘	2	Ch. 13
뒤	"behind," "after"	Ch. 20
드레스	"dress"	Ch. 11
드물다	"to be rare"	Ch. 9
듣다	"to listen"	Ch. 6
들어가다	"to go in"	Ch. 17
들어오다	"to come in"	Ch. 17
등	"back (of body)"	Ch. 10
등산	"mountain climbing," "hiking"	Ch. 2
따뜻하다	"to be warm" (weather, or to the touch)	Ch. 9
딸	"daughter"	Ch. 18
딸기	"strawberry"	Ch. 10
땅	"earth," "dirt"	Ch. 13
때때로	"from time to time" (adverb)	Ch. 19
떡	"rice cake"	Ch. 8
떨어뜨리다	"to drop (something)"	Ch. 6
떨어지다	"to fall"	Ch. 6
똑같다	"to be exactly the same"	Ch. 11
똑똑하다	"to be smart"	Ch. 13
똥	"poop"	Ch. 13
뛰다	"to fly," "to jump," "to run"	Ch. 8
뜨겁다	"to be hot" (to the touch)	Ch. 9

ㄹ

램프	"lamp"	Ch. 20
레몬	"lemon"	Ch. 4
로션	"lotion"	Ch. 19
리터	"liter"	Ch. 13

ㅁ

마리	animal counter	Ch. 13
마시다	"to drink"	Ch. 6
마일	"mile"	Ch. 13
마지막	"last" (noun)	Ch. 19
마흔	40	Ch. 13
만	"only" (particle)	Ch. 4
만	10000	Ch. 12
만나다	"to meet"	Ch. 13
(만나서) 반갑습니다.	"Nice to meet you."	Ch. 1
만들다	"to make"	Ch. 6
많이	"to be a lot"	Ch. 9
많이	"a lot" (adverb)	Ch. 9
많이 파세요.	"Sell a lot."	Ch. 17
말	"horse"	Ch. 11
말	"word"	Ch. 6
말(을) 하다	"to speak," "to say"	Ch. 6
말리다	"to (make) dry," "to dry (something)"	Ch. 19
맑다	"to be bright and clear" (weather)	Ch. 9
맛	"flavor"	Ch. 9
맛(이) 없다	"to not be delicious," "to not taste good"	Ch. 14
맛(이) 있다	"to be delicious"	Ch. 9
맞다	"to be correct"	Ch. 13
매년	"every year"	Ch. 20
매월	"every month"	Ch. 20
매일	"every day"	Ch. 20
매주	"every week"	Ch. 20
맥주	"beer"	Ch. 13

Glossary

맵다	"to be spicy"	Ch. 9
머리	"head," "hair"	Ch. 10
머리카락	"hair"	Ch. 10
먹다	"to eat"	Ch. 4
먼저	"first (before anything/anyone else)" (adverb)	Ch. 19
먼저 갈게요.	"I'll go first."	Ch. 19
멀다	"to be far"	Ch. 10
멋(이) 없다	"to not be cool," "to be unstylish"	Ch. 14
멋(이) 있다	"to be cool," "to be stylish"	Ch. 9
메시지	"message"	Ch. 17
며칠	"what day"	Ch. 16
며칠입니까?	"What day (of the month) is it?"	Ch. 16
명	person counter	Ch. 13
몇	"how many" (adjective)	Ch. 13
몇 년	"what year," "how many years"	Ch. 16
몇 시	"what time"	Ch. 16
몇 시입니까?	"What time is it?"	Ch. 16
몇 월	"what month"	Ch. 16
모니터	"monitor"	Ch. 11
모르다	"to not know"	Ch. 14
모자	"hat"	Ch. 11
목	"neck," "throat"	Ch. 10
목(이) 마르다	"to be thirsty"	Ch. 9
목소리	"voice"	Ch. 10
목요일	"Thursday"	Ch. 16
목표	"a goal"	Ch. 17
몸	"body"	Ch. 10
무겁다	"to be heavy"	Ch. 10
무례하다	"to be impolite"	Ch. 12
무섭다	"to be scary," "to be afraid"	Ch. 11
무슨	"what" (adjective)	Ch. 11
무엇	"what" (noun)	Ch. 7
문	"door"	Ch. 8
문제	"problem"	Ch. 11
문화	"culture"	Ch. 12
묻다	"to inquire"	Ch. 19
물	"water"	Ch. 6
물고기	"(alive) fish"	Ch. 13
물어보다	"to ask"	Ch. 17
미국	"America"	Ch. 6
미국 사람	"an American (person)"	Ch. 6
미국 음식	"American food"	Ch. 10
미국인	"an American (person)"	Ch. 6
미래	"the future"	Ch. 20
미술	"art"	Ch. 7
미식	"American food" (abbreviation)	Ch. 10
미식축구	"American football"	Ch. 2
미워하다	"to hate" (person)	Ch. 5
미터	"meter"	Ch. 13
믿다	"to believe"	Ch. 6
밀리리터	"milliliter"	Ch. 13
밀리미터	"millimeter"	Ch. 13
밑	"underneath"	Ch. 20

ㅂ

바나나	"banana"	Ch. 4
바다	"ocean"	Ch. 5
바닷가	"beach"	Ch. 5
바람	"wind"	Ch. 13
바르다	"to spread (on)," "to apply"	Ch. 19
바쁘다	"to be busy"	Ch. 10
바지	"pants"	Ch. 20
박물관	"museum"	Ch. 5
박사	"doctor" (someone holding a PhD)	Ch. 8
밖	"outside"	Ch. 20
반	"half"	Ch. 16
반바지	"shorts" (literally, "half pants")	Ch. 20
반지	"ring"	Ch. 20
받다	"to get," "to receive"	Ch. 4
발	"foot"	Ch. 10
발가락	"toe"	Ch. 10
밝다	"to be bright"	Ch. 10
밤	"night"	Ch. 8
밥	"(cooked) rice," "a meal"	Ch. 8

Glossary

밥(을) 먹다	"to eat (a meal)"	Ch. 8
방	"room"	Ch. 8
방법	"method," "way"	Ch. 10
방송	"a broadcast"	Ch. 5
배	"belly"	Ch. 10
배	"boat"	Ch. 4
배(가) 고프다	"to be hungry"	Ch. 9
배구	"volleyball"	Ch. 2
배우다	"to learn"	Ch. 7
백	100	Ch. 12
백만	1000000	Ch. 12
뱀	"snake"	Ch. 11
버리다	"to throw away"	Ch. 17
버스	"bus"	Ch. 16
버터	"butter"	Ch. 8
번호	"number (of something)"	Ch. 12
벌다	"to earn (money)"	Ch. 4
벌레	"bug," "insect"	Ch. 3
벗다	"to take off (clothing)"	Ch. 20
베다	"to cut (into)"	Ch. 11
벽	"wall"	Ch. 11
병원	"hospital"	Ch. 5
보고 싶다	"to miss," "to want to see"	Ch. 16
보내다	"to send"	Ch. 17
보다	"to see"	Ch. 6
보다 (더)	"more than"	Ch. 13
볶음밥	"fried rice"	Ch. 9
봄	"spring"	Ch. 16
부럽다	"to be jealous"	Ch. 17
부르다	"to sing"	Ch. 14
부모님	"parents"	Ch. 18
부분	"part," "portion"	Ch. 5
부엌	"kitchen"	Ch. 10
부터	"from (a time or location)"	Ch. 16
북한	"North Korea"	Ch. 6
분	minute counter	Ch. 16
불	"fire"	Ch. 13
불	dollar counter	Ch. 17
불편하다	"to be uncomfortable"	Ch. 13
비(가) 오다	"to rain"	Ch. 9
비밀	"a secret"	Ch. 12
비밀 번호	"password"	Ch. 12
비슷하다	"to be similar"	Ch. 11
비싸다	"to be expensive"	Ch. 9
비행기	"airplane"	Ch. 16
비행기표	"plane ticket"	Ch. 12
빌리다	"to borrow," "to lend"	Ch. 17
빠르다	"to be fast"	Ch. 10
빨간	"red" (adjective)	Ch. 11
빨간색	"red" (noun)	Ch. 11
빨갛다	"to be red"	Ch. 11
빨래	"laundry"	Ch. 17
빨래(를) 하다	"to do the laundry"	Ch. 17
빨리	"quickly," "fast" (adverb)	Ch. 14
빵	"bread"	Ch. 8
빼다	"to remove"	Ch. 11
뺨	"cheek"	Ch. 11
뿔	"horn(s)"	Ch. 10

ㅅ

사	4	Ch. 12
사과	"apple"	Ch. 10
사다	"to buy"	Ch. 17
사람	"person"	Ch. 6
사랑	"love"	Ch. 4
사랑(을) 하다	"to love"	Ch. 5
사랑에 빠지다	"to fall in love"	Ch. 20
사랑합니다.	"I love."	Ch. 2
사무실	"office"	Ch. 5
사용(을) 하다	"to utilize," "to use"	Ch. 17
사월	"April"	Ch. 16
사이다	"(lemon-lime) soda"	Ch. 6
사자	"lion"	Ch. 13
사장님	"boss"	Ch. 12
사전	"dictionary"	Ch. 3
사진	"photo"	Ch. 6
사진(을) 찍다	"to take a photo"	Ch. 6
사촌	"cousin"	Ch. 18
사탕	"sweets"	Ch. 8
사회	"society"	Ch. 12
산	"mountain"	Ch. 11

Glossary

살 "flesh," "fat"		Ch. 8
살 age counter		Ch. 13
살구 "apricot"		Ch. 11
살구색 "apricot color"		Ch. 11
살다 "to live"		Ch. 5
삶 "life"		Ch. 18
삼 3		Ch. 12
삼겹살 "pork belly"		Ch. 3
삼월 "March"		Ch. 16
삼촌 "uncle"		Ch. 18
상자 "box"		Ch. 13
새 "bird"		Ch. 11
새롭다 "to be new"		Ch. 10
새벽 "past midnight"		Ch. 16
색(깔) "color"		Ch. 11
샌드위치 "sandwich"		Ch. 20
생각 "an idea," "a thought"		Ch. 10
생각(을) 하다 "to think"		Ch. 10
생선 "(dead) fish"		Ch. 15
샤워(를) 하다 "to take a shower"		Ch. 17
샴푸 "shampoo"		Ch. 17
서다 "to stand"		Ch. 7
서른 30		Ch. 13
서울 "Seoul"		Ch. 8
섞다 "to mix"		Ch. 11
선물 "present"		Ch. 11
선생님 "Sir," "Mr.," "teacher"		Ch. 7
선택(을) 하다 "to choose," "to select"		Ch. 20
설거지 "(dirty) dishes"		Ch. 17
설거지(를) 하다 "to do the dishes"		Ch. 17
설탕 "sugar"		Ch. 8
섬 "island"		Ch. 6
성격 "personality"		Ch. 6
성적 "(school) grade"		Ch. 10
세 3 (adjective)		Ch. 13
세계 "world"		Ch. 13
세수(를) 하다 "to wash one's face and hands," "to wash up"		Ch. 17
센티미터 "centimeter"		Ch. 13
셋 3		Ch. 13
셔츠 "shirt"		Ch. 11
소 "cow"		Ch. 13
소개(를) 하다 "to introduce"		Ch. 7
소금 "salt"		Ch. 8
소리 "sound," "noise"		Ch. 10
소시지 "sausage"		Ch. 7
소주 "(Korean) alcohol"		Ch. 13
속옷 "underwear"		Ch. 11
손 "hand"		Ch. 10
손가락 "finger"		Ch. 10
손녀 "granddaughter"		Ch. 18
손님 "guest," "customer"		Ch. 12
손목시계 "wristwatch"		Ch. 20
손자 "grandson"		Ch. 18
쇠고기 "beef"		Ch. 13
수업 "lesson," "course," "class"		Ch. 20
수영 "swimming"		Ch. 2
수영(을) 하다 "to swim"		Ch. 9
수영장 "swimming pool"		Ch. 5
수요일 "Wednesday"		Ch. 16
수프 "soup"		Ch. 9
수학 "math"		Ch. 7
숙제 "homework"		Ch. 7
숙제(를) 하다 "to do homework"		Ch. 7
술 "alcohol"		Ch. 9
숫자 "an integer," "a number"		Ch. 12
숲 "forest"		Ch. 13
쉬다 "to rest"		Ch. 10
쉽다 "to be easy"		Ch. 10
슈퍼(마켓) "supermarket"		Ch. 5
스무 20 (adjective)		Ch. 13
스물 20		Ch. 13
스테이크 "steak"		Ch. 7
스페인어 "Spanish (language)"		Ch. 6
스포츠 "sports"		Ch. 2
슬프다 "to be sad"		Ch. 12
시 "o'clock"		Ch. 16
시 "poetry"		Ch. 2
시간 "time"		Ch. 11
시간 hour counter		Ch. 16
시계 "clock," "watch"		Ch. 17

Glossary

시다	"to be sour"	Ch. 10
시대	"a period," "an age," "a generation"	Ch. 11
시원하다	"to be cool" (weather, or to the touch)	Ch. 9
시월	"October"	Ch. 16
시작	"beginning," "start"	Ch. 20
시작(을) 하다	"to begin," "to start"	Ch. 20
시험	"test"	Ch. 7
시험(을) 보다	"to take a test"	Ch. 10
식당	"restaurant"	Ch. 9
식초	"vinegar"	Ch. 8
신	"god"	Ch. 6
신다	"to wear (on feet)"	Ch. 20
신뢰	"trust"	Ch. 11
신문	"newspaper"	Ch. 6
신발	"shoes"	Ch. 13
실례하다	"to do a discourtesy"	Ch. 17
실례하지만...	"Excuse me but..."	Ch. 17
실례합니다.	"Excuse me."	Ch. 17
싫어하다	"to dislike" (person/thing)	Ch. 5
싫어합니다.	"I dislike."	Ch. 2
심심하다	"to be bored"	Ch. 14
심장	"heart"	Ch. 10
십	10	Ch. 12
십만	100000	Ch. 12
십이월	"December"	Ch. 16
십일월	"November"	Ch. 16
싸다	"to be cheap"	Ch. 10
싸우다	"to fight"	Ch. 7
쌀	"(uncooked) rice"	Ch. 8
쓰다	"to be bitter"	Ch. 10
쓰다	"to use," "to write"	Ch. 17
쓰다	"to wear (on head)"	Ch. 20
쓰레기	"garbage," "trash"	Ch. 17
씨	"Mr," "Ms./Mrs."	Ch. 5
씹다	"to chew"	Ch. 17
씻다	"to wash," "to bathe"	Ch. 17
ㅇ		
아	"Ah"	Ch. 7
아기	"baby"	Ch. 18
아내	"wife"	Ch. 18
아니다	"to not be"	Ch. 14
아니요	"no"	Ch. 1
아들	"son"	Ch. 18
아르바이트 (or 알바)	"part time job"	Ch. 4
아름답다	"to be beautiful"	Ch. 9
아마(도)	"maybe," "possibly"	Ch. 20
아버지	"father"	Ch. 18
아빠	"dad"	Ch. 18
아이	"child"	Ch. 18
아이고!	"Oh my!"	Ch. 13
아이스크림	"ice cream"	Ch. 4
아주	"very" (adverb)	Ch. 9
아침	"morning"	Ch. 16
아침 (식사)	"breakfast" (literally, "morning meal")	Ch. 8
아파트	"apartment"	Ch. 6
아프다	"to be in pain," "to be painful," "to be sick"	Ch. 10
아홉	9	Ch. 13
악하다	"to be evil"	Ch. 9
안	"inside"	Ch. 20
안 되다	"to not become," "to not be okay," "to not work"	Ch. 17
안녕하세요.	"Hello."	Ch. 1
안녕히 가세요.	"Goodbye." ("Go in peace.")	Ch. 1
안녕히 계세요.	"Goodbye." ("Stay in peace.")	Ch. 1
안녕히 주무세요.	"Goodnight." ("Sleep well.")	Ch. 7
앉다	"to sit"	Ch. 7
알겠다	"to know," "to understand"	Ch. 8
알겠습니다.	"I see.," "Understood."	Ch. 8
알다	"to know"	Ch. 14
앞	"in front of"	Ch. 20
야구	"baseball"	Ch. 2
약	"medicine," "drugs"	Ch. 15
약국	"pharmacy"	Ch. 15

Glossary

약속(을) 하다	"to promise"	Ch. 18
약하다	"to be weak"	Ch. 9
양	"sheep"	Ch. 11
양말	"socks"	Ch. 13
양복	"a suit"	Ch. 13
양파	"onion"	Ch. 7
어깨	"shoulder"	Ch. 10
어둡다	"to be dark"	Ch. 10
어디	"where"	Ch. 8
어떤	"what kind of" (adjective)	Ch. 10
어떻게	"how"	Ch. 8
어떻게 됩니까?	"Tell me about…"	Ch. 15
어떻게 지내세요?	"How are you doing?"	Ch. 17
어떻다	"to be how"	Ch. 10
어렵다	"to be difficult"	Ch. 10
어른	"adult"	Ch. 18
어머니	"mother"	Ch. 18
어제	"yesterday"	Ch. 8
억	100000000	Ch. 12
언니	"older sister" (used by females)	Ch. 18
언어	"language"	Ch. 15
언어학	"linguistics"	Ch. 15
언제	"when"	Ch. 8
얼굴	"face"	Ch. 11
얼마입니까?	"How much does it cost?"	Ch. 12
엄마	"mom"	Ch. 18
없다	"to not exist"	Ch. 14
에	"to," "at," "in" (particle)	Ch. 5
에게	"to (a person)"	Ch. 17
에게(서)	"from (a person)"	Ch. 17
에서	"from," "at," "in" (particle)	Ch. 13
여기	"here"	Ch. 11
여기요.	"Over here." ("Excuse me.")	Ch. 17
여덟	8	Ch. 13
여동생	"female younger sibling"	Ch. 18
여드름	"pimple," "acne"	Ch. 11
여름	"summer"	Ch. 16
여보세요?	"Hello?" (on the phone)	Ch. 19
여섯	6	Ch. 13
여자	"girl," "woman"	Ch. 6
여자 친구	"girlfriend"	Ch. 6
여행	"travel," "a trip"	Ch. 15
여행(을) 하다	"to travel," "to take a trip"	Ch. 15
역사	"history"	Ch. 2
역시	"(just) as expected" (adverb)	Ch. 20
역할	"(acting) role"	Ch. 5
연극	"performance," "play"	Ch. 5
연습(을) 하다	"to practice"	Ch. 17
연필	"pencil"	Ch. 4
열	10	Ch. 13
열다	"to open (something)"	Ch. 6
열쇠	"key"	Ch. 8
열심히	"diligently," "hard" (adverb)	Ch. 20
열차	"(ordinary) train"	Ch. 16
영	0	Ch. 12
영국	"England"	Ch. 6
영국 사람	"English (person)"	Ch. 6
영어	"English (language)"	Ch. 6
영화	"movie"	Ch. 3
영화관	"movie theater"	Ch. 5
옆	"beside," "(right) next to"	Ch. 20
예	"an example (of something)"	Ch. 11
예(를) 들면…	"For example…"	Ch. 11
예쁘다	"to be pretty"	Ch. 9
예의(가) 바르다	"to be polite"	Ch. 12
오	5	Ch. 12
오늘	"today"	Ch. 8
오다	"to come"	Ch. 5
오랫동안	"for a long time" (adverb)	Ch. 16
오렌지	"orange"	Ch. 4
오빠	"older brother" (used by females)	Ch. 18
오월	"May"	Ch. 16
오전	"before noon," "A.M."	Ch. 16
오후	"after noon," "P.M."	Ch. 16
올해	"this year"	Ch. 20
옮기다	"to move (something)"	Ch. 20
옷	"clothing," "clothes"	Ch. 11

Glossary

와/과 함께 "together with"		Ch. 14
완벽하다 "to be perfect"		Ch. 19
왜 "why"		Ch. 8
외국 "foreign country"		Ch. 6
외국어 "foreign language"		Ch. 6
외우다 "to memorize"		Ch. 14
요리 "cooking"		Ch. 11
요리(를) 하다 "to cook"		Ch. 11
요즘 "lately," "nowadays," "these days"		Ch. 7
우리 "we," "us"		Ch. 8
우리나라 "Korea" (literally, "our country")		Ch. 8
우산 "umbrella"		Ch. 11
우유 "milk"		Ch. 6
우주 "universe"		Ch. 13
운동 "exercise"		Ch. 15
운동(을) 하다 "to exercise"		Ch. 13
운전(을) 하다 "to drive"		Ch. 13
울다 "to cry"		Ch. 4
움직이다 "to move"		Ch. 20
웃기다 "to be humorous," "to be funny"		Ch. 20
웃다 "to smile," "to laugh"		Ch. 4
원 "Won" (Korean currency)		Ch. 12
원숭이 "monkey"		Ch. 3
원하다 "to want"		Ch. 5
원하지 않습니다. "I don't want..."		Ch. 4
원합니다. "I want..."		Ch. 4
월 month name counter		Ch. 16
월요일 "Monday"		Ch. 16
웨이터 "waiter"		Ch. 9
위 "above," "on top of"		Ch. 20
위 "stomach"		Ch. 10
유럽 "Europe"		Ch. 6
유리 "glass"		Ch. 20
유명하다 "to be famous"		Ch. 14
유월 "June"		Ch. 16
육 6		Ch. 12
은행 "bank"		Ch. 5
을/를 Object Marker		Ch. 2
(을/를) 더 주세요. "Please give me more..."		Ch. 17
음 "Hm"		Ch. 7
음식 "food"		Ch. 2
음악 "music"		Ch. 2
의 Possessive Marker		Ch. 11
의견 "opinion"		Ch. 6
의미 "meaning"		Ch. 6
의사 "(medical) doctor"		Ch. 8
의자 "chair"		Ch. 9
이 "this" (adjective)		Ch. 11
이 2		Ch. 12
이(빨) "tooth," "teeth"		Ch. 10
이/가 Subject Marker		Ch. 8
이것 "this thing"		Ch. 11
이기다 "to win"		Ch. 7
이다 "to be"		Ch. 6
이런 "this kind of" (adjective)		Ch. 10
이렇다 "to be this way"		Ch. 10
이름 "name"		Ch. 11
이모 "aunt" (mother's side)		Ch. 18
이미 "already" (adverb)		Ch. 16
이번 달 "this month"		Ch. 16
이번 주 "this week"		Ch. 16
이상하다 "to be strange"		Ch. 19
이야기 "story"		Ch. 14
이야기(를) 하다 "to chat," "to gossip"		Ch. 14
이웃 "neighbor"		Ch. 12
이월 "February"		Ch. 16
이제 "(from) now"		Ch. 6
이틀 "two days"		Ch. 16
이해(를) 하다 "to understand"		Ch. 14
인간 "human"		Ch. 6
인기 "popularity"		Ch. 14
인기(가) 없다 "to be unpopular"		Ch. 14
인기(가) 있다 "to be popular"		Ch. 14
인상 "impression"		Ch. 19
일 "work," "job"		Ch. 4
일 1		Ch. 12
일 day counter		Ch. 16

Glossary

일(을) 하다	"to work"	Ch. 4
일곱	7	Ch. 13
일본	"Japan"	Ch. 6
일본 사람	"a Japanese (person)"	Ch. 6
일본 음식	"Japanese food"	Ch. 10
일본말	"Japanese (language)"	Ch. 6
일본어	"Japanese (language)"	Ch. 16
일본인	"a Japanese (person)"	Ch. 6
일식	"Japanese food" (abbreviation)	Ch. 10
일어나다	"to wake up," "to get up"	Ch. 8
일요일	"Sunday"	Ch. 16
일월	"January"	Ch. 16
일찍	"early" (adverb)	Ch. 14
읽다	"to read"	Ch. 6
입	"mouth"	Ch. 10
입니다	"am," "is," "are," "equals"	Ch. 1
입다	"to wear (on body)"	Ch. 20
입술	"lips"	Ch. 10
있다	"to exist"	Ch. 6

ㅈ

(자동)차	"car"	Ch. 4
자르다	"to cut (off)," "to sever"	Ch. 11
자리	"a seat," "space (for something)"	Ch. 7
자연	"nature"	Ch. 12
자연스럽다	"to be natural"	Ch. 12
자유	"freedom"	Ch. 12
자전거	"bicycle"	Ch. 16
자주	"often" (adverb)	Ch. 19
작가	"author"	Ch. 3
작년	"last year"	Ch. 20
작다	"to be small"	Ch. 9
잔디	"grass," "lawn"	Ch. 13
잘	"well" (adverb)	Ch. 7
잘 가요.	"Go well."	Ch. 19
잘 지내세요?	"Are you doing well?"	Ch. 7
잘생기다	"to be handsome"	Ch. 10
잘생긴	"handsome" (adjective)	Ch. 10
잠	"sleep"	Ch. 8
(잠[을]) 자다	"to sleep"	Ch. 8
잡다	"to grab," "to catch"	Ch. 10
장	flat item counter	Ch. 13
장미	"rose"	Ch. 13
재미(가) 없다	"to not be fun," "to not be entertaining"	Ch. 14
재미(가) 있다	"to be fun," "to be entertaining"	Ch. 10
저	"I," "me"	Ch. 1
저	"that (farther)" (adjective)	Ch. 11
저	"Uh..."	Ch. 7
저것	"that thing (farther)"	Ch. 11
저기	"there (farther)"	Ch. 11
저기요.	"Over here." ("Excuse me.")	Ch. 17
저녁	"evening"	Ch. 16
저녁 (식사)	"dinner" (literally, "evening meal")	Ch. 8
저는 ____(이)라고 합니다.	"My name is ____."	Ch. 15
저는 ____입니다.	"I am ____."	Ch. 1
저렴하다	"to be inexpensive"	Ch. 10
저의 이름은 ____입니다.	"My name is ____."	Ch. 11
전	penny counter	Ch. 17
전자 사전	"electronic dictionary"	Ch. 3
전화	"telephone call"	Ch. 12
전화(를) 받다	"to answer the phone"	Ch. 12
전화(를) 하다	"to telephone," "to call"	Ch. 12
전화기	"telephone"	Ch. 12
전화번호	"phone number"	Ch. 12
점심 (식사)	"lunch" (literally, "afternoon meal")	Ch. 8
젓가락	"chopsticks"	Ch. 7
정말(로)	"really" (adverb)	Ch. 7
정부	"government"	Ch. 12
정오	"noon"	Ch. 16
정원	"garden"	Ch. 6
정치	"politics"	Ch. 12
제주도	"Jeju Island"	Ch. 13

Glossary

조금 "a little"	Ch. 9
(조금) 깎아주세요. "Please give me a discount."	Ch. 17
조금 더 "a little more" (adverb)	Ch. 17
조금만 "only a little"	Ch. 9
조카 "niece," "nephew"	Ch. 18
졸리다 "to be sleepy"	Ch. 10
종이 "paper"	Ch. 13
좋다 "to be good"	Ch. 9
좋아하다 "to like"	Ch. 5
좋아합니다. "I like."	Ch. 2
좋은 아침입니다. "Good morning."	Ch. 16
좋은 하루 되세요. "Have a nice day."	Ch. 16
죄송하다 "to be sorry"	Ch. 9
죄송합니다. "I'm sorry."	Ch. 9
주다 "to give"	Ch. 17
주름 "wrinkle(s)"	Ch. 11
주문(을) 하다 "to order (something)"	Ch. 17
주방 "kitchen"	Ch. 10
주세요. "Please give me…"	Ch. 4
주소 "an address"	Ch. 5
주일 week counter	Ch. 16
주제 "topic," "theme"	Ch. 14
죽다 "to die"	Ch. 4
죽음 "death"	Ch. 18
준비(를) 하다 "to prepare"	Ch. 16
중 "center"	Ch. 20
중국 "China"	Ch. 6
중국 사람 "a Chinese (person)"	Ch. 6
중국 음식 "Chinese food"	Ch. 10
중국말 "Chinese (language)"	Ch. 6
중국어 "Chinese (language)"	Ch. 16
중식 "Chinese food" (abbreviation)	Ch. 10
중요하다 "to be important"	Ch. 10
중학교 "middle school"	Ch. 8
쥐 "mouse," "rat"	Ch. 13
증조할머니 "great grandmother"	Ch. 18
증조할아버지 "great grandfather"	Ch. 18
지갑 "wallet"	Ch. 15
지구 "the Earth"	Ch. 13
지금 "(right) now"	Ch. 6
지금부터 "from now"	Ch. 16
지난 달 "last month"	Ch. 16
지난 주 "last week"	Ch. 16
지다 "to lose"	Ch. 7
지도 "map"	Ch. 6
지루하다 "to be boring"	Ch. 14
지리 "geography"	Ch. 7
지붕 "roof"	Ch. 8
지역 "an area," "a region"	Ch. 5
지하철 "subway"	Ch. 16
직원 "employee"	Ch. 12
진실 "truth"	Ch. 6
진실(을) 말하다 "to tell the truth"	Ch. 6
질문 "question"	Ch. 11
질문(을) 하다 "to ask a question"	Ch. 11
집 "home," "house"	Ch. 5
집 주소 "home address"	Ch. 5
짧다 "to be short (in length)"	Ch. 10
쪽지 "note"	Ch. 17

ㅊ

차 "tea"	Ch. 4
차갑다 "to be cold" (to the touch)	Ch. 9
차다 "to kick"	Ch. 7
차다 "to wear (on wrists)"	Ch. 20
차이 "difference"	Ch. 6
참치 "tuna"	Ch. 4
창(문) "window"	Ch. 11
찾다 "to look for," "to find"	Ch. 10
채소 "vegetables"	Ch. 4
책 "book"	Ch. 3
책상 "desk," "(writing) table"	Ch. 20
처음 "first" (noun), "for the first time" (adverb)	Ch. 19
처음 뵙겠습니다. "Nice to meet you."	Ch. 1
천 1000	Ch. 12
천만 10000000	Ch. 12
천만에요. "You're welcome."	Ch. 16

Glossary

천장 "ceiling"	Ch. 8	컴퓨터 게임 "computer game"	Ch. 15
첫 "first" (adjective)	Ch. 19	컵 "cup"	Ch. 13
첫인상 "first impression"	Ch. 19	케이크 "cake"	Ch. 10
초 second counter	Ch. 16	켜다 "to turn on"	Ch. 19
초대(를) 하다 "to invite"	Ch. 13	코 "nose"	Ch. 10
초등학교 "elementary school"	Ch. 8	코트 "coat"	Ch. 20
초록색 "green" (noun/adjective)	Ch. 11	콜라 "cola"	Ch. 7
초밥 "sushi" (vinegared rice with fish, etc.)	Ch. 7	크다 "to be big"	Ch. 9
최고 "(the) best"	Ch. 15	키 "height," "stature"	Ch. 13
최악 "(the) worst"	Ch. 15	키(가) 작다 "to be short (height)"	Ch. 13
추가(를) 하다 "to add (to something)"	Ch. 11	키(가) 크다 "to be tall (height)"	Ch. 13
추하다 "to be ugly"	Ch. 10	키우다 "to raise"	Ch. 6
축구 "football"	Ch. 2	킬로(그램) "kilo(gram)"	Ch. 13
축하(를) 하다 "to congratulate"	Ch. 18	**ㅌ**	
축하합니다. "Congratulations."	Ch. 18	타다 "to ride"	Ch. 16
출발(을) 하다 "to depart"	Ch. 6	탁구 "table tennis," "ping-pong"	Ch. 2
춤(을) 추다 "to dance"	Ch. 7	태극기 "the Korean national flag"	Ch. 11
춥다 "to be cold" (weather)	Ch. 9	태어나다 "to be born"	Ch. 4
취미 "hobby"	Ch. 15	택시 "taxi"	Ch. 16
치과 "dentist"	Ch. 5	턱 "chin"	Ch. 11
치과 의사 "dentist"	Ch. 15	털 "hair (not on head)," "fur"	Ch. 10
치다 "to hit"	Ch. 7	테니스 "tennis"	Ch. 2
치약 "toothpaste"	Ch. 17	텔레비전 "television"	Ch. 6
치즈 "cheese"	Ch. 5	토마토 "tomato"	Ch. 4
친구 "friend"	Ch. 6	토요일 "Saturday"	Ch. 16
친절하다 "to be nice"	Ch. 9	톤 "ton"	Ch. 13
칠 7	Ch. 12	특히 "especially" (adverb)	Ch. 19
칠월 "July"	Ch. 16	틀리다 "to be incorrect"	Ch. 13
침대 "bed"	Ch. 8	티비 "television" (abbreviation)	Ch. 6
침실 "bedroom"	Ch. 8	티셔츠 (or T 셔츠) "T-shirt"	Ch. 11
칫솔 "toothbrush"	Ch. 17	팀 "team"	Ch. 17
ㅋ		**ㅍ**	
카메라 "camera"	Ch. 6	파 "green onion"	Ch. 7
카페 "café"	Ch. 5	파란 "blue" (adjective)	Ch. 11
칼 "knife," "blade"	Ch. 13	파란색 "blue" (noun)	Ch. 11
캔디 "candy"	Ch. 8	파랗다 "to be blue"	Ch. 11
커피 "coffee"	Ch. 9	파스타 "pasta"	Ch. 7
컴퓨터 "computer"	Ch. 10	파티 "party"	Ch. 13
		팔 "arm"	Ch. 10
		팔 8	Ch. 12

Glossary

팔다	"to sell"	Ch. 17
팔월	"August"	Ch. 16
패다	"to beat," "to bash"	Ch. 11
펜	"pen"	Ch. 6
편지	"(written) letter"	Ch. 17
편하다	"to be comfortable"	Ch. 13
포도	"grape"	Ch. 4
포크	"fork"	Ch. 7
표	"ticket"	Ch. 12
풀	"glue"	Ch. 7
프랑스	"France"	Ch. 7
프랑스어	"French (language)"	Ch. 6
프로 선수	"professional athlete"	Ch. 17
프로그램	"a program"	Ch. 5
피곤하다	"to be tired," "to be exhausted"	Ch. 10
피구	"dodge ball"	Ch. 2
피부	"skin"	Ch. 19
피자	"pizza"	Ch. 7
필요하다	"to be necessary"	Ch. 13

ㅎ

하나	1	Ch. 13
하늘	"sky"	Ch. 13
하다	"to do"	Ch. 4
하루	"one day"	Ch. 16
하얀	"white" (adjective)	Ch. 11
하얀색	"white" (noun)	Ch. 11
하얗다	"to be white"	Ch. 11
하지만	"but," "however"	Ch. 4
하키	"hockey"	Ch. 2
하하	"Haha"	Ch. 7
학교	"school"	Ch. 5
학생	"student"	Ch. 7
한	1 (adjective)	Ch. 13
한 번 더	"once more" (adverb)	Ch. 16
한국	"(South) Korea"	Ch. 6
한국 사람	"a Korean (person)"	Ch. 6
한국 음식	"Korean food"	Ch. 10
한국말	"Korean (language)"	Ch. 6
한국어	"Korean (language)"	Ch. 16
한국인	"a Korean (person)"	Ch. 6
한복	"Hanbok"	Ch. 20
한식	"Korean food" (abbreviation)	Ch. 10
할머니	"grandmother"	Ch. 18
할아버지	"grandfather"	Ch. 18
항상	"always" (adverb)	Ch. 19
해	"the sun"	Ch. 13
해	"year"	Ch. 16
해변	"seaside," "seashore"	Ch. 5
핸드폰	"cell phone" (literally, "hand phone")	Ch. 4
햄버거	"hamburger"	Ch. 7
행복하다	"to be happy"	Ch. 12
행운(을) 빌다	"to wish (someone) good luck"	Ch. 20
행운(을) 빌어요!	"Good luck!"	Ch. 20
허리	"waist"	Ch. 10
헉	"My gosh"	Ch. 7
혀	"tongue"	Ch. 10
현재	"the present"	Ch. 20
형	"older brother" (used by males)	Ch. 18
호수	"lake"	Ch. 6
혹시	"by chance" (adverb)	Ch. 19
화요일	"Tuesday"	Ch. 16
화장실	"bathroom"	Ch. 8
환자	"a patient"	Ch. 6
환전(을) 하다	"to exchange money"	Ch. 5
회	"sashimi" (raw fish)	Ch. 7
회사	"company"	Ch. 12
후식	"dessert"	Ch. 8
후추	"pepper"	Ch. 8
훌륭하다	"to be wonderful"	Ch. 12
훔치다	"to steal"	Ch. 20
휴	"Phew"	Ch. 7
흔하다	"to be common"	Ch. 9
희망	"hope"	Ch. 11
흰	"white" (adjective)	Ch. 11
흰색	"white" (noun)	Ch. 11
힌트	"a hint"	Ch. 4
힘	"strength," "power"	Ch. 7

Made in United States
Orlando, FL
12 December 2022